FINISHED FROM THE START AND OTHER PLAYS

FINISHED FROM THE START AND OTHER PLAYS

Juan Radrigán

Translated from the Spanish by
Ana Elena Puga with Mónica Núñez-Parra

NORTHWESTERN UNIVERSITY PRESS
EVANSTON, ILLINOIS

Northwestern University Press
www.nupress.northwestern.edu

The Spanish versions of these plays were originally published in *Teatro de
Juan Radrigán: 11 obras,* by Juan Radrigán in 1984 by CENECA-University
of Minnesota, Santiago, Chile: Editorial Universitaria.

Printed in the United States of America

10 9 8 7 6 5 4 3 2 1

Library of Congress Cataloging-in-Publication Data

Radrigán, Juan, 1937–
    [Plays. English Selections.]
    Finished from the start and other plays / Juan Radrigán ; translated from
the Spanish by Ana Elena Puga with Mónica Núñez-Parra.
    p. cm.
    "The Spanish versions of these plays were originally published in Teatro de
Juan Radrigán : 11 obras, by Juan Radrigán in 1984 by CENECA-University
of Minnesota, Santiago, Chile."—T.p. verso.
    Includes bibliographical references.
    ISBN-13: 978-0-8101-2342-7 (pbk. : alk. paper)
    ISBN-10: 0-8101-2342-8 (pbk. : alk. paper)
    I. Puga, Ana Elena. II. Núñez-Parra, Mónica. III. Title.
PQ8098.28.A3A6 2007
862'.64—dc22

                                    2007026853

Dedico estas traducciones a Víctor,
por su apoyo con cariño

CONTENTS

ACKNOWLEDGMENTS

From the time I first traveled to Santiago to meet them, in 2001, Juan Radrigán and his partner, Silvia Marín, have unreservedly shared their invaluable store of memories, photos, and knowledge. Mónica Núñez-Parra and David Preiss were also there since the beginning, inspiring me to learn more about Chile and about Chilean theater.

Thanks to Radrigán's introduction, I met Martín Balmaceda, Pietro González, and Berioska Ipinza, whose work on an innovative Spanish-language production of *Hechos consumados* in New York City in 2001 motivated me to join them in forming our own theater company, LaMicro, dedicated to staging Latin American theater in bilingual and English-language productions. As translator and dramaturg for the LaMicro productions of *Isabel Banished in Isabel* and *Finished from the Start,* I was lucky enough to watch directing and acting that did justice to Radrigán's vision.

Meanwhile, as a graduate student at the Yale School of Drama, I depended on the kindness and intelligence of Moira Fradinger and Sylvia Mitraud. Moira read early drafts of several of these translations, as did my dissertation adviser, Diana Taylor.

Colleagues, research assistants, and students—both inside and outside the Department of Theatre at Northwestern University—gave me the sustenance to complete this anthology. Susan Manning's intellectual and emotional support made the introduction possible. Steve J. Stern, at the University of Wisconsin, provided an invaluable reading of the introduction from the perspective of a historian of Chile. Independent scholar Beatriz J. Rizk also read the introduction and offered many helpful suggestions. In Santiago, María de la Luz Hurtado, of the Escuela de Teatro at the Pontificia Universidad Católica, provided me with access to a rich archive of material.

Harvey Young was always available for friendly consultations and, along with Heather Schoenfeld, organized a very useful reading of *Testimony to the Deaths of Sabina.* In Harvey and Heather's living room, Mary Poole, as Sabina, and Leslie A. Hinderyckx, as Rafael, skillfully brought the text to life in English for the first time. Several graduate students also gave me excellent feedback on that early draft: Oona Kersey, Stefka Mihaylova, Emily Sahakian, and Christopher Van Houten. The translation of *The Beasts* was well served by an informal reading by my colleagues Mary Poole, Linda Gates, and Gail Shapiro, along with acting student Joshua Penzell. Mary and Linda offered detailed suggestions on how to improve the translation. Lighting designer Joseph Appelt helped me analyze the video of the production of *Hechos consumados* by the Teatro Nacional Chileno (Chilean National Theater). Shawn Douglass kindly read *Without Apparent Motive;* Jonathan Berry offered useful feedback.

When LaMicro collaborated with Northwestern University theater undergraduates in a 2004 production of *Finished from the Start,* we were primarily supported by a grant from the Center for Interdisciplinary Research in the Arts. Tracy C. Davis, director of the Interdisciplinary Ph.D. in Theatre and Drama; Lucille Kerr, chair of the Department of Spanish and Portuguese; and Mary Weismantel, of the Latin American and Caribbean Studies Program, also supported the production. Research trips to Chile were supported by two university research grants in combination with leave time granted by Department of Theatre chair Rives Collins and School of Communication dean Barbara O'Keefe.

Some of my undergraduate students, in particular Robert Karol, Dillon Porter, and Colin Gillespie, have offered some wonderful suggestions on the wording of particular phrases.

Christina McMahon was more than a research assistant: she read and commented helpfully on the entire manuscript, from acknowledgments to bibliography, saved me from several potentially embarrassing mistakes, and dug up priceless information. Another research assistant, Daniel Smith, substantially furthered my early work on the project. Brett J. Janecek ably assisted with its completion.

Finally, on the home front, my parents, Marta and William, gave me Spanish; my niece Anna Maria lent me her fine ear for language; she and my sisters Laura and Maria were there for me.

—*Ana Elena Puga*

TRANSLATOR'S NOTE

Translation from Page to Page

Juan Radrigán challenges spectators to bear witness to the trauma dictatorship inflicts upon its victims in his native Chile. His repeated recourse to theatrical testimony—a process I would describe as experiencing trauma, either directly or indirectly; grasping a certain truth from the experience; and then restaging that truth so that others may also grasp it—leads me to reflect on my own moral obligation.[1] As a translator, do I too have a duty to bear witness? And in translating from page to stage, do dramaturgs, directors, and actors who bring these works to life outside of Chile also have a duty to bear witness? Or would feeling such an obligation encumber productions with so much moral freight that they would sink into didacticism?

For better or for worse, as solemn and as bereft of postmodern irony as it sounds, I do feel a duty to bear witness, to bear witness to events that I did not directly experience in a country in which I have never lived and only traveled to for the first time in 1990, as a twenty-nine-year-old newspaper reporter for the *Houston Chronicle* writing articles about the end of Augusto Pinochet's rule (though it was far from the end of the Pinochet era) and about the uphill battle of the families of the disappeared to have the crimes against their relatives exposed, prosecuted, and punished. The experience of speaking, for instance, to a woman who had lost both her husband and her son to political disappearance no doubt affected my attitude toward the translation of Radrigán's dramas when I first undertook this project a decade later, in 2000.

Above all, after a certain amount of vacillation, I came to feel an obligation to keep the plays set in Chile, with Chilean characters confronting Chilean realities. But how to best accomplish that? Susan Bassnett and André Lefevere sum up the dilemma that faces translators of narrative and theater alike: "We need to find out how to translate the cultural capital of other civilizations in a way that preserves at least part of their own nature, without producing translations that are so low on the entertainment factor that they appeal only to those who read for professional reasons."[2]

Two contradictory strains of theory offer very different approaches to translation. One theory argues that in order to make a work meaningful in a new language and culture it is necessary to make sometimes radical changes both to the formal elements of the original, such as syntax, rhythm, and punctuation, and to the expressions of cultural context that may prove meaningless to outsiders: song lyrics, television shows, brand names, proverbs, puns, and so forth. A prominent translator of Latin American novels, Suzanne Jill Levine, for instance, reasons along deconstructionist lines that it is not only permissible but is also the translator's moral obligation to continue the process of "subversion" that the author began in his or her own language. Levine, who often works in collaboration with the authors, argues that "the literary translator can be considered a subversive scribe. Something is destroyed—the form of the original—but meaning is reproduced through another form. A translation in this light becomes a continuation of the original, which already always alters the reality it intends to re-create."[3] In translating for theater, the pressure to make a translation playable exacerbates the need for accessibility so much that some translators cross the line from translation to adaptation. David Johnston, for instance, uses the term *transubstantiation* to describe his versions of Spanish classics for the British stage.[4] Other translators, such as Kirsten Nigro, have asked Latin American playwrights to modify characters for English translations in order to make them more appealing to audiences with different cultural norms and thus perhaps increase the probability that the play will be produced outside Latin America.[5]

A second group of theorists, such as Gayatri Chakravorty Spivak and Lawrence Venuti, stresses the importance of maintaining the differences found in minority cultures. Spivak warns against what she calls "a sort of with-it translatese, so that the literature by a woman in Palestine begins to resemble, in the feel of its prose, something by a man in Taiwan."[6] While Spivak and other postcolonial theorists are primarily concerned with how European languages swallow up Indian or African languages, their insights also apply to translations of works from Spanish to English, though these are, of course, both originally European languages. After all, Latin American countries have, to various degrees, functioned as colonies of the United States—militarily, economically, and, to a certain extent, culturally. As I work on translating and staging Radrigán's plays in the United States, I try not to forget the paradoxical fact that I am handling something intended as a weapon of resistance to U.S. colonialism in Latin America.

Venuti offers some specific guidelines on how to preserve the foreign quality of the source text in English translation, which he calls "foreignizing" or "minoritizing," in contrast to what he considers the less-preferable "domestication."[7] Foreignizing should not be confused with those word-for-word literal translations that can provoke great mirth for their lack of common sense. Rather, Venuti calls on translators to invent a language of their own that may combine language from different periods, genres, and styles in order to remind readers that they are reading a work that was originally written in another language. Instead of bringing the text to the reader, such translations ask the reader to embrace an unfamiliar culture.[8]

When faced with specific challenges in translating Radrigán, I found myself trying to create an accessible, entertaining play for a U.S. reader/spectator without falling into the easy trap of effacing the characters' nationality, which I felt would perpetuate the kind of cultural colonialism that Radrigán so opposes. Following what has become fairly standard practice in translation these days, I didn't Anglicize the characters' names. I didn't add an *h* to *Marta* or turn *Miguel* into *Michael*. And I left the names of towns, neighborhoods, and streets intact.

A greater challenge was deciding how to render the thick slang of the Chilean underclass—rural in *The Beasts* (*Las brutas*) and urban in the other five plays. There is no readily recognizable Chilean-immigrant dialect in English, as there is with, say, Italian or Mexican working-class immigrants. Even more troubling, any generalized Latino dialect could lead spectators to confuse the characters with members of whatever Hispanic minority prevails in their region of the United States: Puerto Rican or Dominicans (New York City), Cubans (Miami), or Mexicans (Chicago). Finally, I didn't want anyone to mistake the characters for African Americans, because that seemed to fall too easily into a stereotype: they're poor, they're struggling, so they must be black. As the translator Louise B. Popkin has observed, "By definition, very colloquial language tends to be linked to a specific time, place, and social setting."[9] Popkin's solution in her elegant translation of Mauricio Rosencof's *Las cartas que no llegaron* (*The Letters That Never Came*) was to elevate the register of the characters' speech into a more neutral terrain. I resisted that solution, however, because it would neutralize the core of Radrigán's political thrust, to depict the lives of the poor and socially marginalized. In the end, inspired by those theatrical costumes that hint at an era or region without fastidiously reproducing every detail of its apparel, for the five plays set in Santiago, I created an argot of underclass usage common to any number of ethnicities: *ain'ts*, malapropisms, double negatives, slang expressions, incorrect use of the past tense. For the most part, I aimed at using slang appropriate to the period in which the plays originally took place, the eighties, except for the older couple in *Testimony to the Deaths of Sabina* (*Testimonio de las muertes de Sabina*), who I imagined would also continue to use some expressions from their youth in the forties and fifties.

Because of its rural setting, *The Beasts* required a different approach. I was taken by how much the desolate geography of the area of northeastern Chile at the foot of the Andes, where the three sisters eke out their isolated existence, resembles the sparsely populated Rocky Mountain ranges of Wyoming. Though the Rockies tend to be more verdant than the dry, barren mountains near the Atacama Desert, there are several remarkable similarities between the mountain people of the two areas. Among these are a rugged individuality, a reliance on physical strength, an intimate relationship with the land, and a Wild West style of rural violence fictionalized in Annie Proulx's short stories and brought to the cinema in the adaptation of her story "Brokeback Mountain." In fact, the rape Justa recounts in such matter-of-fact detail seems like it could have come from a Proulx story, though in fact it was written years earlier. Moreover, the work of the three sisters—raising goats, ranching, and mining—is also typical of Wyoming.

Rocky Mountain speech, I discovered, was influenced by Spanish and French, as well as various Native American languages. Words like *wrangler, corral, chicken feed, horse sense,* and *high-tail* seemed like they might come out of the mouths of the Quispe Cardozo sisters.[10] Even certain patterns of migration, namely the import of Chinese laborers, are similar enough in South and North American contexts that certain derogatory expressions, such as "China boy" to describe the Chinese workers in Northeastern logging camps here match up to certain expressions, such as "I ain't nobody's China girl" (meaning something like "I ain't nobody's slave"), used by the sisters. (In the end, I eliminated the superfluous reference to ethnicity and translated the phrase as "I ain't nobody's slave.") Besides vocabulary and colorful expressions, I adopted certain Western U.S. grammatical constructions, most obviously the use of *a* instead of *to* or *of,* as in "I jumped on top a him."

Rocky Mountain speech alone, however, is not distinctive enough to capture the idiosyncratic dialect of the Quispe Cardozo sisters. And so I found myself reaching for certain Southern expressions, grammatical patterns, and pronunciations, particularly those used by the inhabitants of the Smoky Mountains in Appalachia; for example, *hollow* became *holler.*[11] In a first draft, the sense of doubt expressed by *might* was intensified with the expression *might could;* the plural of *you* became *y'all; afraid* became *afeared.* When actors read the draft aloud, however, it became clear that the Southern turns of phrase were too powerful. Almost without meaning to, the actors were drawn to adopt a Southern accent, which would lead a spectator to forget that, in fact, the play takes place at the foot of the Andes and that it need not, perhaps should not, be transposed to any particular region of the United States. I took out many of the Southernisms, in the hope that directors and actors will not be tempted to equate ignorance and poverty with the South.

In all the translations, guiding myself by native speakers' readings of the plays in Spanish, I tried to preserve the rhythm of the original. As much as possible, I tried to keep the punctuation and sentence lengths more or less the same as in the Spanish. At first, I tried to find word-for-word equivalents for Chilean interjections, such as the ubiquitous *po,* a contraction of *pues* ("well"), that seems to end almost every phrase. But the more I experimented with *huh,* or *you know,* or *see,* or *man,* the clearer it became that many of those *po*s would have to go. Actors reading the text in English made it obvious that any *po* equivalent could prove intrusive and distracting to a U.S. listener.

In certain instances, which I identified primarily by instinct, it seemed appropriate to engage in what Venuti might condemn as "domestication" destructive of the source culture. The only logically consistent test for when to domesticate and when to foreignize seemed to be the limits of what I thought I could get away with without losing the theatrical spectator's attention. References to television shows always pose a dilemma: does one simply translate the title of a television show unfamiliar to U.S. audiences or does one try to find an equivalent television show? In *The Guest* (*El invitado*), I translated word for word the title of Radrigán's parodic twist (*Cheer Up, Ms. Dying-of-Hunger!*) on the Chilean television segment "Buck Up, Buddy." I could have substituted a similar parody of a U.S. television show, say, changing *Wheel of Fortune* to *Wheel of Famished* or *The Dating Game* to *The Dying Game*. But Radrigán's title seemed just as amusing in English, despite the fact that the link to an actual show, with all the emotion and cultural memory that such links engender, was lost.

On the other hand, in *Finished from the Start* (*Hechos consumados*), references to a Mexican comedy that was very popular in Chile in the eighties, *El Chavo del Ocho* (*The Kid from Number Eight*), came complete with a specific gesture—a cue to an actor—*la garrotera,* a physical paralysis, performed in a comic manner, that the character suffered whenever frozen with fear. When Marta says she suffered "la garrotera" as she accidentally caught a glimpse of what appeared to be a kidnapping or assassination, it gives a touch of hilarity to a life-threatening matter. Because a *garrotero* is a brakeman, my first, more literal, translation rendered her temporary disability as a "brake attack." But when the actor playing Marta, Eva C. Vásquez, performed the "brake attack" in a workshop production at Northwestern University in the spring of 2004, not a single person in an audience of about one hundred people laughed. The humor seemed to depend on a common cultural memory that was missing from the overly literal, though perhaps foreignizing, version of *la garrotera*. Chastened, I decided that this was a moment for domestication. Internet surfing, combined with my memories of my own sixties and seventies television viewing, led me to the Mel Brooks comedy *Get Smart* and Agent 86's "invisible wall." When I saw Vásquez perform her invisible-wall routine the following fall during a production at New York City's Centro Cultural Julia de Burgos, the audience's wave of laughter confirmed my decision.

Similar challenges were presented by uniquely Chilean foods and drinks, well-known songs, national heroes, popular writers, sports teams, and the titles of the plays themselves. To give just one example, the Spanish title of what I've rendered as *Finished from the Start* (*Hechos consumados*) has a poetic ring of doom in Spanish. The literal translation would be *Consummated Acts,* which has no poetic ring and would mislead English speakers into thinking of sex. Just about the only time one hears the word *consummate* is when one speaks of consummating a marriage. And the context for the title is not a discussion about marriage or sex, but rather the speech in which Emilio says that we are all "hechos consumados" fated to die, and before we die, fated to either have money and power or not. In the 1986 film version by director Luis Vera, the title was translated as *An Accomplished Fact.* This seemed accurate but flavorless. Looking for flavor, I lurched from the legalistic *Perfected Deeds* to the businessy *A Done Deal,* to the soap opera–like *Creatures of Destiny.* Reading the character Emilio's speech closely, one realizes that the implied creator of humanity is neither a single God nor a vague concept like fate or destiny. The creator is either gods, in the plural sense, or more likely, given the context of the rest of the play, other people who have power and money. "*They* made us . . . ," "*They* told us . . . but *they* didn't tell us why," Emilio says (italics mine). The unfairness of the system brought to mind a rigged sporting event, much like Pedro's boxing match in *The Guest, or Tranquility Is Priceless* in which the contenders never stand a chance of determining their own outcome. Hence, *Finished from the Start.*

Because of my determination to see the plays staged, certain aids that scholarly translators sometimes employ, such as glossaries and footnotes, were anathema to me. An audience can hardly be expected to view the play with glossary and footnotes in hand. And yet, in a very few instances, I resorted to footnotes, primarily to supply information to production teams that might use it to create visual or sound effects that would complete a cultural translation. For instance, Pedro sarcastically remarks on the Santiago soccer team Colo Colo as a tool of the authorities used to distract the public from more pressing issues. I resisted substituting the name of a U.S. sports team because that would too abruptly wrench the characters from their Chilean setting. From the context, the spectator should be able to understand that Colo Colo is a sports team of some sort. In production, visual cues such as a poster or a pennant, combined with aural cues such as cheering crowds or the voice of a soccer announcer whooping "gooooooool" in typical Latin American fashion could offer the spectator more hints as to the nature of Colo Colo without having to read the endnote.

Though translators cannot rely on directors and actors to fill in any gaps in the text, the knowledge that a work may live on stage as well as on the page can lead to certain liberating foreignizations, to riff on Venuti's term. For example, in the Spanish version of *Hechos consumados,* Marta and Emilio are constantly drinking tea from something called a *choca,* which is an empty tin can filled with water that can be heated over an open fire. With a single tea bag, one can make endless cups of weak tea. For *Finished from the Start,* my first thought was that since poor people in the United States would be more likely to drink coffee than tea, and since, conveniently, there are many slang terms for coffee in American English—*joe, java, mud*—I would just have Marta and Emilio drink coffee. But several Chilean colleagues, including Mónica Núñez-Parra and the director Martín Balmaceda, convinced me that a U.S. reader would understand from the stage directions and a U.S. spectator could glean from the staging decisions that the Chilean poor drink tea. Marta and Emilio went back to drinking tea.

Translation from Page to Stage

Staging, it has often been noted, is a kind of translation, and staging of a foreign work is a kind of cultural translation. Together, translation and staging are two parts of a single process of cross-cultural theatrical representation. In the move from page to stage, the production team encounters dilemmas parallel to those of the translator: When do you foreignize and when do you domesticate? How do you represent a Latin American drama that is supposed to be, in part, a weapon of resistance against capitalist exploitation of workers in the land and in the language that epitomizes the export of that exploitation to Latin America? How can we (the translator and production team) serve as witnesses to crimes we never experienced and convey the emotional truth of a historical trauma that most of our spectators did not live through? In short, how do you stage a Latin American play of resistance in the United States without eviscerating it?

In 2001, several Chilean immigrants to the United States, Balmaceda and actors Pietro González and Berioska Ipinza, had worked together on a Spanish-language production of *Hechos consumados* at Teatro SEA in New York City. The production was so successful that the group wanted to take Radrigán to English speakers as well. Radrigán put them in touch with me, and the ensuing collaboration led to the birth of a new U.S. Latino and Latina theater company, LaMicro. My involvement as translator and dramaturg in LaMicro's first two productions—*Isabel Banished in Isabel* (2003) and *Finished from the Start* (2004)—forced me to grapple with the questions articulated previously as more than theory, as practical problems that affect every element of a production, from the set design to the postshow discussion. While both productions had elements of foreignization and domestication, *Isabel,* it seems to me, succumbed more than *Finished from the Start* to the pressure of the dominant culture.

LaMicro's *Isabel* opened on June 17, 2003, at the Workshop Theater in New York City. An element of the production that was distinctly foreignizing, bringing the Chilean nature of the work into this culture, was how Balmaceda divided the role of Isabel between two actors, a younger, Chilean Isabel, played by Berioska Ipinza, and an older, Anglo Isabel played by Valerie Cihylik. The age difference between the actors mirrors the relationship between the Spanish and English versions of the play: the original Chilean production is forever "younger" because it was staged first; the Anglo version is more contemporary yet "older" in that it is more distant from the circumstances under which the work was first produced. Ipinza, as the younger Isabel, wears a fifties-style sky-blue dress, a strand of pearls, matching pearl earrings, and high heels, thus embodying the character's memories of an earlier, better-off, happier self. She slowly emerges from the garbage bag (Balmaceda "translated" the garbage can from Radrigán's stage directions as a bag) to which Cihylik talks, lending her the ethereal quality of embodied memory. Cihylik, as the older, more downtrodden Isabel, wears a green head scarf, a faded blue housecoat, and slippers with socks; a cloth parrot hangs from her neck, an allusion to the silenced birdsong for which she yearns.

A second foreignizing element of the staging pertains to language: Ipinza occasionally repeats in Spanish a phrase that Cihylik has said in English, or vice versa:

IPINZA: L'hambre, compadre, es larga y negra, es como un hoyo aonde una no termina nunca de caer.

CIHYLIK: Hunger, my friend, is long and black, like a hole you never stop falling into.

Ipinza also delivers one short speech, lamenting her loneliness, entirely in Spanish. Even to non–Spanish speakers, the uniquely Chilean pitch and intonation of the accent were clear. In Chilean phrasing, about a dozen syllables remain at a more-or-less steady pitch before one syllable suddenly rises to higher pitch and then drops back down on the next: "Dicen qui'una se puee volver loca pen*san*do, que no se da ni cuenta cuando empieza a hablar sola" ("They say that you can go crazy thinking, that you don't even notice when you start talking to yourself"). Spectators were provided with an English-language version of the speech in their programs, which they could refer to after the performance. But during the show, in the darkened theater, those spectators who could not understand the Spanish were, perhaps even more than the Spanish speakers, able to focus on the language entirely for its sound texture and rhythm. Rather than completely surrender the production to the dominant language, we followed a foreignizing impulse to expose spectators to at least a few morsels of Chilean Spanish.

Despite this impulse, however, it became clear from postshow discussions that a play that had been written in Santiago as a cry against the silence imposed by the dictatorship had been transformed in New York City into a work of solidarity with the homeless. During a postshow discussion one spectator even asked accusingly, "Have any of you ever been homeless? Do you have any homeless friends?" as if to imply that our work lacked authenticity because of our lack of experience with New York City homelessness. Actually, Isabel states that she is not homeless, that she does have a room to sleep in. But in New York City, a character on the verge of mental illness who talks to a garbage bag is quickly associated with the issue of homelessness.

Balmaceda, as the director, and I, as the dramaturg, debated how obvious to make the play's antidictatorship stance. He feared being too obvious; I feared not being obvious enough. Certain symbols, such as the wooden Pinocchio dolls that Ipinza and Cihylik hung around their necks like miniature albatrosses, could only be understood by those familiar enough with Chile under Pinochet to know that *Pinocchio* was a derogatory term for the dictator. I suggested explicating, or at least hinting at them, by including on the construction-site set a back wall with scrawled graffiti that would read both "Down with Pinochet!" and "Down with Pinocchio!" Balmaceda replied that he preferred to leave the Pinocchio dolls as a kind of subtle joke for Chileans and others in the know. While a graffiti-covered wall was used as a backdrop, because we didn't want to twist Radrigán's work into a dogmatic lesson play, we ended up deciding against using a direct message such as "Down with Pinochet!" As Balmaceda correctly noted, to give Pinochet that much prominence seemed counter to the spirit of Radrigán's work, which never mentions the dictator by name. Instead, we created graffiti messages that contained strong hints as to the play's political origins, such as "¿Dónde están?" ("Where are they?"), the rallying cry of relatives of the disappeared. But judging from postshow discussions, these messages depended too much on a store of cultural memory that many audience members at our productions lacked.

When LaMicro staged *Finished from the Start* in April 2004 at Northwestern University outside of Chicago, and again the following November in New York City, we were united in our determination not to allow the motif of disappearance and the allusions to the coup that pervade the work be lost on our U.S. audience. We did not want the play to be mistaken for nothing more than a protest against poverty. Balmaceda spoke of preserving "the memory of the play," by which he meant both the drama's potential to testify to the traumatic historical events to which it alludes and the cluster of memories emanating from earlier productions of the work—memories preserved in reviews, in other documented accounts of those productions, in oral anecdotal accounts, or only in the minds of those earlier spectators who still live. Staging all of the above would be impossible; the attempt would result in a production *about* previous productions, which was not our intention. Yet we hoped to create a good-enough substitute for the common store of experience that had made the work so aesthetically and politically potent to Santiago spectators in 1981, when the work was first staged. To this end, we devised three primary aides to memory: the staging of the characters described in the stage directions as offstage presences invisible to the spectators, the use of video to give historical background and to trigger emotional associations, and the incorporation of a much higher percentage of Spanish language in a more experimental fashion than in *Isabel*.

At Northwestern, the victims of political persecution were played by a silent chorus of six actors, clearly identified on the program as "the disappeared."[12] During the moments when Marta and Emilio see the disappeared, the chorus of four men and two women, accompanied by eerie music and bathed in golden light, slowly crossed the stage in a stately rhythm that brought to mind ghosts or zombies. Their seventies costumes, designed by Anna Maria Carvallo, represented a spectrum of social class, from a worker in a knit cap and heavy boots to an executive woman in a business suit and pumps. All the clothes were torn and dirtied, the actors' faces and bodies caked with stage blood and "dirt," to suggest that the victims had been beaten and/or tortured. The goal was to spur the memory, or the imagination, of an audience that may have read or heard about the disappeared in Latin America but that would not necessarily recall any specifics about their plight. A time line in the theater program explained that between 1973 and 1988 the secret police detained and tortured an estimated thirty-five thousand people, of whom some three thousand permanently disappeared, their bodies clandestinely buried or burned or dumped at sea. A historical exhibit in a reception area of the theater offered more information, including listening stations with taped interviews with military officials, Catholic Church workers, and family members of the disappeared who gave individual accounts of political kidnappings and assassinations.[13] While many audience members took advantage of the supplementary information to make the connection between the chorus and Chile's disappeared, in spite of all the cues, at least one spectator missed the reference. "Who were those *Night of the Living Dead* types supposed to be?" one Northwestern student asked me after a performance.

The video, designed by Jill Wissmiller, functioned both as an informational frame that precedes the play and as a series of more abstract images that add emotional texture to certain key moments. The introductory two-and-a-half minutes of black-and-white footage culled from several documentaries shows Socialist president Salvador Allende's inaugural parade, supporters marching arm in arm, a fist in the crowd raised in triumph as the slight, bespectacled Allende, presidential sash draped across his torso, rides by on a float. Cut to clouds of smoke rising from the crumbling presidential palace, underscored by the sounds of bombs exploding. A voice-over of Allende's last speech announces the air force's rebellion and prophesies "moral punishment" for the insurgents. Cut to the aftermath of the coup: Soldiers round up men, patting them down as they stand with their hands behind their necks or up against a wall, feet spread. A woman's voice lists family names: "my son Óscar Arturo Ramírez, my brother . . . , my sister-in-law . . . , my nephew . . ." Each name is followed by the refrain "desaparecido." As the word is repeated it develops an ominous power, and its meaning, "disappeared," becomes obvious. The screen stands next to a makeshift clothesline on which Marta's clothes are drying, the physical juxtaposition of the big picture to the individual belongings suggesting a connection between the coup and the troubles of the characters.

After the documentary, the brief segments (thirty seconds or less per segment) of color video images interspersed throughout the play offer far more abstract emotional texture, alluding to both disappeared people and a disappeared time: a handheld camera pans across a muddy grassy area and lingers on an abandoned work boot, a dress shoe, the rubber sole of an overturned shoe; there is a close-up of a hand fingering a rootless tooth, as if examining human remains; happy colors appear in psyche-delic flashes as Marta waxes nostalgic about the gardening work she used to do with the long-gone Mario. The theme of loss was underscored by the music: a haunting contemporary baroque oratorio, *Lost Objects,* by Michael Gordon, David Lang, and Julia Wolf, which laments a long list of losses—from socks to people to resistance.

Along with video, touches of Spanish language helped remind spectators that the play is set in another time and place—with a different set of collective experiences and memories—and that understanding the work requires that they bridge a gulf between that culture and this culture. Like English translations that foreignize, bilingual productions can help bring the spectator toward the work—as opposed to serving up the work to the spectator. Bilingual productions may function in tandem with translations to at least temporarily dislodge English from its position as dominant language, so that those who comprehend only English might at least for a few moments experience the sense of disorientation and powerlessness that subordinates, in terms of the linguistic and the often-related economic disadvantage, live with every day. Paradoxically, both translation and bilingual production may help familiarize spectators with the Spanish language, perhaps making the language seem less foreign in the future, a future likely to involve further encounters with Spanish, since Latinos have become the largest minority in the United States.

A translation such as this one might, then, serve as the basis for what, for want of a better term, I have dubbed *countertranslation*, or the process of working backward from a translated text to the source language in order to decide what portions of the original to include in a bilingual theatrical production. Some of Venuti's ideas about how translation should be conducted—highlighting rather than concealing cultural difference, foreignizing so as to maintain awareness of the source's linguistic identity even in the target language—may be fruitfully applied to countertranslation in the service of bilingual production. Once Radrigán's text was translated into English, many of the decisions about when and how to revert to Spanish paralleled the decisions a translator must make when deciding when and how to preserve a source text's original syntax or its punctuation or any one of its many distinguishing features, even though these may be perceived as awkward in the target language.

It was the directors and the actors, in rehearsal, who decided which lines would be uttered solely in Spanish, which would be repeated in both Spanish and English, and which would be spoken only in English translation. In the end, though Spanish was interspersed throughout the eighty-minute running time, it totaled only about 10 percent of the dialogue. Balmaceda and the lead actors, Pietro González (Emilio) and Eva C. Vásquez (Marta), agreed that the places where the text should be spoken in Spanish emerged intuitively. Vásquez, a native of Puerto Rico, studied the Chilean accent and tried to adopt it as much as possible. Roberto Cambeiro (Miguel), the son of Spanish immigrants to the United States, spoke the fewest lines in Spanish and was the only one of the three main actors who spoke English without a Spanish accent. His unaccented English added an allegorical component to the juxtaposition of Anglo and Hispanic cultures, since his character was also the most powerful and belligerent.

To summarize, through rehearsal and production, we discovered that performing certain lines in both Spanish and English, or in Spanish alone, served to

1. remind the spectator that the play is set in another time and place— with a different set of collective experiences and memories—and that understanding the work requires that he or she bridge a gulf between that culture and this culture (this was also underscored by scenic design, sound design, and costumes);

2. dislodge English from its position as dominant language, so that those who comprehend only English would at least very temporarily experience the sense of disorientation and powerlessness that subordinates, in terms of linguistic and often related economic disadvantage, live with every day;

3. familiarize some spectators with Spanish, perhaps making the language seem less foreign in the future; and

4. share the poetry of the language as uttered in Chilean-accented Spanish, with the unique rhythms of its phrasing, colloquialisms, elisions, omissions, and other peculiarities of pronunciation.

I would encourage theater practitioners to continue to experiment with bilingual production of Radrigán's work. Bilingualism adds a welcome level of complexity to representation: it simultaneously testifies to the Latino life of a play translated from Spanish and to its current life in a culturally complex country. It reminds us of the moral imperative to attempt the impossible: to undertake the undone task of the absent witness.

—*Ana Elena Puga*

Notes

1. I am indebted to Dori Laub's "Bearing Witness" for this definition.
2. Bassnett and Lefevere, *Constructing Cultures*, 11.
3. Levine, *Subversive Scribe*, 7–8.
4. Johnston, "Valle-Inclán," 86.
5. See Nigro, "Getting the Word Out," 124, for a discussion of her collaboration with Mexican playwright Sabina Berman on the translation of *Muerte súbita* (*Sudden Death*).
6. Spivak, "Politics of Translation," 400.
7. Venuti, *Scandals of Translation*, 11.
8. The contrast in translation approaches that Levine and Venuti advocate interestingly parallels the debate surrounding choices made by transcribers of illiterate *testimonio* narrators. For instance, Elisabeth Burgos-Debray decided to correct Rigoberta Menchú's mistakes in gender pronouns to keep her from appearing "picturesque" (xxi). Burgos-Debray's choice can be interpreted either as a way to maintain Menchú's dignity in English or as an example of pernicious domestication that erases her individuality and minority status. For more on minoritizing translation, see Venuti, *Scandals of Translation*, 8–20.
9. Popkin, "Translator's Note," xix.

10. For foreign language influences on Rocky Mountain speech, see Dillard, *Towards a Social History of American English*. For vocabulary that recalls the Quispe Cardozo sisters, see Hendrickson, *American Talk*. Editor Rick Newby's *Rocky Mountain Region* also was a valuable resource.
11. For Appalachian dialect, I relied heavily on Montgomery and Hall, *Dictionary of Smoky Mountain English*.
12. In the New York City production, a single actor, I-Cheng Chen, embodied the disappeared.
13. The exhibit was organized by Greg Egan, Matthew Mazurowski, and Andrew Whatley.

INTRODUCTION

The Missing Witness

Juan Radrigán (b. 1937) is one of Chile's best-loved and most prolific playwrights. He has written almost forty plays, two novels, and a collection of poetry. Now nearing age seventy, he continues to produce at least a play a year, many of them popular and critical successes. He has gone from scraping together a few pesos to rent a hall and put together a basic set to winning commissions for lush productions in established venues such as the Teatro Nacional Chileno (Chilean National Theater) and the Pontificia Universidad Católica (Pontifical Catholic University) in Santiago. A film was made of his 1981 masterpiece *Hechos consumados* (*Finished from the Start*). During its thirteen-year existence (1980–93), his tiny theater company toured Europe and South America. With almost no formal education, he has crafted some of Chile's most enduring poetic language. His works have been translated into English, French, German, Portuguese, Swedish, and even Slovenian. Yet it is hardly a rags-to-riches narrative that defines Radrigán. He still rents a cramped fourth-floor walk-up in a working-class neighborhood of Santiago dotted with auto repair shops, which he shares with his longtime companion Silvia Marín, their eight-year-old daughter Rocío, and his twenty-three-year-old stepson Rienzi. While his days of manual labor are over, Radrigán still cobbles together a modest living from various part-time teaching jobs, commissions, royalties, and private theater workshops. Out of both economic necessity and artistic ambition, retirement is out of the question.[1]

Radrigán wrote many of his finest plays under dictatorship, years ago and in a faraway country. Yet their protest of poverty, injustice, and indignity still matters today in flawed democracies around the world, including our own. It matters not only because many of the same evils exist here in the United States today, almost thirty years after Radrigán began to write in Chile—indifference to the suffering of others, silence in the face of injustice, excessive obedience to authority, worship of the almighty dollar—but also because it is the rare playwright who can lash out at social ills without obvious preaching or teaching. Radrigán's blend of humor and working-class poetry instead seduces us to listen to long-ignored people and to see them as human beings instead of as issues or problems. What we do afterward is up to us.

The plays Radrigán wrote during the dictatorship, from 1973 to 1990, of General Augusto Pinochet differ markedly in style and content from the plays he wrote after the end of the dictatorship. His earlier plays depicted the lives and the language of the marginalized: from the working poor and their hungry children to prostitutes, pimps, homeless drunks, petty criminals, and murderers. His recent plays often explore the existential crises of more middle-class protagonists, including famous literary figures such as the poet Vicente Huidobro and the playwright Samuel Beckett, who, as might be expected, employ more standard speech.

As a graduate student at the Yale School of Drama, I began to work on translations of the early plays, both because their colloquial language posed a stiff artistic challenge and because their beauty and enduring potential for political impact made the challenge feel worthwhile. A Chilean friend with a background in sociology and a fine ear for language nuances, Mónica Núñez-Parra, soon began to assist me in my effort to decipher urban Santiago slang. She later read the plays aloud with me to help me absorb their rhythms, carefully checked the Spanish against my English renditions, and occasionally offered assistance in word choice. Two of the translations have now been staged by a theater company that I cofounded with some friends, LaMicro. My hope is that other contemporary directors, actors, and audiences in the English-speaking world will also find these plays compelling and give them the attention they merit.

Radrigán's early plays interlock like pieces of a giant dramatic puzzle: the prostitute with a limp from *El loco y la triste* (*The Crazy Man and the Sad Woman*) is resuscitated as an offstage character in *Without Apparent Motive*. The protagonist and plot of *La felicidad de los García* (*The Happiness of the García Family*), about a thief who pretends to win at the races so that he can treat his family to the luxuries for which they long, resurface in *Hechos consumados* (*Finished from the Start*) as an anecdote Marta tells about her father.[2] Marta and her friend Emilio evolve into Micaela and Diego in *Islas de porfiado amor* (*Islands of Stubborn Love*). Reading or watching a series of Radrigán plays offers a pleasure similar to that of the traditional Latin American children's game of *lotería*, in which stereotypical images on cards are matched with their corresponding images on a board. As with the *lotería* cards, certain identifiable Radrigán character types recur regularly: the prophet, the drunk, the lonely man, the self-doubting creator, the woman hungry for love. However, it is as if the images on the cards were to vary slightly each time they come up: the differences among the later reincarnations make the game more interesting.

A Tragic Sense of Life

Radrigán calls himself a "tragic optimist," and his tragic sense of life may be traced to an individual history marked by personal hardship coupled with his experience of a terrible period in Chile's national history.[3] The problem of evil was more than an abstraction to him as he and his three older siblings grew up in poverty, without the opportunity to attend school regularly. His father, Samuel Radrigán López, led a nomadic existence, taking his wife and four children around South America in an old truck, supporting them with whatever work he could find repairing tractors and other farm equipment. A lively conversationalist, he was an avid ballroom dancer and a womanizer who regularly had to be dragged out of brothels. When Radrigán was seven years old, his family lived in a rented room in a small town in Bolivia while his father worked repairing carnival equipment in a nearby village. One day his father drove away in his truck, as if to go to work, but never came back. He had abandoned the family. Radrigán's mother, Blanca Ester Rojas Liberona, though trained as an elementary school teacher, could not find a teaching job and was forced to take in laundry to support Radrigán, his older brother, and his two older sisters. One of his earliest memories is the sadness in his mother's eyes, which he saw mirrored in the faces of many other Chileans during the family's nomadic period.[4] At age twelve, Radrigán began to work to help support the family: he ran errands, helped out in stores or factories, took any job he could find.

For many Chileans in the forties, the Communist Party represented the best hope to improve working conditions and to provide the poor with necessities such as food, drinkable water, adequate housing, electricity, and education. Within Chile's system of proportional representation, however, smaller political parties such as the Communists primarily exert influence indirectly, by forming coalitions with larger parties. In the presidential elections of 1946, the Communist Party gave its support to Gabriel González Videla, a member of the left wing of the Radical Party.[5] In return, González Videla (president from 1946 to 1952) was expected to support the demands of coal and copper miners, urban workers, and agricultural laborers. Instead, he cracked down on labor, violently repressed strikers, and outlawed the Communist Party altogether in 1948, in order to curry favor with the United States, which in the wake of World War II was just beginning to shape its cold war policies.[6] Many Communists were imprisoned, forced underground, or sent into exile, including, most infamously, the prominent poet Pablo Neruda.[7] It was not until 1957 that the law banning the Communist Party was overturned and the Communists were allowed back into official political life.[8] Though Radrigán's family was not politically active, his firsthand experience as a child laborer earning dismally low pay under deplorable working conditions quickly developed his awareness of class inequities and social injustice in Chile's highly stratified society.

Taught to read and write by his mother, Radrigán at first indiscriminately consumed any book he could get his hands on, then set himself a reading plan that progressed country by country through Latin America: Peru, Uruguay, Argentina, and so on. He wrote his first short story at age sixteen. And he continued to struggle to write poetry and short stories while working at a variety of temporary jobs, including carpenter, painter, dent fixer, loading dock worker, and door-to-door salesman. At the age of twenty-five, in 1962, he published a collection of short stories, *Los vencidos no creen en Dios* (*The Defeated Don't Believe in God*), a passionate but sentimental series of portraits of the powerless that did not win much attention. "Luckily, not too many people read it," Radrigán remarks with his usual dry sense of humor. A novel, *El vino de la cobardía* (*The Wine of Cowardice*), pubished in 1968, and a collection of poems, *El día de los muros* (*The Day of the Walls*), published in 1975, met with similar indifference from the public. Though less sophisticated than his plays, all three works demonstrate the preoccupation with the fate of the marginalized that was to mark his dramatic oeuvre as well.

For many years the struggle to earn a living, support a family, and find time to write consumed Radrigán's energy. While some of his friends were inspired, like so many Latin Americans, by Fidel Castro and Che Guevara's triumphant march into Havana on January 1, 1959, Radrigán rarely even found time to attend a street rally. "I didn't like public speaking. I didn't like politics. I liked reading and writing more," he recalls. At the age of twenty-eight he married Yolanda Josefina Araya Quiroga and soon had two small children to raise, Flavia (b. 1967) and Juan (b. 1969). He worked his way up from sweeping the floors in textile mills, learning from other workers how to repair the machinery, and soon earned decent wages as a mechanic. His fellow workers often elected him president of their union, which more than once led to his being fired. Though he still disliked politics, he felt compelled to fight for compliance of labor laws and to counter daily assaults on workers' dignity. For instance, he once successfully organized a short strike to protest the practice of always having a worker open the door for the factory owner. From then on, at least at the Julio Israel Textile Factory, Julio Israel opened his own door.

In 1970, when the Socialist Salvador Allende was elected president by a slim margin, Radrigán was thrilled. Like many Chileans, Radrigán thought that Allende's Popular Unity government would finally bring a measure of social justice to urban and agricultural workers alike. As the first democratically elected Marxist leader in the world, Allende promised to follow a democratic path to socialism.

Meanwhile, the United States, which had been unsuccessful in covert attempts to prevent Allende's election, did all it could to prevent him from taking office.[9] The Nixon administration's policy toward Chile was neatly summed up by the infamous quote from Henry Kissinger: "I don't see why we need to stand by and watch a country go communist because of the irresponsibility of its own people."[10] On the economic front, the United States cut aid and blocked loans from international banks, denying Chile badly needed foreign exchange at a time when both foreign and domestic investors were pulling their capital out of the country.[11] State Department officials encouraged large U.S. corporations deeply invested in Chile, such as Ford Motor Company, Bank of America, and International Telephone and Telegraph Company, to leave the country.[12] Meanwhile, under the direction of National Security Adviser Kissinger, the Central Intelligence Agency crafted a plan to foment a military coup.

At first, the plan included kidnapping General René Schneider, the commander of the army who had vowed to stay out of civilian politics, in order to clear the way for the less scrupulous retired General Roberto Viaux to seize power. But when Schneider was killed in the attempt, the plot was abandoned and Allende took office as scheduled on November 3, 1970.[13] The new president quickly nationalized a wide variety of foreign enterprises, including the copper industry, and implemented land reform far more aggressively than had the previous Christian Democratic government. Allende's administration held down prices and raised wages, spurring an economic boom that lasted just a year before a dramatic crash. Price controls failed; inflation spiraled crazily; shortages of consumer goods, including food, soon followed; and a black market flourished. Strikes began to paralyze the country—organized by the very workers who were the intended beneficiaries of Allende's policies. Opponents on both the Left and the Right undercut his authority: the extreme Left agitated for armed revolution; the extreme Right called for a military coup.[14] In the countryside, a guerrilla group, Movimiento de Izquierda Revolucionaria (MIR, Revolutionary Left Movement), organized illegal land seizures to "accelerate the reform process," thus pitting Allende against both the landowners and the peasants.[15] From Washington, the Nixon administration secretly assured military leaders of support in the event of a coup.[16]

On the morning of September 11, 1973, Radrigán was getting ready to go to work at the textile factory when he received a phone call from a friend who told him that a military coup had taken place. Despite earlier pledges of loyalty to the Allende government, the army commander, General Pinochet, had seized power. Radrigán knew that as a labor leader he was in danger of arrest. Labor leaders were Allende's natural allies, and anyone who supported Allende was now the enemy. He decided not to go to work that day and soon realized that he would never be able to return to the factory. As the morning progressed, the armed forces, commanded by Pinochet, fired a round of rockets into the government palace and then attacked the building with tanks and infantry troops. Allende broadcast his last speech to the nation and then took his own life.[17]

Repression was harshest during the first three years following the coup. Roundups and summary executions eliminated any possible resistors before they had a chance to act.[18] The national stadium in Santiago was used to imprison thousands of civilians, including, most famously, the guitarist and folk singer Victor Jara, whose fingers were broken before he was executed. Labor activists, academics, psychologists, and journalists were all targeted for investigation as suspected Communists. Torture became a standard practice in interrogation. In 1976, Pinochet's secret police assassinated Allende's former ambassador to the United States, Orlando Letelier, and his American aide Ronni Moffit on the street in Washington, D.C.[19] After the dictatorship, a Chilean government commission documented 3,197 cases of murder and disappearance, a total that human rights activists say is far lower than the actual number of deaths.[20] Radrigán watched in helpless horror as some of his friends were killed or disappeared by the secret police. One friend, an actor and a teacher who was active in the left-wing guerrilla group MIR, Ana María Puga Rojas, was shot and killed along with her husband, Alejandro de la Barra Villarroel, by government agents on December 3, 1974, as the couple went to pick up their son from nursery school.[21] Thirty years later, Radrigán still finds it difficult to speak about what he or those close to him suffered during that era, both because he was fortunate compared to others and because in retrospect some Chileans now exaggerate their supposed opposition to the regime. "People whose grandmothers weren't even chasing them are now claiming that they were persecuted during the dictatorship," Radrigán says. "I don't want to talk about it. It was a terrible disgrace that was visited upon us. That's all." And yet not all Chileans, perhaps not even the majority of Chileans, agree with Radrigán. A plebiscite in 1980, while tainted by charges of fraud, appeared to confirm that a majority of those Chileans who voted were willing to keep Pinochet in power until 1989.

Theater during the dictatorship was knocked out for a time but stumbled to its feet within a few years. During what some have dubbed a "cultural blackout," university theaters and theater departments were closed or reorganized.[22] Some actors and directors were arrested; others fled the country. The new government imposed a 22 percent tax on any work that could not win the government stamp of approval: "cultural." Theater historian Juan Andrés Piña recounts that among those works deemed unworthy of the cultural classification was Beckett's *Waiting for Godot*.[23] The strict enforcement of a nine-o'clock curfew further discouraged theatrical activity. And, most important, self-censorship kept many playwrights, directors, and producers cautious for fear of triggering repression: no organized oppositional theater movement such as Argentina's *teatro abierto* ("open theater") appeared in Chile.[24] One theater company, Aleph, that in 1974 dared to defy the dictatorship with *Y al principio existía la vida* (*And in the Beginning There Was Life*), a transparent allegory depicting the nation as a sinking ship, quickly found itself raided and disbanded, and its members detained by the secret police, some imprisoned and others forced into exile. One actor, Juan McCleod, was never seen again after his detention. Piña identifies a rebirth of theater, however, by 1976, just three years after the coup, with the appearance of the first works that explore taboo themes: unemployment, censorship, political corruption, and human rights abuses.[25] David Benavente's 1976 collaboration with the company ICTUS, *Pedro, Juan y Diego,* was the first antidictatorship theater to escape persecution. The work cautiously alluded to misguided government policy with an ambiguous allegory about three construction workers forced to build a wall in the wrong position.

Even if it had been safe for Radrigán to return to work, he might have found that his job no longer existed. After the Pinochet government adopted ultra-free-market economic policies, a flood of foreign imports decimated the domestic textile industry.[26] Radrigán became a street vendor of new and used books, running a bookstall by day and writing by night until the early morning. In 1979, he completed his first play, *Testimonio de las muertes de Sabina* (*Testimony to the Deaths of Sabina*), based on the experiences of some fellow street vendors who had lost their fruit stall as a result of a nightmarish city bureaucracy. It alludes to the dictatorship only through the atmosphere of terror endured by the protagonists. Though Radrigán had almost no contacts in the theater world, and rarely went to the theater himself, he had heard of the young director Gustavo Meza, who founded Teatro Imagen in 1974 in an attempt to produce theater that would loosen the dictatorship's death grip on cultural life. A prominent actor and mutual friend, Tennyson Ferrada, passed the text along to Meza, who quickly staged it in a small Santiago theater.[27] Radrigán was forty-two.

As if to make up for his late start, a creative torrent of work followed: a dozen plays in the next five years, some short and others full length. In 1980, he wrote *¡¡¡Viva Somoza!!!* with Meza, contributing a darkly humorous vignette, "A Question of Placement" ("Cuestión de ubicación"), in which a young girl dies of malnutrition while her family squabbles about where to put the new television set. The drama slyly poked fun at consumers who grabbed at the cheap electronic imports flooding the country while ignoring the long-term consequences of the economic policy that allowed in the goods: unemployment and hunger for many Chileans. The same year, Radrigán wrote two full-length dramas: *Las brutas* and *El loco y la triste*. *Las brutas* (*The Beasts*) is based on the true story of three sisters found hanged in 1974 in a remote area of northern Chile, where they eked out a meager living by raising goats, cattle, and sheep. In *El loco y la triste*, a drunk and a prostitute holed up in a shantytown hut resist the authorities' determination to raze their dwelling in the only way they can: a suicidal dance of death amid the bulldozers demolishing their shack. Despite the harsh ending, the play displays the dark poetic humor that often rescues Radrigán's work from sentimentality: "Seems like I swallowed an earthquake," says Huinca as he tries to control his morning shakes.

In November 1980, Radrigán started his own theater company, Teatro Popular El Telón (The People's Curtain), together with the actor-director Nelson Brodt. Later they were joined by Pepe Herrera, Carlos Alberto Muñoz, Nancy Ortiz, Mariela Roi, Jaime Wilson, and Silvia Marín, who became Radrigán's longtime companion. The following year, El Telón staged the last four plays translated in this collection, the trilogy *Redoble fúnebre para lobos y corderos* (*Funeral Drums for Lambs and Wolves*) and *Hechos consumados* (*Finished from the Start*). Linked by the themes of isolation, loneliness, loss, poverty, despair, violence, and fear, each of these works involves a different kind of witnessing. The first play of the trilogy, the monologue *Isabel desterrada en Isabel* (*Isabel Banished in Isabel*), exposes the insides of a soul-shattering silence among Chileans under dictatorship. The second play, the monologue *Sin motivo aparente* (*Without Apparent Motive*), draws us into the mind of a criminal who speaks as a witness to his own crime, a crime spurred by the secret police. The third play in the trilogy, *El invitado* (*The Guest*), consists of a dialogue not only between its two characters but also between the characters and the audience, shattering the fourth wall by posing the unspoken question on many Chileans' minds during the eighties: why do we put up with the dictator? Radrigán's best-known play, *Hechos consumados*, draws on his experiences in the textile industry to depict an unemployed factory worker's fatal battle in defense of his dignity as a human being. The three main characters are witnesses to an endless stream of humanity invisible to the spectator—a clear allusion to the nation's disappeared.

In the early eighties, El Telón developed a system of touring and a staging aesthetic suited to resisting dictatorship. Advertising in newspapers and other media was out of the question, both because of the prohibitive cost and because of the fear of reprisals. Even handing out flyers was dangerous because the company had learned from personal experience that the authorities imposed stiff fines on distributors of unofficial propaganda. Besides, none of the company members wanted to risk having their names in print. Instead, the cast, director, and playwright would walk around a neighborhood knocking on doors and telling people there would be *teatro* later that day. In order to gather the largest possible audiences in church halls, gymnasiums, or outdoor plazas, as well as to avoid the 22 percent tax on profits, the company charged very little or granted free admission. An El Telón handbill from January 1982, typed in faded ink on Radrigán's old manual typewriter, promises free admission for two to a performance of *Redoble fúnebre para lobos y corderos* at the Teatro Bulnes in Santiago but pleads for donations from those who can afford to make them.

Radrigán's emphasis on character and on the spoken word, rather than on visual effects, has led some critics to compare his work to Jerzy Grotowski's poor theater.[28] But Radrigán was only vaguely aware of Grotowski when he began to develop his aesthetic and says he was shaped more by the exigencies of Chilean life under dictatorship than by European theories. For instance, the makeshift sets and costumes that never cost more than a total of five thousand pesos (about one hundred dollars)—a table, a bench, a boulder—allowed for quick setup and hasty departure, if necessary. The not-entirely-intentional result was an extraordinary emphasis on the actors, their words, their bodies, and their relationship with the spectators.

While mass media was heavily censored throughout the almost seventeen years of dictatorship, by the eighties the secret police tended to ignore theater, perhaps dismissing it as a harmless way of letting off steam or perhaps fearing that a crackdown would only mobilize opposition. With the exception of the imposition of fines for leafleting or hanging posters, and the occasional anonymous telephone threat, the authorities tolerated Radrigán's theater. In fact, the year 1982 brought Radrigán recognition by critics and mainstream journalists alike, as the Chilean Circle of Arts Critics awarded the prestigious award for best play of 1981 to *Hechos con-sumados.*[29] The next year, *El toro por las astas* (*The Bull by the Horns*) won both the Circle of Arts Critics award and the city of Santiago's prize for literature.[30] Chilean newspapers published profiles of the newly dis-covered playwright but refrained from any mention of his antidictator-ship message. Similarly, in interviews, Radrigán himself, asked about the "mission" of his theater, would say only that El Telón hoped to make people think, so that they would leave the theater internally changed.[31]

El Telón was prevented neither from touring Europe, twice, nor from making excursions to other parts of South America. In 1983, financed in part by the French government, the company traveled for two months through Italy, Sweden, France, Germany, Switzerland, and Holland, performing *Hechos consumados* and *El toro por las astas.*[32] The highlight of the trip was the company's three performances of *Hechos consumados* in a crowded 450-seat theater at the international theater festival in Nancy, France. After one of the shows, French journalists tried to elicit opin-ions about the dictatorship from Radrigán and the actors: Pepe Herrera, Nancy Ortiz, Mariela Roi, and Jaime Wilson. Company members cir-cumspectly replied that it wasn't their role to comment on their country's political situation.[33] El Telón's second European tour, between January and August 1988, featured sixty-two performances of a single play, *La contienda humana* (*The Human Struggle*), on a tour that took the com-pany through Germany, Switzerland, Italy, Sweden, France, England, Scotland, and Luxembourg. Radrigán himself directed the two-character play, which featured Hugo Medina as Eladio, a writer stricken with guilt over his inability to protect his wife from being disappeared from their own home, and Pepe Herrera as José, the writer's character animated in the form of a life-size doll. *La contienda humana* opened in Chile only after the European tour, on October 17, 1988.

Ironically, Pinochet's defeat in a 1988 plebiscite and the subsequent return of democracy to Chile in 1990 contributed to the demise of Radrigán's theater company. While under dictatorship, El Telón's com-pany members had been willing to sacrifice economic security for the sake of subverting authoritarian rule; under democracy, the actors began to feel the need to take better-paying work. Some career opportunities took company members far from Chile: One actor, Jaime Wilson, moved to Australia. Another, Carlos Alberto Muñoz, relocated to Sweden. Radrigán, meanwhile, was deeply disturbed by the terms under which Pinochet manipulated his own departure from power. The former dictator declared himself commander in chief of the army until 1998; neither could the other military commanders be replaced before then.[34] During his last months in office, Pinochet packed the supreme court with his allies, making it seem doubtful that many human rights violations would ever be prosecuted.[35] Many Allende supporters viewed the newly elected president, the Christian Democrat Patricio Aylwin, who led a coalition of fourteen parties called La Concertación, as a Judas who had betrayed Allende at the last minute by withdrawing support from the beleaguered leader's failing government. While much of the country was celebrating the return of democracy, Radrigán felt depressed rather than jubilant. Sensing that the new political reality called for a different dramatic style but uncertain of how to respond creatively, he went into what he calls his period of self-exile, during which he holed himself up in his apartment and stopped writing.

Between 1989 and 1993, El Telón remained dormant. Its final production, in 1993, was *Islas de porfiado amor,* in which a man and a woman who, for twenty years, have exiled themselves in a remote, uninhabited desert are so isolated that they wonder whether Allende won the presidential election. They have so little to do that their primary form of entertainment is to dress up and go watch a train speed by them. Like the train, time, life, and history itself have passed them by. While the protagonists are perhaps emblematic of Radrigán's psychological state as he wrote in the aftermath of the return to democracy, they also epitomize the exclusion from history of many Allende supporters, who struggled with the reality that a president as determined to lead the nation into socialism was unlikely to ever come to power in Chile again. In the spirit of many Radrigán characters, the female protagonist, Micaela, laments: "Since God is all that he is, doesn't he understand that something happened that no one can forget? Doesn't he understand that there are things a person cannot forgive, because she would cease to be a person?"[36] In Chilean history, for someone of Radrigán's political bent, the unforgivable includes the coup that deposed Allende and led to his suicide; the torture, exile, and disappearance of thousands of civilians; and the imposition of a neoliberal economic program that produced a "miracle" in terms of economic growth but proved catastrophic for the poorest 20 percent of the population.[37]

Radrigán fully emerged from his self-imposed seclusion in 1995 with the play *El encuentramiento* (*The Match*), a radical departure in form from his earlier works. A popular opera in verse set in colonial Chile, with music composed by Patricio Solovera, the play highlights the class and ethnic antagonisms between Europeans and Mapuche Indians present since the foundation of the nation. One of its last lines, "el duelo no ha terminao," puns on the double meaning of *duelo* as both "duel" and "mourning": "The duel/mourning is not over yet." Neither the battle for social justice that Allende's government represented for many nor the national mourning for the atrocities committed under dictatorship seemed over to Radrigán.

While the past decade has not brought economic justice to the poorest Chileans, it has renewed hopes of some measure of social justice for victims of human rights abuses and their families. Aylwin was succeeded first by another Christian Democrat, Eduardo Frei, and then by the nominally Socialist Ricardo Lagos, all of whom in fact, for the most part, continued the neoliberal economic program started under the dictatorship.[38] For years after the return to democracy, even some of the worst human rights abuses went unprosecuted. For a long time, the former head of the secret police, Manuel Contreras, was one of the few high-level Pinochet officials imprisoned, for plotting the murder of Letelier, Allende's former U.S. ambassador. In 1998, however, Pinochet was arrested in London and held under house arrest for fourteen months, until British authorities released him on the grounds that the then eighty-four-year-old former dictator was too ill to stand trial. Upon his return home in 2000, Chilean authorities finally began legal proceedings against him for human rights abuses. Yet once again, in 2002, he was found unfit to stand trial, this time on the grounds of mental deterioration.[39] According to the organization Human Rights Watch, 311 former military men, including twenty-one army generals, have been charged or convicted of human rights violations. Yet a 2004 government report ordered by Lagos confirmed that some twenty-eight thousand people, of the thirty-five thousand who claimed to have been tortured under detention, were indeed tortured.[40] This means, as Radrigán notes, that hundreds of police agents and former military men who tortured their prisoners are still in positions of social responsibility, some in government employ.

As of this writing, in 2006, another Socialist, Michelle Bachelet, Lagos's former defense minister, has recently won election to the presidency. Bachelet's father, an air force general who served in the Allende government, was subjected to torture despite a cardiac ailment and died in prison in 1974, after being refused medical care. The following year, Bachelet and her mother were also imprisoned briefly and then permitted to leave the country.[41] Despite her personal experience of political repression, however, it is unclear whether the election will give her the mandate necessary to vigorously pursue prosecutions of human rights abusers.

Two recent Radrigán plays express pessimism about the prospects for justice. In *Exilio de la mujer desnuda* (*Exile of the Nude Woman*), 2001, Radrigán personifies truth as a nude woman whom everyone is afraid to look at. His latest short monologue, a cross between a rant, a prayer, and a poem, *El desaparecido* (*The Disappeared*), 2004, fuses the image of a single victim of a political kidnapping with the idea of a vanished communal love. The protagonist, Victoria Torres, openly assaults the spectator with the losses she has suffered under dictatorship: a husband and two sons. Victoria's answer to her rhetorical question about herself, "When the hell will this crazy shit be quiet?" could easily represent Radrigán's answer to the question of when he will stop writing, or more precisely, since all men are mortal, when his characters will stop speaking to us: "Never."[42]

Theatrical *Testimonio*

The Radrigán plays collected here all undertake, in different ways, to bear witness. In so doing, they contribute to a Latin American genre that has come to be known as *testimonio*. Though rooted in actual political injustice, *testimonio* may be fictional: it may take narrative or theatrical form, and it may use poetic language to help position the individual character as a synecdoche for his or her community.[43] Sometimes, though not always, *testimonios* are narrated by illiterate protagonists to academics who then transcribe and edit the narratives, adopting the speaker's persona in order to write the story in the first person. While in the sixties and seventies *testimonio* was lauded for its potential to give expression to working-class, female, illiterate, and other disenfranchised voices, more recently the genre has been criticized for various reasons, including a supposed propensity to create a falsely homogeneous image of the community for which the testimonial subject speaks and an alleged tendency to "confirm stereotypical notions of the Third World subaltern as Other."[44] While those criticisms may be true of some works, in my view, the enduring power of Radrigán's dramas demonstrates that *testimonio*, at least in the theater, nevertheless demands that we listen to voices we might otherwise ignore.

The most significant difference between *testimonio* and autobiography, Doris Sommer notes, is that testimonial subjects see themselves as speaking for a class or community. "The important thing is that what has happened to me has happened to many other people too," Sommer quotes Rigoberta Menchú.[45] Menchú's landmark *testimonio, I Rigoberta Menchú: An Indian Woman in Guatemala* (1984), was narrated to the anthropologist Elisabeth Burgos-Debray and translated into English by Ann Wright. Another classic *testimonio*, the 1966 *Biografía de un cimarrón (The Autobiography of a Runaway Slave*, was written by Miguel Barnet and based on the life of a Cuban former slave, Esteban Montejo, who was more than one hundred years old when he told his story to Barnet. While the term *testimonio* has subsequently expanded from as-told-to narratives transcribed by academics to include the first-person writings of literate narrators as well, these writers also tend to identify with a larger, often persecuted, group, such as people who were imprisoned, tortured, and/or exiled under dictatorship.[46] "While sharing this part of my experience, I pay tribute to a generation of Argentines lost in an attempt to bring social change and justice. I also pay tribute to the victims of repression in Latin America. I knew just one Little School but throughout our continent there are many 'schools' whose professors use the lessons of torture and humiliation to teach us to lose the memories of ourselves," writes Alicia Partnoy in the introduction to *The Little School,* her 1986 first-person memoir of her illegal detention in an Argentine torture center.[47]

When *testimonio* is performed, rather than presented through a text—a documentary novel, an ethnography, an autobiography, or some hybrid of these genres—the confrontation between actor and spectator provides greater opportunity to challenge and subvert the official stories propagated by dominant elites. For one thing, it is much easier for a reader to close a book than it is for a spectator to leave a theater in the midst of a performance. The audience is held captive in a way that the reader is not. Radrigán has said that he began to write theater precisely because under dictatorship it seemed like the most effective way to reach people directly, with a minimum of mediation or censorship.[48]

The theatrical effectiveness of *testimonio* stems from what John Beverley describes as its potential for giving one "the sensation of *experiencing the real*."[49] If textual *testimonio* derives some of its potential for resistance from its strong link to oral tradition, then performed *testimonio* has even more resistant potential. The oral, and ephemeral, nature of performance creates the illusion that one is actually face-to-face with a previously voiceless voice, unedited and unencumbered by anthropologists or novelists or other intellectual helpers. In the theater, because there is no permanent text for the spectator to leave and return to, the mediation of the written text is hidden, relegated to the rehearsal process. The theatrical focus on the voice and the body eliminates the apparent contradiction of reading something supposedly "written" by someone who is illiterate and backgrounds the troubling questions raised by the relationship between the "native informant" and the writer: How much of this did the informant actually say, and how much of it did the mediator invent? What was changed or eliminated? In fact, much like the ghostwriters of narrative *testimonios*, the playwright has artfully selected and crafted a theatrical text. The characters cannot entirely deceive the spectators, who are, of course, aware that they are observing theatrical conventions and watching actors. Yet the physical presence of the actor nevertheless creates a greater sense of immediacy and urgency, a higher level of suspension of disbelief, and a genuine sense of excitement about the disclosure in a communal forum of what may be a societal secret, a widely known truth that is nevertheless usually voiced only to trusted friends. The excitement of the revelation may be accompanied by a heightened sense of responsibility, as spectators begin to see themselves as witnesses to a significant event, witnesses with a duty to acknowledge its significance and respond accordingly.

Just as important, performance has the advantage of being able to create the illusion that buried truth is being publicly revealed *for the first time*. This phenomenon is analogous to what political scientist James C. Scott describes as moments of open refusal to comply with social superiors: "the declaration of the hidden transcript."[50] In other words, what some people have been thinking or whispering to one another privately suddenly erupts in a public sphere, creating what Scott says is "an enormous impact . . . on the person (or persons) who makes the declaration and, often, on the audience witnessing it."[51] Radrigán's theater is full of these revelatory moments, moments that had an electrifying impact on audiences fed up with Pinochet's long rule but fearful of publicly expressing dissent. His plays revealed hidden transcripts so brazenly that at the conclusion of some performances, Radrigán recalls, spectators would sometimes shout obscenities and death threats to Pinocchio or *el hijo de puta* (the son of a bitch), as the dictator was referred to in popular code.[52] The political slogans that were eventually shouted in the streets were first symbolically stated in the theaters at least five years earlier, maintains Chilean sociologist María de la Luz Hurtado.[53] Some of the people who, in the late eighties, ventured from the safety of their homes to gather in the avenues and plazas, braving tear gas and bullets to chant, "He will fall! He will fall!" were the spectators who, in the late seventies and early eighties, not only filled theaters but also attended clandestine performances of music known as *peñas* and secret showings of films, circulated banned texts, and generally swam in a stream of oppositional discourse.

Testimonio has been criticized by scholars who note that the voice of an illiterate narrator must necessarily be mediated by that of the literate transcriber, who may err by either standardizing speech patterns and grammar, resulting in a neutralized and whitened language, or by reproducing idiomatic language, resulting in a folkloric caricature of a narrator.[54] It is difficult to see how the interlocutor, however well intentioned, can win. Yet I would argue that Radrigán pulls off a delicate balancing act, creating characters that are neither folkloric caricatures nor artificially articulate versions of the subaltern. He always treats his characters with the respect accorded to social equals: he lovingly pokes fun at times, but he never condescends or denigrates them. Whether confronting poor spectators in neighborhood gymnasiums or confronting middle-class audiences in comfortable theaters, whether in South America or in North America, these characters retain the capacity to change the way we conceive of social class and to challenge our assumptions about our right to economic privilege.

Because of his own working-class experience, unlike many university-educated Chilean playwrights, Radrigán doesn't have to do research to replicate the speech patterns of the poor. On my way to meet him for the first time, in the summer of 2001, I found myself lost in downtown Santiago and borrowed a map from a newsstand vendor, a stout man wearing an apron over his clothes. "I want to see where I am," I told him as I scanned the confusing jumble of crisscrossing lines on the large sheet of paper unfolded before me. "You standin right there. Can't you see yourself?" he said and burst into laughter at his own cleverness. My jaw dropped, too, not in amusement, but with the shock of recognition. He had just spoken a line from Radrigán's play, *Isabel desterrada en Isabel*. And what is more, he had spoken it with the same missing syllables, with the exact intonation that Mónica, my Chilean collaborator, had used when reading the work aloud to me.

Radrigán's theater, however, provides more than accurate transcription of the street slang of the urban poor—rich as it is with grammatical mistakes, missing consonants, added vowels, and meaningless interjections used as verbal exclamation marks. To that brew he adds his own invented malapropisms, humorous colloquialisms, piercing metaphors, and violent similes. "Thinking is the same as if they was to slash hope's throat right in front of your eyes," says Isabel. In this image, thought is not only personified but also given the corporal presence of a murderer. Yet Isabel, who barely feeds herself by cleaning houses and is so lonely that she makes friends with a garbage can, is neither neutralized nor folklorized (to make another clunky verb out of an adjective) by her obviously poetic, nonnaturalistic speech. If anything, the poetic image gives her tragic status, imbuing her despair with a dignity that transcends the grubbiness of her daily struggle, which is all that a spectator might see if she were to look and talk exactly like a "real" woman on the verge of homelessness and mental illness.[55]

As Beverley notes, the word *testimonio* evokes the idea of telling the truth in a legal or religious context, as in testifying in court or testifying to the presence of God.[56] The irony of Radrigán's theater is that while his characters search endlessly for a God, because that God is always silent, indifferent, or cruel, in the end they testify only to his absence. Radrigán's characters—whether they are homeless, close to homeless, hungry children, working poor, petty criminals, drunks, prostitutes, or murderers—yearn for divine intervention to bring them love, or at least justice. But the ultimate Witness doesn't seem to be paying adequate attention. Some of the funniest and most achingly beautiful moments in Radrigán's plays stem from his characters' attempts to articulate overwhelming pain and win salvation. But there is no salvation to be had from the false prophets, blank bureaucrats, and dutiful repressors who are always lurking in the background, usually relegated to offstage roles. It is the victims, not the victimizers, who are privileged with a stage presence, even though their hopes are usually frustrated. Emilio, in *Hechos consumados*, decides to take a heroic last stand against repression: he pays for it with his life. Luciana, in *Las brutas*, begs her older sister Justa to tell her what sensual love is like: Justa responds by describing her one-and-only experience of sex, which turns out to have been a rape. The isolated Isabel, in *Isabel desterrada en Isabel*, entertains herself by pretending to give God a good talking-to: "Damn, if I was God's wife, I'd say 'Listen up, Old Man, you're so into the miracle thing, open the eyes of the dopes down there. They're making a mess of the life you gave them. They dished out the laughter and bucks to a few, and to the others they gave silence and kicks in the ass.'" God does not respond.

Testimony to the Deaths of Sabina (*Testimonio de las muertes de Sabina*), 1979

The one-word cliché to sum up *Testimony to the Deaths of Sabina* is *Kafkaesque*. Yet the parallels between the bureaucratic maze in which the old fruit sellers Sabina and Rafael find themselves trapped and the plight of K. in *The Trial* cannot go unremarked. "Someone must have been telling lies about Josef K., for without having done anything wrong he was arrested one fine morning," begins Kafka's novel.[57] One fine morning, as she hawks her fruit from her street stall, Sabina is issued a citation, leading to a chain of events almost as grim as K.'s fate. Like K., Sabina and Rafael have no idea what they have done wrong. But, as in Kafka's universe, lack of guilt is no defense against punishment. More salient than situational similarities between the novel and the play, however, is the atmosphere of terror evoked by both, the sense of frustration and impotence in the face of a mysterious, superior, malevolent bureaucracy. Radrigán creates that atmosphere with a single eerie sound effect repeated at the end of each of three acts: heavy footsteps drawing closer and more threatening each time.

The authentic witness in *Testimony* is as absent as a real trial in *The Trial*. Sabina's tragedy is that no one but she herself is capable of testifying to her despair. Rafael doesn't understand her. Their grown children don't come to visit. The neighbor she yells at through the wall doesn't respond. Each failure to witness leads to another one of her metaphoric deaths. Sabina's lament for herself uses deceptively simple words to express profound existential anguish: "No, no one's gonna remember me. No one's gonna go see me or talk about me; I'm gonna die more than everyone else! I'm gonna die so much when I die!" In an interview published the day after the play opened, Radrigán enumerated Sabina's deaths as the deaths of faith, hope, and future.[58]

What Radrigán and the reviewers who lauded the play in the heavily censored press could only hint at was that the work strongly suggests that these deaths represented more than an individual trauma: they were a social consequence of the 1973 coup. When Gustavo Meza directed Ana González and Arnaldo Berríos in the premiere of the play at Santiago's Teatro de los Comediantes, all three were conscious of that subtext. One of Meza's directorial decisions underscored a sense of lost time: at several key moments, the actors would freeze, as if a snapshot were being taken of them on the brink of an abyss.[59] At the same time, according to what reviewers did publish, González and Berríos skillfully maneuvered the full range of emotions related to their mutual blend of love and personal betrayal, from tenderness to rage. One reviewer praised the depiction of the marriage but complained that the actors tended to break the intimacy of that relationship by directing too many of their lines to the spectators.[60] It is precisely those moments that break the fourth wall that implicate the spectators for their failure to function as effective witnesses, not just on Sabina's behalf, but on behalf of the economically disadvantaged they encounter in daily life. The play's final lines, for instance, could easily be directed toward the spectator as a commentary not only on the loss of a fruit stand but also on the loss of Allende and the hope he represented for many poor people:

> SABINA [*emptily*]: If they don't respect us, they don't listen to us, we can't live . . . I've lived my whole life in a pipe dream; I couldn't never have nothing that was mine forever . . . They could come any day and take it all away . . . What world do we live in? What shitty world do we live in?

The other significant allusion to the Pinochet dictatorship that audiences in 1979 would have immediately recognized is Sabina and Rafael's economic reality. Though, on the one hand, Pinochet's government attempted to address some of the problems of the very poor, on the other hand, the authorities suspected the economically disadvantaged, particularly if they betrayed any tendency toward labor activism, as a possible Communist threat.[61] Meanwhile, economic shock treatment administered in order to shift the economy from the road to socialism to the road to free-market capitalism caused unemployment and underemployment to skyrocket. Constable and Valenzuela describe an informal sector composed of vendors of every conceivable product and service: "People invented an astonishing array of survival tactics: raising plants to barter for used clothes, cooking empanada meat pies to sell at soccer games, playing the guitar on buses at rush hour. A society of peddlers sprang up, lining the downtown Ahumada Promenade and chanting out their prices as they scanned the block for foot patrolmen. At the sound of a whistle, they snatched up their displays of socks or nail files and vanished into the crowd."[62]

As Constable and Valenzuela note, women tended to fare better than men in the informal sector, exacerbating tension between couples who held traditional gender-role expectations.[63] Radrigán depicts the excruciating humiliation of the man who is not living up to his role as provider in Sabina's lapses into contempt for Rafael. "You're the man!" she reminds him, as if it were his responsibility to save their livelihood. When angry, she calls him a pimp, because the fruit stall was originally her business: he only began to work there with her after losing his job as a textile worker.

In the *lotería* deck of Radrigán characters, the image of the unemployed textile worker will come up again as Emilio in *Finished from the Start,* in which the thieving Rafael has morphed into a far more noble character defeated not by his own dishonesty but by free-market economic policies beyond his control.

The Beasts (*Las brutas*), 1980

Set in the mountains of northern Chile, *The Beasts* is based on the actual story of three sisters—Justa, age fifty-three; Luciana, forty-three; and Lucía Quispe Cardozo, forty—who were found hanged from a boulder on December 4, 1974. Though they did not leave behind a note and no one could explain why they would have taken their lives, the deaths were ruled a suicide.[64] Radrigán's play accepts that premise and builds on it to portray the sisters as both victims of their own fears of state repression and of their inability to face a grim life of urban poverty, should they relocate. At the same time, they face a difficult truth: as they grow older they will soon be too weak to do the manual labor necessary to survive alone in the wilderness tending their cows and goats. While Chekhov's three cultured sisters yearn for the lost glamour of Moscow, Radrigán's *brutas*—meaning "coarse," "rough," or "unpolished," as in a "diamond in the rough"—live in terror of the city.[65] They have no television, no radio, and can neither read nor write. Lucía, the middle sister, suggests going to find the government to verify the alarming rumor they have heard, that the military police are coming to kill all their animals as a way of combating land erosion caused by grazing. Yet her younger and older sisters reject the idea as impossibly far-fetched. The Government (capitalized in the text), to them, is a mysterious abstraction beyond human contact:

> LUCIANA: And how we gonna meet up with that there Government if we don't know where he's at? Didn't you hear how Mr. Javier said he ain't in Copiapó, that he's in some other place real far off? . . . What are we gonna do, Justa?
>
> JUSTA: Don't know. Been thinking about it for a long time, but I don't know what we can do . . . They say that they come in a big bunch, that you can't do nothin against them.

The sisters are so far outside the reach of "civilization" that they cannot even begin to imagine how they would appeal to the sort of bureaucracy that so bedevils the urban poor in *Testimony*.

Besides explicitly alluding to the threat of military repression, the drama more indirectly alludes to the punishment of internal banishment that the government inflicted on many of its imagined or actual dissidents. Exile to a remote rural area far from the capital city of Santiago was a way of rendering potential critics impotent. Student leaders, left-wing teachers, military officers insufficiently enthusiastic about the coup, and a host of others were sentenced from days to years in isolated areas intended to perpetuate what Jacobo Timerman called a "culture of fear."[66] While such fear could pervade urban as well as rural areas, in centralized nations such as Chile, in which cultural and political life tends to revolve around the capital city, being wrenched from one's Santiago home and sentenced to live in a remote region of the country is particularly terrifying. The experience engenders what Timerman describes as an extreme sense of vulnerability, a state of constant alert, a feeling of individual impotence, and a loss of contact with reality such that "it comes to seem practically impossible to verify what is objective fact as against subjective experience."[67] While the sisters in *The Beasts* are not formally sentenced to live alone, their society has equipped them for little else and breeds all the symptoms of the culture of fear, including an inability to distinguish subjective anxieties from objective realities: rumors about authorities killing off their cattle send them into panic.[68]

The Beasts moves toward its morbid finale as inexorably as a Greek tragedy. Perhaps the most tragic of the three characters is Luciana, because she displays a hunger for life and a curiosity about sensual experience that distinguishes her from her older sisters. Luciana personifies a contest in which fate conquers free will: while she does not want to die, once her sisters have made up their minds to kill themselves, her future is sealed. Like Antigone or Iphigenia, who lament dying as virgins, Luciana realizes that she would have enjoyed sexual experience, would have liked to have had children—in short, would have liked to have lived more. Though in Radrigán's drama Luciana is forty-seven years old, she has "the soul of an adolescent," said Odette Cortesi, the actor who played Luciana in Teatro el Rostro's 1982 staging, one of the play's earliest and most significant productions. "Of the three, she is the most romantic, tragic, and immature."[69] Gradually, her sisters convince Luciana that she has no choice but to follow their lead and die along with them.

The oldest sister, Justa, is the leader of the pack. From the start of the play, the opening stage directions describe her already braiding a rope, the rope that she will eventually use to tie her sisters together and hang them. Like Madame Defarge's knitting in *Tale of Two Cities*, the rope acquires the sinister aura of inevitable death. Justa's name, which means "just," raises the question of whether in fact she is just in her sentence of death. Underlying Justa's logic of suicide lurks a bitterness born of frustrated hopes: for years, she and her father fruitlessly searched the hills for a deposit of gold ore; the one man she might have loved raped her. Yet Justa is no cold-blooded executioner. She does not physically force her sisters to participate in her plan: she convinces them with the strength of her arguments. If what she says is true, that she walked for two days searching for people and found that everyone had abandoned the region, then they are indeed doomed to starvation or death from the cold, sooner or later. The decision to take matters into their own hands may therefore be interpreted as a sign of defiance rather than of resignation.

The middle sister, Lucía, at first seems the most conformist of the three. Whatever Justa orders, Lucía obeys. Neither as embittered as Justa nor as naive as Luciana, Lucía nevertheless cannot face change. She would rather die than break her routine of knitting woolen clothing, caring for the animals, and completing her chores. She, not Justa, is the first to voice the thought of suicide: "If something happens that we gotta go, I'd rather kill myself: I ain't scared of that."

Justa's rape and the sisters' suicides exemplify both the horror of crimes without witnesses and the process of identification by which testimony can belatedly create witnesses.[70] As Justa recounts her violation to her sisters in stark, matter-of-fact language, her pain becomes their pain to such an extent that Luciana reacts with anger rather than with sympathy. Radrigán in turn makes himself, along with his readers or spectators, the only witnesses to the deaths of the three women, who died as alone as they lived. He forces us to feel their anguish, not in the service of our own catharsis but for the sake of their memory.

The first two productions of *The Beasts*, appropriately enough, opened in smaller cities far from the urban capital of Santiago: Valparaiso and Concepción. The Valparaiso production was the earliest (August 1980), directed by Arnaldo Berríos, who the year before had played Rafael in *Sabina*. Because *The Beasts* was staged in Valparaiso's Chilean–North American Institute of Culture, one review from the era cautiously refrains from praising the production directly, instead citing the U.S. cultural attaché Guy Burton, who compared the play to works of Chekhov and noted its exploration of the relationship between humanity and nature. No mention was made of any of the drama's more subversive themes.[71] Over the years, the play has been restaged in countries as far flung as Sweden (1987), France (1999), Uruguay (2002), and Slovenia (2003).

Isabel Banished in Isabel (Isabel desterrada en Isabel), 1981

The first of two monologues and a dialogue collected under the trilogy *Funeral Drums for Lambs and Wolves* (*Redoble fúnebre para lobos y corderos*), *Isabel Banished in Isabel* underscores the human craving to speak and to be heard. As the title indicates, the protagonist is exiled within herself and from the mainstream of society. A survivor of the Pinochet dictatorship, Isabel, like the survivors of an earlier disaster, the Holocaust, described by Shoshana Felman and Dori Laub, needs to tell her story and needs a witness to listen to it: "The survivors did not only need to survive so that they could tell their stories; they also needed to tell their stories in order to survive. There is, in each survivor, an imperative need to tell and thus to know one's story, unimpeded by ghosts from the past against which one has to protect oneself. One has to know one's buried truth in order to be able to live one's life."[72]

As isolated as Sabina and the Quispe Cardozo sisters, Isabel reincarnates the figure that a Radrigán *lotería* game card might title "the lonely woman." Even more violently than Sabina rejects her husband, Isabel turns against her boyfriend, Aliro. His habit of mortally injuring the birds they sell to earn a living, his way of trying to ensure a steady supply of return customers, proves too much for her to tolerate. Isabel reports him to the police in hopes of preventing further deterioration of her world into a place where no birds sing: "Now no one talks, no one laughs, no one says hello; the birds are the only ones that sing. If they're quiet, all of life will be quiet, and us that don't have nothin, we's gonna die crushed by the silence." But after Aliro's imprisonment, which as sometimes occurred under dictatorship, continued for a mysteriously long time, Isabel's fear becomes her reality: like the birds, she is slowly crushed by silence. When, at the monologue's conclusion, she kicks and screams at a garbage can because it will not speak to her, it is unclear whether her fit of rage is temporary or whether loneliness has finally driven her mad.

Isabel's address to the garbage can, a reflection of her degradation, also reveals a desperate desire to tell her truth. Her steady stream of speech, unbroken by pauses, combats the general silence she complains of, a silence, the work hints, imposed by dictatorship's culture of fear. In response, like Radrigán himself, producing play after play, Isabel talks relentlessly; she speaks, therefore she is. She talks to herself, she talks to the garbage can, she talks to God, she tries unsuccessfully to talk to a stranger, and she talks to the audience.

The compulsion to speak, however, also recalls Felman's description of how, despite the need to talk in order to reestablish a sense of self, Holocaust survivors and other trauma victims may also suffer a loss of language, a sense that language is incommensurate with their experience.[73] If Isabel's speech represents a failed attempt to compensate for loss, then her silences indicate an even more dire victimization. At several key points in her life, the spectator learns, Isabel endures abuse without being able to speak in her own defense. She doesn't know how to respond to the employer who wants to pay her for house cleaning with a bottle of wine instead of the food she needs. Words are inadequate for the task of righting wrongs. Words fail to describe emotional longings or physical hunger. When she looks into the eyes of a hungry child eagerly devouring a rotten apple, words prove insufficient: "She just stared at me; didn't say nothing to me. And what did she need to talk for, cuz her eyes was screaming everything that was happening to her." The child's silent hunger mirrors Isabel's own muted childhood and her inability to find language that fully redresses the injury suffered. No matter how much she speaks, what she says, or how eloquently she says it, like many Chileans under dictatorship, Isabel is destroyed by a series of losses—of her parents, of her life partner, of her ability to earn a living—none of which lament can restore.

In the tradition of *testimonio*, the silence Isabel complains of extends beyond her individual world to Chilean society at large. When she tries to bum a cigarette from passersby, they ignore her. When she responds to a stranger who she thinks is talking to her, he curses her. Near the end of the play, the stage directions indicate that she breaks the fourth wall to look at the audience as she asks: "How could we let this happen? How could we let it happen?" The trauma is social rather than individual; the blame must be shared with the spectators. Presumably already listening, and looking, by virtue of their role as spectators, the audience members are implicitly asked to keep their senses alert after they leave the performance and to assume the responsibility of listening to people like Isabel.

The mute public is depicted in Isabel as something new, something that is happening *now* as opposed to during some unspecified time in the past. The implicit comparison is between a "then" before dictatorship and a "now" under dictatorship, when talking might lead to one's imprisonment or imprisonment of a loved one. The birdsong that Isabel protects at great cost to herself recalls the voices of protest to dictatorship, in particular folksingers, who were especially prominent in Chile.[74] Chilean voices of dissent were sometimes ignored, sometimes brutally repressed, and sometimes self-censored. Though Isabel is no folksinger, no savvy political leader agitating from exile against dictatorship, her voice nevertheless poses a threat to the prevailing order. By focusing on the symptom, the silence, she encourages the spectator to consider the disease, dictatorship. The simple act of drawing attention to the silence in a public forum breaks it. Isabel's voice, and Radrigán's drama, then becomes a kind of birdsong that pierces the general stillness.

Isabel is one of Radrigán's most frequently staged plays, with more than a dozen different productions in Chile, Uruguay, Argentina, Sweden, Belgium, Australia, and the United States. The earliest productions, beginning with the El Telón version in 1980 directed by Nelson Brodt and featuring Gloria Barrera and Miriam Pérez alternating as Isabel, tended to stress the pathos of the protagonist. Later versions tend to depart from realistic portrayals. One particularly whimsical Isabel, Alexandra Von Hummel directed by Mariana Muñoz, performed the play in the parking lot of the University of Chile's theater school in 2000. Reviewers found Von Hummel refreshing for her lack of self-pity and youthful energy.[75] Yet that superficial cheer may have been intended to impart more than a hint of irony about contemporary consumer society: Von Hummel entered on a giant tricycle, wearing a Barbie-doll pink dress and waving as if she were a beauty queen greeting the crowds from her parade float. The use of pop music, along with a circuslike wealth of kitschy props and costume elements, further transformed the play from a critique of Chile as a terrorist state to a comment on the terror of Chile today as an ultracapitalist state.

Without Apparent Motive (*Sin motivo aparente*), 1981

The monologue *Without Apparent Motive* undertakes the difficult task of depicting the mind of a criminal without judging him and without sentimentalizing or romanticizing him either. The apparent senselessness of an act of random violence is peeled away to reveal that it is not in fact senseless, but rather a product of the dictatorship. Like Isabel, Pedro speaks to an inanimate object: the corpse of a stranger he has murdered, in retribution for the killing of his friend. He recounts to the corpse the tragicomic story of the events leading up to both deaths. After learning that his hard-drinking loner of a buddy is dying of cirrhosis of the liver, he devises an elaborate plan to "marry" him off to a prostitute in a sham wedding ceremony. To his horror, he then discovers that his friend would rather not marry but prefers to remain in solitude. The wedding plans canceled, the friend, drunk again, is reaching into his pocket to get some cash when he is shot by a man we are given to understand is a member of the security forces. Enraged, Pedro vents his fury on the first passing stranger he encounters.

Witnessing, I have been arguing, on the basis of the work of theorists of both *testimonio* and the Holocaust, has a redemptive value: it can feed the viewer's determination to survive, strengthen his or her identity, speed the psychic healing process, and disseminate evidence of atrocity to the entire world. But seeing has its dangers, too. In *Without Apparent Motive,* Radrigán depicts witnessing as a corrosive force that can destroy the viewer's ethical core. On the one hand, Pedro mocks the physical contortions that some will engage in to avoid acknowledging an act of violence: "Haven't you noticed that when something happens in the street, people turn their heads away and start walking like they was glued to the wall? Some people seem like they turned into hunchbacks all of a sudden, they walk so bent over." But on the other hand, the work itself recognizes that there are good reasons why people fear confrontations with violence, reasons that transcend the desire to avoid an unpleasant experience. Witnessing, in this case, far from giving Pedro insight into his own buried truth, turns him into a killer.

Pedro is a witness, but he is neither an innocent survivor nor a worker in what Primo Levi calls "the gray zone," forced to serve a repressive regime in order to survive.[76] Instead, he is at once a victim and an alienated product of such a regime: touched by the machinery of violence, he, too, learns to kill as casually as if the lives of others hold no value. More marginal than even the lowest rung in the official structure of repression, he maintains his independence, freelancing violence, so to speak, without any control from above. Felman divides witnesses of the Holocaust into three groups: those who witnessed it as victims, those who witnessed it as perpetrators, and those who witnessed it as bystanders.[77] Pedro embodies the complexities of all three vantage points: he is a victim and a bystander to his friend's killing, yet also a perpetrator of his revenge killing. Like Isabel, and like most Radrigán characters, Pedro witnesses from the perspective of the subaltern: uneducated, impoverished, and underemployed in casual, unskilled labor. And like many Radrigán characters, Pedro fails as a witness in that his testimony neither redeems nor heals. Although at one point Pedro begs his victim for forgiveness, in the end he assumes a defiant attitude, refusing even to give the corpse the dignity of a proper burial.

The irony of Pedro's stance is heightened by what he says about the friend we meet only through his narrative. The nameless friend seems like a cross between one of Sam Shepard's urban cowboys and a more traditional Christ figure. To Pedro's schemes to dupe people seeking taxis, he responds with lofty maxims about how "you gotta . . . live fighting, but fighting a clean fight." When confronted with the consequences of rioting after the coup, the friend preaches nonviolence on all sides. The character is so exaggeratedly loving and morally upright that he might prove unbearably self-righteous if it weren't for his tragicomic flaw—his drunkenness. His fondness for the bottle gives him a Falstaffian vulnerability that softens the edges of his probity. His lessons of honesty, nonviolence, love, and rugged independence are lost on Pedro, however, as he stubbornly employs all manner of underhanded scheming to find his pal a mate. Much like those who kill in the name of religious icons, Pedro violates all of his would-be spiritual leader's teachings. His friend would not have approved of revenge killing, he concedes. The character who couldn't hate is the one who must die, leaving as witnesses a much less loving and lovable sort. Despite the friend's Christ-like demeanor, he was no martyr and his death was not a sacrifice: nothing was gained by it.

The nameless friend fits a type that can be found in at least two other Radrigán works, Moisés in *Pueblo del mal amor* (*The People of Twisted Love*), 1986, and a character called the Miracle Worker in *El toro por las astas:* the powerless prophet to whom others look in vain for salvation. Far from leading his people to the Promised Land, Radrigán's version of Moses fails to prevent their massacre. The ironically named Miracle Worker is another comic Christ figure—a carpenter with a girlfriend named Magdalena, who has no wisdom to impart to his disappointed and angry would-be followers other than, "Life is inside of you, and if you don't live it, who can? There are no miracles." Perhaps Radrigán's characters must testify to their own despair because neither other mortals nor supernatural forces will ever serve as the perfect witness that one might hope for. Much as Allende's promise never came to fruition, the longed-for savior is always elusive. The witnesses who matter most to Radrigán are not the characters but rather the spectators, who are always implicitly invited to assume responsibility for improving the world the characters depict. In a 1989 essay introducing *La contienda humana*, Radrigán explained: "When we portray the country as broken and heartbreaking, we are saying that that is the actual state of things, that we should start to build from there; we are not saying that we should keep licking our wounds for all eternity."[78]

The Guest, or Tranquility Is Priceless (El invitado, o la tranquilidad no se paga con nada), 1981

More than any other Radrigán work, this last play of the *Funeral Drums* trilogy openly confronts the spectators with their responsibility to witness. The dialogue between Pedro and Sara consistently breaks the fourth wall between actor and audience, as the performers turn the tables on the spectators and make them the object of their scrutiny. Under the actors' gaze, the spectators become conscious of themselves as performers:

SARA [*calling*]: All right then, come in.

[PEDRO *enters unwillingly, not at all tranquil.*]

Speak. [*Gesturing toward the audience*] There they are.

The middle-aged couple, we learn, has something to ask us. But before they can bring themselves to do so, Sara and Pedro must first tell us the story of their relationship's decline. They perform a series of flashback skits that speak to various episodes in their struggle to survive since a mysterious, malevolent character called the Guest invaded their lives, robbing them of their paychecks, their desire to have children, their hope for a better future. The flashbacks are such discrete entities that one could imagine them staged Brechtian style, with placard titles: THE TELEVISION APPEARANCE, THE BOXING MATCH, THE WELFARE JOB OFFICE, HIDING FROM THE GUEST, FIGHTING, THE DAY WE MET. In the flashbacks, we see the couple struggle to find an adequate witness to their humiliation: they fail each other; the media fails them; the Guest's perverse spying destroys them; and, finally, they invite the spectators to testify to their own experience of the Guest.

In typical testimonial fashion, Sara and Pedro underscore their connection to the other working poor of their socioeconomic class:

PEDRO [*stubbornly*]: From the beginning.

[PEDRO *strikes a pose and addresses the audience.*]

>One day a man that worked on construction met a woman that worked in a factory: that's when I was born. My name is Pedro, like my father; but if I go passing by anywhere and someone says José, Mario, Guillermo, Pancho, Tito, or Antonio, I turn my head and look, because it's me they're calling. I'm the one who never went to school, the one who only got up to sixth grade, cuz he had to go out and earn a living; the one who falls from the top of the scaffolding and the one who picks him up . . .
>
>SARA: My name is Sara, but it's the same as if it was Carmen, Rosa, or María, and it's the same as if I was smaller or bigger, more black or more white; it's just the same, cuz inside my bones is stuck the same laughter and the same troubles . . . I ended up this way after a miracle, an economic miracle, I've heard em call it.

The long list of common names with which the characters identify indicates that they speak for the common woman and the common man. The wide variety of occupations and the range of physical attributes they describe, however, also counters a tendency to lump all the poor together. The poor are at once "the same," all victims of Pinochet's right-wing economic policies, and different, individuals with different identities involved in an alienating struggle for survival.

The media, heavily censored under Pinochet, is mocked as a laughably inadequate witness to the grim reality experienced by people like Sara and Pedro. Radrigán parodies the escapism of an actual television program of the era and its facilely cheerful segment, "Buck Up, Buddy." Sara competes on a television game show with the ludicrous title of *Cheer Up, Ms. Dying-of-Hunger!* The game show is interrupted by an emergency news flash that turns out to be nothing more than a society wedding announcement, the playwright's jab at how government-controlled media slighted reporting on dire economic news in favor of lighter fare. The media machine pretends that the obscene gap between rich and poor does not exist, that the lives of the rich and famous are the general rule. At the same time, the media engages in flat-out exploitation: if he wins his boxing match, Pedro will be beaten up rather than rewarded, because it is his opponent who is being promoted as the rising star. And television's illusory glamour may easily seduce the disenfranchised: a woman who mixes martinis on a television commercial fuels Pedro's sexual fantasies. Yet the characters are not totally duped. Alluding to one of the regime's favored opiates, the cult of soccer, Pedro jokes that if five hundred lives were lost in an earthquake, the headlines would trumpet the national soccer team's "heroic deed" in winning despite having five hundred fewer fans.

An even more inadequate witness than the media is the Guest himself. Asked who or what the Guest symbolizes, Radrigán answers with a refreshing lack of authorial coyness: "Pinochet." To call Pinochet "the Guest" emphasizes a single fact about the dictator's rule, that a large percentage, perhaps the majority, of Chileans at least initially supported the coup that brought him to power. Furthermore, the 1978 and 1980 plebiscites, though deeply flawed as exercises in democracy, showed that some voters did indeed welcome his leadership.[79] The same public that "invited" him, the play suggests, has the responsibility to oust him. At the same time, the moniker "the Guest" ironically underscores how dislodging the military dictator would prove far more difficult than ridding oneself of unwanted company. Finally, the play implicitly asks, "Whose guest is he anyway?" calling attention to how the vast majority of Pinochet's supporters came from the upper-middle and upper classes.

The Guest prods us to consider the role of an adequate witness versus that of a repressive spy. Both the witness and the spy rely on their sense of sight and hearing. Yet while the former uses information gathered to tell the truth of what happened to a victim, to attempt to redress the injury, the latter uses information to further victimize. During his long self-appointed reign, Pinochet appeared to have eyes and ears everywhere, a sinister presence dramatized by the scene in which Sara and Pedro move their chest of drawers to try to block his view of their bed, thus ending his intrusion into their most intimate moments. The play both denigrates Pinochet as a Peeping Tom and magnifies him as an Orwellian force that makes privacy obsolete. A big man with a well-trimmed mustache that evoked Hitler to his detractors and Grandpa to his supporters, Pinochet's image was ubiquitous: on television, in the media, on billboards, and even in unflattering graffiti depicting him as a pig or as Pinocchio, as opponents nicknamed him. His incongruously thin, high voice could often be heard on the radio.[80] On the one hand, the middle-of-the-night raids in working-class neighborhoods, the house-to-house searches, and the beatings and arrests of "vagrants" begging for food were all associated with Pinochet. On the other hand, the free candy handed out to poor children, the cartoons shown to entertain them, the makeshift jobs organized to keep their parents busy, and the enforced order in the streets were also linked to him.[81] As Catherine Boyle notes, Sara and Pedro's home serves as a metaphor for a nation under surveillance.[82] Chilean opponents of dictatorship, like the inmates in the prison cells arranged around a central spy tower, the panopticon famously described by Michel Foucault, might never know for sure whether they were being observed at any particular moment, but they always had the sense that someone might be checking up on them.

The most important witness in *The Guest,* however, is neither the Guest nor the characters, but rather the spectator. The frame of the action implicates the spectator. At the beginning the characters announce that they have a question for the spectator; at the end they finally spit out their concern: "We want you to tell us how you got used to living with the Guest." In effect, they demand that the spectator testify to his or her own experience. During the dictatorship, according to Radrigán, the vast majority of audience members simply responded with silence, implicating themselves as absent would-be witnesses. Yet in one more recent postdictatorship production staged by the tiny No Más (No More) theater company in Santiago in August 2005, some members of the audience of fewer than a dozen people felt moved to actually call out and respond with brief, disjointed confessions such as "I left the country," and "I became a poet."[83] In the wake of physical and psychic violence, sometimes testimony, however awkward, may be the only possible self-defense.

Finished from the Start (*Hechos consumados*), 1981

Finished from the Start adds a mystical complication to the problem of witnessing: Who will serve as witnesses to the disappeared victims of political repression? And are we witnesses to them or are they witnesses to us? Where are the souls of those who were executed and hastily disposed of, never to be seen again, or to be identified only years later when their remains are recovered from unmarked graves? A surreal motif—a constant stream of mysterious people who walk by for no apparent reason—laced through an otherwise naturalistic plot reminds us that the disappeared have never been erased from social memory. The stage directions describe the parade of humanity as invisible to the spectators. They are, however, visible to the main characters, who react with a blend of wonder, fear, and empathy. The spectators can only "see" the disappeared through the descriptions of Marta and Emilio, two homeless strangers squatting on an empty lot. Yet Marta and Emilio's testimony proves insufficient: they describe the invisible essences only in the most general terms—male and female, young and old—leaving the spectators free to picture them as they will. Asked to witness something they cannot literally see, the spectators are therefore challenged to consider how they can use their imagination to testify to violence that most of them never experienced directly.

Besides being asked to witness the atrocity of disappearance, the spectator to *Finished* is also prodded to acknowledge the less spectacular violence inflicted by the dictatorship's neoliberal economic policies. Both the male protagonist, Emilio, and his antagonist, Miguel, come from an underclass that grew larger and more desperate even as the national economy's growth and low inflation won international recognition as a supposed economic miracle. The two characters share a history of work in textile factories, an industry that Radrigán knew intimately from years of experience on its machinery and in its unions, an industry devastated by sudden elimination of tariffs on cheap foreign imports and by new probusiness labor laws. Suddenly union organizing was banned; wages were slashed; working days extended at times to twelve hours; and high unemployment made it easy to replace any workers who protested.[84] Emilio is the worker who has already lost everything. Since many firms, especially those that had made the decision to train workers on new technologies, refused to hire workers over the age of thirty, a middle-aged man like Emilio faced a lifetime of unemployment.[85] When a factory went bankrupt, as many did (particularly in 1982–83, making Radrigán's play seem prophetic of a devastating trend), workers could lose severance pay and pensions overnight. Miguel is the worker who is barely hanging on, working longer and longer hours only to fall further and further behind. Though he clearly feels some sympathy toward the defiant Emilio, their very similarities terrify him. Miguel dreads ending up like his counterpart: hungry and humiliated despite a savage defense of his dignity as a human being. Under different circumstances, they might have been friends. Instead, when Emilio defies Miguel's order to move along, economic desperation pushes them into mortal conflict.

Though Emilio proves perceptive and courageous, he cannot serve as the play's ideal witness because he is marked for death, and in a sense he has already died. He exists in a kind of purgatory, neither fully alive nor truly dead, yet already identifying strongly with the dead, bringing to mind the ghostly characters in the Latin American classic *Pedro Páramo,* by Mexican novelist Juan Rulfo. When Emilio and Marta recount the loss of their loved ones and livelihood, the folksy lyricism of their language, though inflected by urban Chile rather than rural Mexico, nevertheless recalls how Rulfo's characters use deceptively simple turns of phrase with heavy symbolic and emotional loads. For example, the narrator of Rulfo's 1953 short story "Nos han dado la tierra" ("They Gave Us the Land") takes a look around at the barren stretch of earth his people have been deeded by the government and laments: "No, the plain is no good for anything. There are no rabbits or birds. There's nothing. Except a few scrawny huizache trees and a patch or two of grass with the blades curled up; if it weren't for them, there wouldn't be anything."[86] Radrigán's characters similarly speak in short, repetitive sentences that cut to the heart of whatever matter they discuss. In an urban variation on the use of geography as a metaphor in *The Beasts, Finished from the Start*'s setting on an empty lot on the outskirts of the capital city also uses barren land as an image for a people bereft of hope:

EMILIO: Gardens? . . . There any left?

MARTA: Almost none. [*Pause.*] That's what makes me real mad at people: they locked themselves up in their houses and let the gardens die.

EMILIO: If only that was all they did.

MARTA: But it was the worst . . . This was the time for the carnations, for the mums, and the dahlias, afterwards came the time for the gladiolas and the giant mums. Everything looked so pretty, full of color . . . But they let the gardens dry up. And I say: what's folks gonna do when spring comes and there ain't no flowers?

Rulfo's influence shows in both the plaintive tone and the importance placed on the relationship with nature, as evidenced by the repetition of the key word *gardens*. For Radrigán, too, the desiccated earth serves as a figure for the inner death of the characters.

Emilio's physical death ensues from his adamant refusal to compromise his principles, recalling Salvador Allende, who refused to abandon the presidential palace even as Pinochet's troops bombed and invaded it. In a similar act of suicidal defiance, Emilio refuses to budge, refuses to move even a few feet to the other side of a property line. Yet it would be a stretch to read the penniless Emilio as a figure for Allende, who was a cultured politician, an eloquent speaker from Chile's privileged class. Similarly, Miguel is no Pinochet. A victim of forces more powerful than he, if anything, his inadequacy as a witness stems from his habit, like the lowest-ranking soldier, of following immoral orders without question.

The prophetic figure of Aurelio cannot witness because he focuses on the future, not the past, foretelling the death of Emilio. Besides, he speaks in such Cassandra-like conundrums that ordinary people could not understand his testimony.

That leaves Marta, the woman Emilio rescues from drowning. Accidental witnessing almost costs Marta her life, as she is thrown in a canal by some men whom she accidentally spies disposing of a body. As in *Without Apparent Motive*, witnessing has its dangers. Nevertheless, in the end, Marta once again assumes the function of a witness, watching powerlessly as Miguel clubs Emilio to death, screaming the final question to the audience: "What did they do to us? What the hell did they do to us?" The most comprehending witness of the disappeared has himself disappeared, leaving Marta as a witness, who then turns to the audience, passing the responsibility along to them and planting the question in the spectators' mind: who will be the next victim?

El Telón performed the original production of *Finished from the Start* in some of the poorest shantytowns of Santiago: La Victoria, La Pintana, Lo Hermida, San Gregorio. Under the direction of Nelson Brodt, with a production budget of less than one hundred dollars, there was no set, sound, or lighting design. The stage properties consisted of a clothesline, a few items of clothing, two large cloth sacks, four logs set in a square and surrounded by stones, and a couple of empty tin cans from which the characters drink their tea. When the play was performed outdoors, if a stray dog wandered onto the playing area, the actor playing Emilio (Pepe Herrera) would improvise and pretend that the dog was part of the play. When the play was performed indoors, the company indulged in a single low-tech "special effect": a black wire to hang the clothes across the stage so as to suspend them in the air as if by magic. Silvia Marín, who played Marta, prepared for the role by spending some time with a couple who were homeless yet nevertheless took the trouble to gather rainwater to carefully hand wash their clothes in a nylon bag dug into a hole in the ground. Despite their difficult circumstances, the woman had an air of optimism about her that Marín admired. On stage, Marín recalls, she tried to reproduce that optimism, down to the woman's gesture of clasping her hands in front of her lap as she spoke, as if she were respectful of her husband and respectful of life itself.

In 1999, the Chilean National Theater staged a well-funded and technologically sophisticated production of the play. Directed by one of Chile's most innovative and well-respected young directors, Alfredo Castro, *Finished from the Start* was thus consecrated as part of the national dramatic canon. Castro's production adopted a minimalist aesthetic that gave the production a sleek, clean look.[87] Rodrigo Vega's set consisted of a bare raked stage and a slanted ceiling that mirrored each other, creating the shape of a book on its side, its "spine" upstage, its "covers" opening downstage, toward the audience. The characters entered and exited from upstage, where a moat allowed the security guard, Miguel, to approach while visible only from the waist down. His work boots and the club he carried in his hand, as well as the threat they posed, were thus emphasized. The moat was also used as a trench along the entire back of the stage to "float" past black-and-white drawings of heads and hands symbolizing the disappeared. The gulf between the world of the disappeared and the world of the living thus appeared simultaneously tiny and infinite.

Since the stage was devoid of any furnishings or other properties, except for a pile of Marta's clothes, the lights, designed by Sergio Contreras, took on great significance. Light on the stage floor and ceiling emphasized a warm ocher floor that recalled both earth and sun. Blue light along the gap created the effect of a horizon. The warm stage colors contrasted with costumes, designed by Pablo Núñez, that assigned each character a symbolic color: black for Emilio, white for Marta, and gray for Miguel.

Perhaps the most remarkable change from the original staging was in the portrayal of Aurelio, the prophet of Emilio's death who speaks entirely in poetic metaphors that recall one of Shakespeare's fools on a flight of wordplay. Played by Benjamín Vicuña in Castro's production, Aurelio was dressed as a schoolboy in a tattered school blazer and short pants and made to look as if he'd been beaten and bloodied. Aurelio had become one of the disappeared, a directorial decision underscored by having his image flash in black and white across the stage, in the same manner as those of the rest of the victims. The character thus lost his otherworldly dimension and became more tightly integrated into the rest of the play. The tighter knitting of the plot created a more naturalistic, apparently less random and less chaotic theatrical universe, which may have made the work more accessible but sacrificed some of its strange beauty.

In accordance with the scenic design, rather than attempt a realistic depiction of poverty, the actors represented stylized indigence. Amparo Noguera was a glamorous Marta, with beautifully groomed tresses that dangled to her waist, her hands and bare feet perfectly manicured. As Emilio, José Soza wore a white shirt and a black suit; his polished black leather shoes only revealed holes in the soles when he sat down on the stage floor, his feet stretched out ahead of him. As he delivered the play's climactic speech, Emilio (Soza) clutched Marta (Noguera) to him and spoke his lines over the back of her shoulder, as if they were the leads of a television soap opera: "We're finished from the start; we didn't have no say in ourselves; they made us and they told us: 'Here you are, go over there,' but they didn't tell us why they had made us or why we had to go over to that side that we didn't know . . . to that side where the only sure thing was that we had to die." Marta's retort, "What you delusionating bout now?" which could be delivered in a light, offhanded manner, was instead loaded with the weight of forced emotion underscored by heart-string-tugging music. Poverty was cleaned up and sentimentalized, making it more attractive but requiring less of the spectator-as-witness.

—Ana Elena Puga

Notes

1. All the information about Radrigán's life and quotes from Radrigán not attributed to other sources come from a series of personal interviews with Radrigán and his longtime companion, Silvia Marín. The first interview, with both Radrigán and Marín, took place on August 31, 2005, in Santiago. Two subsequent telephone interviews took place on October 21 and 23, 2005.
2. *La felicidad de los García* also enjoyed a reincarnation as a video of resistance after the ICTUS Theater Company adapted it for film and released it under a new title, *El 18 de los García*. In the mideighties, when ICTUS sponsored alternative video screenings and discussion groups in and around Santiago, *El 18 de los García* was the second-most requested video. I am grateful to Steve J. Stern for calling this video, and its popularity, to my attention. For more on ICTUS's work and an analysis of the video, see Stern, *Hearts and Minds*, 307–32.
3. Radrigán, *Crónicas*, 19.
4. Ibid., 15–16.
5. The Chilean Radical Party began in the nineteenth century as a liberal, anticlerical movement. But during its rise in the twentieth century, from 1938 to 1952, it exhibited a chameleonlike ability to reinvent itself as more populist or more conservative, depending on which way the political wind was blowing. For more on the rise and fall of the Radical Party, see Collier and Sater, *History*, 235–63. For a comprehensive study of the role of the party system from Allende's election to the end of Pinochet's rule, see Yocelevsky, *Chile*.
6. Collier and Sater, *History*, 246–51.
7. Neruda's exile, from 1948 to 1952, is dramatized in a 1984 film directed by Michael Radford, *Il Postino*.
8. Piña, *Teatro chileno*, 64.
9. For a thoroughly documented account of the extent of U.S. efforts to prevent Allende from coming to office and to destabilize his government once he was in power, see Kornbluh, *Pinochet File*.
10. Qtd. in Seymour M. Hersh, "Censored Matter in Book About CIA Said to Have Related Chile Activities; Damage Feared," *New York Times*, September 11, 1974.
11. Williamson, *Penguin History*, 501.
12. Kornbluh, *Pinochet File*, 18–19.
13. Ibid., 30.
14. Drake, *Chile*, 47–51.
15. Collier and Sater, *History*, 337–38.
16. Kornbluh, *Pinochet File*, 114.
17. Constable and Valenzuela, *Nation of Enemies*, 15–16.
18. For details on the aftermath of the coup, see Constable and Valenzuela, *Nation of Enemies*.
19. Halperín Donghi, *Contemporary History*, 350.
20. The complete *Report of the Chilean National Commission on Truth and Reconciliation*, also known as the Rettig Report, after Raúl Rettig, the former Radical Party senator who chaired the commission, is available online at http://www.usip.org/library/truth.html (accessed March 8, 2006).

21. Because my last name also happens to be Puga, the first time I met Radrigán, in August 2001, he asked me if I was related to Ana María Puga Rojas (I am not) and told me that my surname had brought her to mind for him.

22. Boyle, *Chilean Theater,* 51.

23. Piña, *Teatro chileno,* 44.

24. For information about *teatro abierto,* see Giella, *Teatro Abierto,* and Graham-Jones, *Exorcising History,* 89–122.

25. Piña, *Teatro chileno,* 85, and 45–50 (rebirth of theater). During Castro's imprisonment, he was among the last people to see the Aleph actor Juan McCleod, who had been beaten and tortured before assassinated. Castro's mother, an apolitical elderly housewife, was also disappeared and assassinated after she came to visit her son. For an account of plays performed in concentration camps, see Lepeley, "Avatares," and Rojo, *Muerte.*

26. For several important studies of how textile industry workers have fared badly under neoliberal economic policies of both Pinochet and the democratic governments that succeeded him, see Winn, *Victims.*

27. *Testimony to the Deaths of Sabina* opened March 23, 1979, at the Teatro de los Comediantes, with the actors Ana González and Arnaldo Berríos in the roles of Sabina and Rafael.

28. Valenzuela, "Shanty Town," 9–10.

29. *Las últimas noticias,* January 2, 1983.

30. Albornoz Farías, "Veinticinco afanosos años," 9.

31. See "El teatro debe hacer meditar para que la gente salga alterada por dentro," *Las últimas noticias,* December 20, 1982. See also "Juan Radrigán: El dramaturgo del año," *Las últimas noticias,* January 2, 1983.

32. "A Francia Viaja 'El toro por las astas,'" *La segunda,* March 1, 1983.

33. "Con éxito se presentó a Radrigán en Nancy," *El mercurio,* June 3, 1983.

34. When Pinochet's term as commander in chief of the army expired in 1998, he bestowed upon himself the title "senator for life," which he claimed guaranteed him immunity from prosecution.

35. Constable and Valenzuela, *Nation of Enemies,* 317–18.

36. Radrigán, *Teatro,* 269.

37. Paul W. Drake, in the foreword to *Victims of the Chilean Miracle,* writes: "From 1990 to 1996 the share of national income of the poorest 20 percent of the population stagnated beneath 4 percent, while that of the richest 20 percent inched up from 56 percent to 57 percent. In other words, in 1996 the top one-fifth of income earners garnered fourteen times the income of the bottom one-fifth. Indeed, the distribution of income was one of the most unequal in the world. In Latin America, only Brazil was worse" (xi).

38. Collier and Sater, *History,* 394–98.

39. Kornbluh, *Pinochet File,* 481.

40. See *Human Rights Overview: Chile;* see also *Informe de la Comisión Nacional sobre Prisión Política y Tortura.*

41. Presidencia de la República, April 6, 2006. http://www.presidencia.cl/view/viewBiografia.asp?seccion=Biografia.

42. Radrigán, *Crónicas,* 25.

43. In the United States, the phrase "testimonial theater" has been used in the popular press and in scholarly articles to describe the work of Emily Mann, Anna Deavere Smith, and Moisés Kaufman's and Tectonic Theater Project's collaboration *The Laramie Project*. These playwrights differ from Radrigán, however, in that their work uses transcribed interviews with actual people. In contrast, although Radrigán usually fictionalizes his characters, his work remains within the *testimonio* tradition, I would argue, because (1) his characters are always drawn from individuals he has encountered, (2) they almost always speak for a class or community and are identified with a social struggle, and (3) they often address the spectator as if speaking directly to someone in their presence.

    In discussing Chilean theater under dictatorship, Catherine Boyle uses the phrase "testimonies of marginalization" to refer to three plays: *Pedro, Juan y Diego* (1976), by David Benavente in collaboration with the company ICTUS; *Los payasos de la esperanza* (Clowns in Waiting; 1977), by the theater collective Taller de Investigación Teatral; and *Tres Marías y una Rosa* (Three Marías and One Rosa; 1979), by Benavente and the *taller*. For Boyle, testimonies seem defined by only the second characteristic enumerated above: characters who speak for their class (*Chilean Theater*, 86).

44. Denegri, "*Testimonio*," 233.

45. Sommer, "No Secrets," 129.

46. Though different kinds of testimonial narratives are found throughout the world, perhaps the most obvious example of the genre outside of Latin America is the huge body of first-person accounts of the Holocaust. An earlier form of testimonial is the nineteenth-century slave narrative.

47. Partnoy, *The Little School*, 18.

48. Valenzuela, "Shanty Town," 9.

49. Beverley, "Margin," 34.

50. Scott, *Domination*, 206.

51. Ibid. Scott gives an apropos example of this phenomenon from Chilean political life. In June 1988, Ricardo Lagos broke the cautious silence among would-be political opponents of Pinochet to condemn the general for seeking another eight-year term of office. During a television report, Lagos rebuffed interviewers who tried to shush him with, "I speak for fifteen years of silence." He pointed a finger at the camera and addressed Pinochet directly: "You promise the country eight more years with torture, assassination, and the violation of human rights. To me, it seems inadmissible that a Chilean is so ambitious for power as to pretend to hold it for twenty-five years" (*Domination*, 207). Several factors created the excitement of the event: the personal risk Lagos took, his defiance of power, and the fact that he had spoken what thousands of people had long been thinking or saying among themselves under less-risky circumstances. In 2000, Lagos was elected president.

52. Though the language with which Radrigán assailed his spectators was among the strongest of its day, it is important to emphasize that he and his spectators nevertheless lived in an era in which coded language had pragmatic and aesthetic advantages. Radrigán never refers to the dictator by name in any of

his works. Even as late as 1988, during the state-tolerated campaign for the vote leading to Pinochet's defeat, opponents avoided pronouncing his name. Everyone knew who "he" was. An anti-Pinochet song frequently played on the radio said only, "No, no me gusta, no. No, no lo quiero, no" ("No, I don't like him, no. No, I don't want him, no"). The object of dislike was obvious to all.

53. Hurtado, "Conjugation of Identities," 13.

54. Denegri, "*Testimonio*," 232.

55. I take exception to Boyle, in her otherwise perceptive study of Radrigán's plays, when she concludes that "life is absurd" in his plays and that his characters are "outcasts and losers" (*Chilean Theater*, 145). Outcasts, yes. And losers, perhaps materially, but never in an existential sense. If life were absurd and the battle were already lost, there would be no point in struggling as much as they do to maintain their human dignity. Radrigán imbues that struggle with enormous significance.

56. Beverley, "*Testimonio*," 3.

57. Kafka, *Trial*, 1.

58. "Anoche debutó un nuevo dramaturgo," *La segunda*, March 24, 1979.

59. Personal interview with Marín, August 31, 2005.

60. Silva, "Crítica," 30.

61. For an even-handed overview of the Pinochet government's attempts to assist the poor, as well as its repression of the underclass, see Constable and Valenzuela, *Nation of Enemies*, 222–46. For a study of the contrast between the memories that rich and poor hold of Pinochet's Chile, see Stern, *Remembering*.

62. Constable and Valenzuela, *Nation of Enemies*, 225.

63. Ibid., 225–26.

64. For a thorough exploration, and debunking, of the idea that the women might have been killed by the military, see Farías, "Tres muertas." The women were Colla Indians, a Quechua-speaking ethnic group that the military in fact persecuted in that region, about one hundred miles northeast of the city Copiapó. But Farías concludes that the military most likely played only an indirect role in the suicides, in that the women, according to their niece, feared that soldiers were going to take away the cattle and goat herds on which they depended for survival. Moreover, the military tended to shoot its victims and was unlikely to go through the trouble of simulating a suicide. Farías suggests, instead, on the basis of a second interview with a local Indian guide, that the sisters saw their suicide as a sacrificial gesture and a protest to the combination of forces—from drought to military repression—that had forced many Indians to abandon their nomadic way of life in the countryside and to relocate to cities, where they lived in shanty towns and begged for spare change to survive.

65. *Bruta* could also mean "stupid," "ignorant," or "animalistic." But Radrigán's tone toward the characters is closer to the more charitable definition.

66. Timerman, *Chile*, 32.

67. Ibid.

68. For an account of one couple's experience of house arrest in southern Chile, in the Osorno Province of the Lakes Region, see Stern, *Remembering*, 73–78.

69. "'Las brutas': Tres mujeres conmueven," *El sur* (Concepción), August 18, 1982.

70. Laub, "Bearing Witness," 57–58.
71. "Elogian obra 'Las brutas,'" *La nación,* August 5, 1980.
72. Laub, "Bearing Witness," 78.
73. Felman, "Education and Crisis," 52–53.
74. For a survey of the role of protest music and song in Latin America during the seventies and eighties, see Matta, "'New Song,'" 447–60. In Chile, the most prominent protest singers were Victor Jara, who was assassinated shortly after the coup; Angel and Isabel Parra; Rolando Alarcón; and Patricio Manns (451). The banned folk group Intillimani toured the world, taking advantage of exile to spread its antidictatorship message.
75. "Un Radrigán Juguetón," *Las últimas noticias,* December 26, 2000.
76. See Levi, "Gray Zone."
77. Felman, "Education and Crisis," 207.
78. Radrigán, *La contienda humana,* 7.
79. The January 4, 1978, plebiscite featured a ballot with a Chilean flag for "yes" and a black box for "no." The text read: "Faced with international aggression launched against our fatherland, I support President Pinochet in his defense of the dignity of Chile and reaffirm the legitimacy of the government" (Constable and Valenzuela, *Nation of Enemies,* 68). Pinochet declared that more than 75 percent of the voters had supported his rule (Drake, *Chile,* 53). In a 1980 plebiscite, boycotted by some leftists and centrists, on Pinochet's "Liberty Constitution," which would keep him in office until 1989, Pinochet said he received 67 percent of the vote (Drake, *Chile,* 55).
80. Timerman, *Chile,* 70.
81. Ibid., 67–77.
82. Boyle, *Chilean Theater,* 128.
83. The audience quotes come from a production I attended in Santiago, Chile, on August 19, 2005.
84. Winn, *Victims,* 127–32.
85. Ibid., 134.
86. Rulfo, *Burning Plain,* 12–13.
87. The description of the 1999 production of *Finished from the Start* is reconstructed from newspaper accounts and from a videocassette recording of a performance provided by the Chilean National Theater.

FINISHED FROM THE START AND OTHER PLAYS

TESTIMONY TO THE DEATHS OF SABINA

Bruno Godoy Araya as Sabina and Rodrigo Reyes as Rafael in the opening of *Testimony to the Deaths of Sabina,* performed by Compañía de Teatro Escuela Ilucion, at Teatro IPA in Valparaiso, Chile, in August 2002. The play was directed by Claudio Vidal Albornoz.

PRODUCTION HISTORY

Testimony to the Deaths of Sabina opened March 23, 1979, and was produced by Teatro de los Comediantes, in the Sala del Ángel in Santiago, Chile, with the following cast and production team:

Director	Gustavo Meza
Sabina	Ana González
Rafael	Arnaldo Berríos
Set and Costumes	Luz María Sotomayor
Lights and Sound	Willy Gangas

CHARACTERS

Rafael
Sabina

ACT 1

[*A room that serves as a dining room, kitchen, and bedroom. Dirt floor, a bed, a table, chairs. In a prominent place: a two-burner paraffin stove, other furniture, and daily utensils, everything well worn. The entrance, which cannot be seen, is to the left. It is winter.* SABINA *and* RAFAEL *arrive, arguing without anger. They are an old couple, still strong, that owns a fruit stand in which they have been working for more than thirty years. She carries a mesh bag with various packages inside it.*]

RAFAEL: Don't be stubborn. Look Sabina, figure it out: we paid five *gambas* for the three boxes of bananas, two more for the avocados, and three for the lemons; a thousand pesos total. How we gonna make two right off? We ain't selling gold you know. And besides, like I told you, bananas don't pay much now.

SABINA [*sitting heavily*]: OK, but I got together more than a boxful, including the green ones; those are leftover too. I had to count those.

RAFAEL [*taking off his jacket*]: How am I gonna count them when we still haven't sold them?

SABINA: But it's capital too.

RAFAEL [*throwing himself on the bed*]: Sure, but it's preinvested capital. It's not the same thing.

SABINA: Preinvested capital? That's a good one you came up with now!

RAFAEL: That's what it's called, see. We shoulda got all apples like I told ya.

SABINA: You don't give up on them apples; you're more stubborn than the guy who wanted to sharpen his pencil with his teeth.

RAFAEL: That's the best deal going now. You can't work any ole way you want; it's the old bags that run the show. How many times did they ask us for apples this morning? What's happening here is that we have a whole lot of chiefs and no Indians, when just one guy should be in charge. Don't you see that otherwise the business gets screwed up?

SABINA: Know what? Tomorrow we'll sell the rest of the bananas and we'll put out the apples. But I know we won't pull it off; you're terrible at hunches.

[SABINA *places the bag on the table.*]

Remember when you got it into your head that we needed to push the chirimoya? We pushed them green and nothing happened, later we worked them ripe and they started to rot, then since you're so thrifty you started to drink them in wine so's not to lose them all. What a great deal that was.

RAFAEL [condescendingly]: Well, I messed up with that one; but that was just once, and you've screwed up tons of times. Remember that little incident with the strawberries!

SABINA: What did I do?

RAFAEL: The same thing you did with the avocados: you didn't weigh the boxes to subtract them, and if I hadn't noticed in time we'd be out begging for handouts now. Oh, and know what else? This morning I caught you, twice, giving the real weight to some women that was waiting for the bus. You know they're all watching their pocketbooks now. If we don't top off the kilos on the ones in a hurry, who we gonna con? You gotta sharpen your skills already.

SABINA: Hey, why don't you just beat them up and take their money? On top of the fixed scale, you want me to cheat on the weighing. I'm the one that's there, you know. Don't you think it's embarrassing when they start complaining in front of everybody?

RAFAEL: That's when you gotta get tough, see; get them before they get you. Don't you see that they get even more embarrassed than us to be shouting in the street?

[SABINA starts to laugh.]

What are you laughing at?

SABINA [laughing]: I remember when you told that old man, "Don't put your finger in the fruit, mister!" And you didn't notice that he was missing a finger.

RAFAEL: So, and how was I supozed to know? I thought he'd stuck his finger in the peach.

[RAFAEL shrugs.]

"Anyone can make a mistake," said the duck, as he got off of the hen.

SABINA [*thoughtfully*]: Hey, *viejo*, what if we brought our lunch from here?*
I could make it the night before; maybe we'd save a few pennies.

RAFAEL: What we gonna take, huh? Plus the headache of heating it up
there.

SABINA: We've got to figure something out; we've gotta save more capital to put in the business. Been a while now we've only been working
with three or four boxes. [*Pause.*] You remember the Stain that had
the stand in front of the shoe repair place?

RAFAEL: What Stain?

SABINA [*annoyed*]: That blondie that had the sickness that stains you.
Why you playing dumb?

RAFAEL: Oh, the one that sold the bootleg liquor.

SABINA: How you gonna sell liquor from a street stand?

RAFAEL: She sold shots to the taxi drivers; course I remember. She got
about five *gambas* outta the bottle of *pisco*.

SABINA: No, she didn't sell no liquor; they woulda closed her down.
First she sold candies, and then she changed to fruit, now she has two
stands in the main station, and this year she's changed coats three
times. The other day she was yakking with the newsstand lady and
she was saying she was gonna get a color TV. Everybody's doing good
and we're going downhill more and more . . . And you still got the
nerve to try to play games with me on the accounts.

RAFAEL: What games did I play with you, *vieja*? The accounts is all
figured out right.

SABINA: Figured out right . . . If I left you working alone in the stand, we
wouldn't even have a pot to piss in, much less cook in.

RAFAEL [*laughing*]: Come on! The only time we did good was when you
were in the hospital. If it wasn't for me, you'd still be selling apples out
of a basket. [*Remembering*] You looked like a duck when you walked
with those baskets.

[RAFAEL *gets up and walks, imitating a duck.*]

Aaaaaples . . . Aaaaaples . . .

[RAFAEL *sits again, laughing.*]

---

* *Viejo* is a term of endearment.

SABINA: There you have it. That's how enterprising I was, thirteen years old and I was already out there with the baskets. And you spent your time lying around in the sun.

RAFAEL: That was when we were on lunch break at the factory, see. I had to air myself out. Don't you see that the smell of the oil that we threw on the wool would stick to my skin?

SABINA: And why didn't you take a bath instead?

RAFAEL: Hmm, if I'd set to bathing, those jerks woulda stolen all the wool. They were already leaving there more loaded up than a bus. Seriously, Sabina; there was some that hada be pushed so's they could get going. Don Alberto would say: "After I let them out for the day, I have to go running back to my office, cuz otherwise when I least expect it one of these losers is gonna rob me."

SABINA: Sure, so you were their stoolie.

RAFAEL: No, not a stoolie. Just a little worker, but one they could trust.

SABINA [*murmuring*]: The bad thing was that afterwards you took too many liberties.

RAFAEL [*alert*]: What's that?

SABINA: That they gave you a lot of liberty.

RAFAEL [*enthusiastically*]: Sure, the boss always told me . . .

SABINA: . . . You're the one in charge here.

RAFAEL: Upstairs. Not in the whole factory, just in the mixing area. But, just so you know . . .

SABINA: You had four guys under you.

RAFAEL: Five, I was also in charge of the old guy who prepared the oil. And once when the carder got sick . . .

SABINA: Don Alberto told you: "Do you know the ropes enough to start up the machine?"

RAFAEL: And I started it up, just like that. [*Self-satisfied*] Hmm, if they'd ever put me on the loom, I would have made it run too!

SABINA: Too bad they threw you out first.

RAFAEL: They didn't throw me out; I quit!

SABINA: And the beating they gave you was cuz they was so grateful?

RAFAEL: Damn, you're a bigmouth. I picked the fight so's I could buy the stand. See, if I'd left on good terms, they wouldn't have paid me a dime . . . How long has it been since then, *vieja*?

SABINA: It's gotta be more than thirty years, cuz I was about to have Rafael when you stopped working.

RAFAEL: Damn, you are ancient. One day they're gonna give you a ticket for being old.

SABINA: A little less old than you, but much better looking . . . Remember that you even cried over this little kitten.

RAFAEL: You, you got a lot of nerve. You know what they called me at the factory? "God's gift to girls." You're the one that was chasing after me like a boob with those baskets . . . Why didn't you leave them at home to chase me? The embarrassment you'd make me go through when you'd turn up at the dances with the baskets full of apples.

SABINA: Sure, cuz them dances was so spiffy.

RAFAEL: They was good, first class, with music and everything. Remember when Armando Bonasco's orchestra played? And Federico Ojeda would go too. No, they weren't just any old thing.

SABINA: Ah, but those dances weren't put on by your union. The club would do those.

RAFAEL: The club and us, see, where were those lowlifes gonna get it together to pay the orchestra? They just came up with the space. [*Pause.*] I remember when we elected the queen of the union and I was the campaign manager for the winner . . .

SABINA: Hmm, the queen had more fleas than a gypsy's mattress. They all thought she was dancing, but she was scratching.

RAFAEL [*almost with sadness*]: Damn, I was cool then! Silk shirt, white, with ruffles on the cuffs, the pants wide on top and tight toward the bottom; [*touching his wrist*] a good watch and [*patting his pocket*] a thick wad in my pocket . . . Oh, and white shoes with black tips. A totally cool cat.

SABINA: I did my hair like Beroneekah Lahkeh.* Remember? And I wore a tight skirt with a ruffle on the bottom and ankle-strap shoes with a cork sole, but good cork, not like they have now.

RAFAEL: Sure . . . Damn, you was a looker. If everybody hadn't known that I was good with my fists, they would have pinched you more than . . .

---

* This is the Spanish-language pronunciation of Veronica Lake.

SABINA [*reminiscent*]: No, in those days people didn't dare.

RAFAEL: They was the same, the thing was they respected you cuz you was with me . . . The looks they gave you when you kicked your leg out to the side for the *sween.** You remember the *sween.* And the hat dance? And the conga?

SABINA: In those days there was the *fostró* † too.

RAFAEL: Sure! "Kalamazoo!" "Mona Lisa!" "Beer Barrel Polka!"

[RAFAEL *leaps up impulsively and dances.*]

I gotta gal, yeah in Kalamazoo.

[RAFAEL *dances and sings, almost ferociously.*]

Don't wanna boast but I know she's the toast of Kalamazoo. Zoo, zoo, zoo, zoo, zoo . . .

SABINA [*going to* RAFAEL, *holding him*]: Hold it, hold it, *viejo.* You're not up to this anymore; it could be bad for you!

RAFAEL [*out of breath*]: They'd leave us alone! [*Anxiously*] You remember how they'd leave us alone in the middle when I'd jazz it up?

[RAFAEL *sits.*]

What were they saying?

SABINA: What was who saying?

RAFAEL: The people—ya know, the ones that was watchin?

SABINA: And how should I know, since I was dancin with you?

RAFAEL: Cuz you dint put so much into it; you dint get inside the music . . . Your whole life was taking care of your baskets.

SABINA: And you. I had to be taking care of you too.

RAFAEL [*interested*]: Me?

SABINA: You made me suffer; you were such a womanizer.

RAFAEL: No, not a womanizer. I didn't look for them; it's just that I had sex appeal. And I had to step up to it; couldn't look like a chump. [*Shrugging it off*] But that's just how it was; I was with you . . . Know why I was with you? Cuz you didn't let me lay a hand on you.

---

* The swing.

† The fox-trot.

SABINA [*hurt*]: Just cuz of that?

RAFAEL: No, not just cuz of that . . . I liked the way you laughed, the way you looked . . . and that thing you had when we kissed, that thing like a cat purr; even if you'd let me go all the way, I still would have married you. But I had this idea in my head that I'd teach you a lesson so's you wouldn't be so stuck up. I'd always say: "This time she's gotta give it up, this time she's not gonna get away." And nothing ever happened, jeez!

SABINA: And what was supposed to happen? You thought I was like them low-class girls from the factory?

RAFAEL: But you sold apples in the street; you wasn't nothing out of this world. Hmm, I once nailed a secretary, ya know. Yeah, I think if your mom hadn't been such a pain, you would have given it up too. Wouldn't you have let me come in your room, if she'd ever gone out?

SABINA: No, even if I'd lived alone I wouldn't have let you come in. You wasn't gonna make a fool outta me.

RAFAEL [*certain*]: Yeah, you would have given it up. Sometimes when we smooched in the doorway you wasn't very shy, remember. Thing was you was scared of your mom. [*Pause.*] Damn, that lady was good at pestering; she wouldn't let you live in peace. You had to be worried and scared all the time. [*Resentfully*] And even though you went through all that, you still had the nerve to fight with me when I'd let Gloria go out for a little while at night. That's why she married the first bum she met.

SABINA: Antonio isn't a bad husband; he's got a good profession. Thing is, is that now nobody sends out their bikes to be fixed. I sure married the first bum I met, cuz you don't know how to do nothin.

RAFAEL: Oh, that's nice; thank you very much.

SABINA: You're welcome. That's what you get for making fun of me with your secretary. Why didn't you marry her when you saw that I was selling apples out of a basket? [*Defiantly*] Go ahead and laugh then.

RAFAEL [*bitingly*]: No, I never laugh at you, the one who laughed was Walleyed Wally.

SABINA [*sighing*]: Poor old Wally's being dragged up again . . . You been hittin the bottle?

RAFAEL: What did you see in him?

SABINA [*evasively*]: In who?

RAFAEL: In Wally, ya know, the guy we're talking about. What good did it do the bum that he looked like a gringo? He wasn't nothing but a loading dock worker in the marketplace. Then when some boss took pity on him and put him in the acids factory, he made himself out to be a chemist. How was he gonna be a chemist when he didn't even know how to read? [*Aggressively*] Are you gonna deny to me that he didn't know how to read?

SABINA: How should I know, I don't even know what you're talking about.

RAFAEL: I was more cool. My whole life I was much more cooler than him!

SABINA: And I ain't said you wasn't.

RAFAEL: . . . Better heat up a little food then; I sure am hungry.

[SABINA *sits again and opens the packages in her bag.*]

SABINA: You were too busy being a ladies' man to eat. Think I didn't notice you this morning changing your shirt cuz you was gonna go see the soda fountain lady? Whaddaya know, the old man's still bitten by the love bug; don't I know it.

RAFAEL [*flattered*]: There's nothing going on, Sabina; I help her with her things cuz she always buys a whole bunch of fruit from us. But that old bag's so dried up that even if you put her in a blender, you couldn't get any juice out of her.

[SABINA *takes out bread and a stick of margarine.*]

SABINA: And still, you look her up and down. [*Emphatically*] I better not catch you, or I'll make it so you won't have nothin to piss with no more.

RAFAEL [*gesturing toward the stove*]: Don't it light?

[SABINA *stands, looks for a bread basket, and arranges the bread.*]

SABINA: It don't work.

RAFAEL [*brusquely*]: Whaddaya mean it don't work? Didn't I fix it yesterday?

SABINA: Sure, you fixed it real good. Now it thinks it's a steam engine; it don't do nothin but smoke.

[RAFAEL *gets up and examines the stove.*]

RAFAEL: You took out the spare part.

SABINA [*innocently*]: What spare part?

RAFAEL: The tin can I put here, ya know [*gesturing*].

SABINA: No, I ain't taken nothing off.

RAFAEL [*taking the stove apart*]: Sure you took it off; I left it good yesterday.

SABINA: Maybe the thing fell off it.

[SABINA *sits and begins to spread butter on the bread.*]

Hey, when you took the package to the old bag, Gloria came by the stand.

RAFAEL [*interrupting his work*]: And why didn't she wait for me?

SABINA [*shrugging it off*]: Cuz she was in a hurry.

RAFAEL [*grumbling*]: She's been in a hurry for a while now . . . Why didn't you tell her to wait for me? . . . Seems like it's been a year since I seen her . . .

SABINA: Just two months. Don't make such a big deal out of it.

RAFAEL: No, since the baptism. I haven't seen her since then.

SABINA: That's right: two months. [*With a certain caution*] You know? Seems like she's afraid of you . . .

RAFAEL [*worked up*]: How could she be afraid of me! Ain't I her father? What did she say to you?

SABINA: Well, nothing. It's just that since you bad-mouthed her husband . . .

RAFAEL: I didn't bad-mouth him. All I said was that I felt like beating the hell out of him.

SABINA [*drily*]: That wasn't none of your business.

RAFAEL: Ah, no? [*Passionately*] Damn, if I ever find out that he raised his hand to her . . . No, don't give me no "it ain't none of my business." If I find out something, I'll throw boiling oil on his . . .

SABINA: But he don't hit her hey; he wouldn't hit her.

RAFAEL [*still excited*]: And if you try and stop me . . .

SABINA [*angered*]: So now no one can say nothin bout your baby. She got married. You understand? She got married.

RAFAEL [*stubbornly*]: I don't care. That don't have nothing to do with nothing.

[RAFAEL *starts working on the stove again.*]

She don't stop being my daughter just cuz she got married.

SABINA [*obviously resentful*]: Why didn't you tie her to your apron strings so they wouldn't take her away from you?

RAFAEL: You didn't want them to live here.

SABINA: And where were we gonna stuff them, bigmouth? Did you ever get me a house? [*Scornfully*] You just better fix that thing.

RAFAEL: You give her money?

SABINA: Yeah, sure. I gived her some.

RAFAEL [*humbly*]: We could buy her a few groceries.

SABINA: And why don't you remember that when you're out drinking?

RAFAEL: Are you a dingbat? You ever heard of anybody who drinks to remember something? We drink to forget. [*Quickly*] The jerk didn't find no work yet?

SABINA: No, just odd jobs.

RAFAEL [*scornfully*]: How's he gonna do odd jobs? He never even learned to walk right!

SABINA: He can't walk right cuz one leg's shorter than the other. Damn, you like to make fun of them's less fortunate than you.

RAFAEL: He's been limp for a while, ya know. Would be great if he'd learn to walk, but that never even dawned on him.

SABINA [*caustically*]: Hey, and what about Rafael?

RAFAEL [*still working*]: Don't know, haven't seen him.

SABINA: Him, you never ask about, do you?

RAFAEL: What's there to ask? He's fine. Course he's fine; he came from me.

SABINA: Sure, the hot stuff. [*Pause.*] If you'da been strict with them from the start, they coulda been somebody. But it was like you was scared of them. They didn't wanna go to school, they just didn't go. If it hadn't a been for me, they never even woulda finished grammar school.

RAFAEL: What more'd you want them to study? We wasn't gonna send them to college. They had to help out with the house too. [*Pause.*] But Rafael's good at everything. Everywhere you put him he does good. [*Counting on his fingers*] He can do carpentry, he can do welding, pipe fitting, shoe repair. Huh, he's almost smarter than I am. Nah, he ain't ever gonna be broke. [*Pause.*] But the one who was really supertalented was Gloria. Remember when she got it into her head to draw?

[RAFAEL *goes to the bed and bends over.*]

SABINA: What you doing?

RAFAEL [*trying to reach something under the bed*]: I have a box put away here with the drawings she used to make.

SABINA: Just leave it there. You've already shown them to me bout a million times.

RAFAEL [*getting up*]: Don't you like em?

SABINA: Yes, but then you get to explaining the pictures to me and you don't know nothing. You give me pure bull.

RAFAEL: No, I do know. I know a little about everything. Damn, if I'da had time to go to school . . .

SABINA: What time was you gonna have, when you spent all your time doing nothing but sucking on a bottle; instead of a baby bottle they used to shove a garden hose in your mouth . . . The only thing you turned out sharp at was accounts.

RAFAEL [*rubbing his hands and pointing to the stove*]: OK, this thing is ready. Matches.

SABINA [*handing them to him*]: Trying to change the subject, right? How'd I end up married to this wine jug with legs? More than thirty years of marriage and you still haven't got me a stove.

RAFAEL: What you want appliances for? The important thing is the love, the joys I've given you.

SABINA [*perplexed*]: Joys?

RAFAEL: Hmm, and all the steaks you've eaten? And the kids? And the movies I took you to? Damn, don't take no offense, but remember that when I met you, you were selling apples out of a basket. And now you have a fabulous stand. Thing is, nothing's enough for you. It takes twenty chocolate bars for you to taste the sweetness. You're very ungrateful, ungrateful and a slob, like my dearly departed mother used to say.

SABINA: Slob? Must be talking bout your grandma.

RAFAEL: Nah, my grandma was so clean it was crazy. The slob was my dad. My mom had to sweep off his face in the mornings to see if he was awake.

[SABINA *starts to laugh.*]

He was such a pig that at his baptism he cursed out the priest that tried to throw water on him. Seriously, Sabina. And he was such a drinker! If a speakeasy was closed, he'd try to suck booze out of the lock so's not to waste the trip.

SABINA [*laughing*]: Cut it out, you old nut.

RAFAEL: You like it when I tell you about my daddy, don't you?

SABINA: Poor old guy, even his bones are gone by now, and you're laughing at him.

RAFAEL: No, he didn't have bones. He was held together by fleas. In the cemetery they wanted to give us a citation because we didn't have no permission from the health department to bury him.

SABINA [*when she can stop laughing*]: You're real slick.

RAFAEL: Why?

SABINA: Cuz I was talking about the stove, about the crappy stove you got for me.

RAFAEL: And I haven't even gotten to your mom yet.

SABINA: Hey, you gonna start with her now?

RAFAEL: No, it's just that now that we're talking about the family, you can tell me the truth: why didn't they bury her in the zoo when she died?

SABINA: Don't go too far, *viejo*. Remember that you get stung real easy.

RAFAEL: But she was so mean to you. Know what I woulda done? I woulda buried her in a round coffin so I could have kicked her all the way to the cemetery.

SABINA: My mother was good!

RAFAEL: At boozing it up!

SABINA: Don't talk about her, loser.

RAFAEL: You mad?

SABINA: You're getting on my nerves . . . She was good . . . And so alone, so, so alone.

RAFAEL: She never went out, not even for earthquakes. And to top it off, she went round all the time dressed in black. Seemed like a crow. Crows are like that: black, sad, and bad. I only saw her go out with you three or four times.

SABINA: No, we went out every week to buy fruit from the orchards. [*Pause.*] You remember my house? It was a closed-up house, old and dark. I'd tell her to let me open the windows, but she'd say no. "What for?" she'd say. "Cuz it's sunny outside," I'd say. She'd shrug . . . She knew she was a pain and sometimes she'd ask me if I hated her. How could I hate her when she didn't have no one but me? I don't know how someone can be so hardened, how she can be so proud that she buries herself alive. She didn't talk, she didn't talk at all . . . But sometimes she'd give me these looks, almost in secret, and her face got so pretty . . .

RAFAEL: She musta been thinking bout him. [*Gesturing toward* SABINA] Was he married?

SABINA: Yeah, married . . . [*Recovering*] Well, we were talking about the stove, smartass.

RAFAEL: Ah, the stove; sure, we're gonna buy one.

SABINA: When?

RAFAEL: This week. [*With certainty*] This week for sure we're gonna get a gas one. [*Pause.*] So it's been a little while now that we've been alone.

[*He falls to thinking.*]

Must be more than a year since Gloria left . . .

SABINA: You still miss her?

RAFAEL: Of course.

SABINA: Why aren't we better off?

RAFAEL: Cuz both the kids have had bad luck. We've had to keep helping them.

SABINA: And us?

RAFAEL: Well, here we are.

SABINA [*looking around*]: Course, here . . .

RAFAEL [*cheering up*]: Well, the winter's almost over and in summer things will pick up.

SABINA [*without conviction*]: Sure.

RAFAEL: Don't you think? It's always gone good for us in summer.

SABINA: And we're always in the same . . . [*Somberly*] Know what I dreamt last night?

RAFAEL: You dreamt? When? You were snoring the whole time.

SABINA [*without paying attention to* RAFAEL]: I dreamt that I came to visit me.

RAFAEL: That they came to visit you? Damn, must be another one of them strange things. You're always having weird dreams. Sometimes they're coming after you and you can't run. Other times you fall in a hole and never reach the ground. Why don't you dream that you win the lottery instead? Dream something first rate. I bet now you dreamed some other complicated thing.

SABINA: No, it's not complicated at all. I dreamt that I appeared to myself.

RAFAEL: See? What was I telling you? Same as that time you dreamt that you were dreaming.

SABINA [*protesting*]: They're dreams, aren't they? I was here and I came to see myself.

RAFAEL: And did you come with wings and all that stuff?

SABINA: No, I was just younger . . . Much younger. I was sitting over there [*pointing out a spot*] sewing your jacket when . . .

[RAFAEL *takes the teakettle.*]

RAFAEL: Hey, you didn't change the tea. We're gonna be drinking tea at mid——

SABINA [*shouting*]: I'm telling you what I dreamed!

RAFAEL: Well, hey, don't yell so much. I'm gonna throw this thing out and come right back.

[RAFAEL *exits.* SABINA *remains immobile for a moment, staring desolately out into space. Her face looks tired and sad. Then she shrugs and stands to place the cups on the table.* RAFAEL *enters in a rush, shaking the teakettle.*]

Well, *vieja*, what did you dream?

SABINA [*drily*]: Nothing.

RAFAEL: Hmm, you get mad again?

[RAFAEL *starts to put tea in the kettle.*]

SABINA [*going to bang on the wall*]: Pedro, you there?

RAFAEL [*good-naturedly*]: Hey, don't be doing that stupid thing again. You're gonna piss off the neighbors.

SABINA [*banging again*]: You there, Pedro? Listen, last night . . .

RAFAEL [*uneasily*]: Hey, hey, get hold of yourself. Take it easy, don't get carried away.

SABINA: Why should I get hold of myself? I have to talk to someone. I'm not gonna talk to myself like a crazy person; that's what the neighbors are for. [*To the wall*] Pedro, listen, last night . . .

RAFAEL: Damn, *vieja*, take it easy, see. [*Conciliatory*] Look, if we sell a
lot tomorrow we'll go to . . .

SABINA: If we sell a lot tomorrow, I'm gonna buy me that radio from
Tight Lips. It's about time I had something for me.

RAFAEL: Don't get involved with that guy, Sabina; they're on to him.

SABINA [*stubbornly*]: I'll buy it from him anyway.

[SABINA *sits again.*]

I'll buy it and I'll buy it . . . I ain't never had nothin. You can't even
scrape up enough to give me a pair of stockings.

RAFAEL [*worried*]: And if he rats?

SABINA: He ain't never ratted.

RAFAEL: Cuz they haven't catched him. But I'm sure that when they get
him, after the very first smack, he'll rat.

SABINA: Don't matter; I'll go to jail.

RAFAEL: Well, it's up to you, but don't come crying to me later.

SABINA: And so how did you buy a watch?

RAFAEL: From a little mouse, not from a big bad rat.

SABINA: Sure, and he picked up that scar he has on his face at the flea
market; or maybe the little orphan kids made it for him.

RAFAEL: That wasn't no scar.

SABINA: No, it was the blessing from his first communion that got stuck
on his big fat face. You're deaf and dumb, when it's something for you
it don't matter at all. [*Sighing*] Goddamn mother . . .

RAFAEL: Hmm, and I thought you'd turned into a lady. It's been a while
since you've said that.

SABINA [*suddenly remembering*]: Hey, know what? I've got a good one for
you.

RAFAEL [*interested*]: What?

SABINA: In the morning, while you were hanging out with that old bag,
they gave me a citation.

RAFAEL: A citation?

[RAFAEL *and* SABINA *fall still, immobile. In the distance can be heard the
footsteps of someone approaching.*]

ACT 2

[*A month later. The same setting. The same entrance.*]

RAFAEL [*annoyed*]: Damn, you sure are sweet. After I put up with the crap of going to Wally's wake, you start goin off like crazy. That dint have nothing to do with nothing, see!

SABINA [*without backing off*]: We had to find out, ya know; that citation ain't right!

RAFAEL [*sitting on the bed*]: Damn, maybe it ain't right, but that guy don't know nothing. Where was Wally gonna get an inspector friend from? [*Pause.*] And dint you catch his getup? He had more threads hanging than an overcooked squash.

SABINA [*taking off her coat, beginning to tidy up the room a bit*]: He was telling me everything we have to do. [*Pause.*] The stand is ours; they can't take it away from us!

RAFAEL: Ain't nobody gonna take it away from you, woman; that man don't know jack. Dint you get it that he was laughing at you?

SABINA [*grouchily*]: Like you care bout that.

RAFAEL: Course I care. If we hadn't been at a wake, I woulda started something right there; I've always stood up for you.

SABINA [*pained*]: Well, but I gotta know.

RAFAEL: But not like this. We can't go nowhere without you goin off about the citation. Next thing you know you'll be asking the bus drivers.

SABINA: Thing with you is that you don't care.

RAFAEL: Whaddaya mean I don't care? What more you want me to do? Can't you see that no one pays us no mind?

SABINA: You lost the paper.

RAFAEL: What paper?

SABINA: That paper they gave us so that we would go ask for that other paper that they wanted down at city hall.

RAFAEL: Damn, but I didn't lose it. The old man that took care of us took it away from me.

SABINA: You should have asked him for a receipt; that's what we went there for.

RAFAEL: They was supposed to give us that at the police station. Don't you get it? No one knows why they turned us in.

SABINA [*anguished*]: So what are we gonna do then?

RAFAEL: Nothing, wait.

SABINA: But what will we wait for!

RAFAEL [*bored*]: What do I know?!

SABINA: You've gotta know; you're the man!

RAFAEL: Goddamn, that's great. It's only when we got trouble that you remember that I'm the man.

SABINA: It's been a month already, a month that we can't even sleep in peace . . . And you can't play the little boy.

RAFAEL [*somberly*]: That's the worse thing: there ain't no one to fight with. We don't know who's got us by the balls; we don't even know what we did . . .

SABINA: And now we can't even sell bags.

RAFAEL: The bags from Taiwan. Not that we made that much on the bags.

SABINA: But it was something, ya know. [*Sighing*] Damn, if you hadn't lost the paper.

RAFAEL: That's enough about the paper. It wasn't good for nothing.

SABINA: It said that they'd wrote us up!

RAFAEL [*keeping his patience with great effort*]: OK, and why had they wrote us up, huh?

SABINA: Don't know.

RAFAEL: You see?

SABINA: Well, it said . . . I remember that it said that we had done something-or-other with the law.

RAFAEL: It said we had transguessed it.

SABINA: Yeah, that! See how you did know?

RAFAEL: But what law?

SABINA: It had a number on there; that number meant what we had done.

RAFAEL: Exactly, but you saw that no one knows what law goes with that number.

SABINA: But the ones that made it gotta know!

RAFAEL: Damn, the ones that makes the laws also dies, ya know.

SABINA: And so who we gonna ask then?

RAFAEL: No one . . . Take it easy, *vieja*. The guy who sends out the inspectors told us already that the citation wasn't wrote up right.

SABINA: But his boss told us that the law don't make mistakes, that we must have done something! [*Pause.*] I ain't done nothing; I ain't done not one thing! [*Exasperated*] Why don't they tell us what they want!

RAFAEL [*going to hug her*]: Don't get so upset, Sabina. This thing has to get cleared up. On the fifteenth we gotta go to court and we'll fix this whole mess there. [*Pause.*] You shoulda put up a fuss with the bastard who wrote you up.

SABINA: But he didn't say nothing to me; he asked for the license and then he begun to write.

RAFAEL: That's when you should've asked him.

SABINA: I asked, but he dint answer me nothing. You know how stuck up they is; they treat us like we was criminals.

RAFAEL: But when they want something they act like little lambs. Just wait for one of them bastards to tell me that he needs a little fruit to take to a sick friend at the hospital, cuz I'll make him swallow the scale.

SABINA: That'll just make things worse, ya know; afterwards they won't let us work in peace. [*Breaking away from the hug and pointing to the stove*] See what's the matter with that thing so we can have a cup of tea before we go to bed.

RAFAEL [*surprised*]: It ain't working right?

SABINA: And when was it ever right?

RAFAEL: But I've fixed it a million times!

SABINA: And you ain't never left it right. [*Murmuring*] You ain't even good for fixin a crappy stove. How you gonna protect the stand?

RAFAEL: What are you talking bout now?

SABINA [*banging things around*]: Like if they take the stand away, you gonna feed me?

RAFAEL: Oh no? Who will feed you then? Garbage mouth.

SABINA [*angrily*]: When have you fed me? You good-for-nothing shit. If it wasn't for the stand, the kids would have died of hunger. How dare you take credit for that, you bastard.

RAFAEL [*tensely*]: Cut it out, Sabina, don't play with me . . .You think that cuz I ain't never hit you I can't beat the hell out of you right now?

SABINA [*disdainfully*]: Go ahead and try it then . . . Alls you'll get is the fun of hitting me. The kids are married, so it ain't no trouble at all for me to get my clothes and dump you. [*Scornfully*] After all, for what you're worth . . .

RAFAEL: And where you gonna go to? Ain't you figured out that you're smelly and old and you have a face like a dog? Who's gonna take you in since all you do is whine and cry? [*Approaching* SABINA *with growing anger*] What was I doing to you? Huh, what was I doing to you that you hada open your mouth?

SABINA [*backing off, frightened*]: And wasn't you wanting to hit me?

RAFAEL: But you started in on me outta sheer craziness. I was gonna fix that crap.

SABINA [*still frightened*]: Fix it then.

RAFAEL: No, I won't fix a single goddamn thing!

[RAFAEL *grabs his jacket with a single swipe.*]

SABINA [*terrified*]: Where you goin?

RAFAEL: To hell! I'm going to hell!

SABINA: You can't go! If they come . . . [*About to cry*] If they come here . . .

RAFAEL: Who's gonna come?

SABINA: Them, the ones from the citation. You can't go!

RAFAEL: Look, they ain't gonna come; we ain't no criminals. [*Swinging the jacket*] You gonna stop talking nonsense?

SABINA [*crying*]: I don't feel like talking about nothing; I don't wanna do nothing . . .

[SABINA *approaches* RAFAEL *and curls up on his chest.*]

I'm scared of that business, *viejo* . . . What's gonna happen to us . . .

RAFAEL [*softening*]: What could happen to us, old lady? Don't be silly, it's just a fine.

SABINA: But no one says nothing. You . . . You can't protect yourself . . . It's like when the kids started falling in love: you had to wait, wait just so you could end up alone.

RAFAEL: Damn, whaddaya mean alone? What am I, invisible?

SABINA: But you've got friends and you go drinking with them on Saturdays and Sundays. You don't have to be thinking all the time . . .

You don't have to be here all the time like me. I wanted to have other things someday, a clean house with a wooden floor and a wardrobe and all them things that other women have . . . I knew I couldn't have them, that they wasn't for me, but I always had dreams . . . And now if they take away the stand, I'm never gonna be able to have no more hope again. They can't steal that from me; they can't!

RAFAEL: Don't be so overdramatic, *vieja;* don't lay it on so thick. Alls they did was give us a citation. How many times have they written us up?

SABINA: Yes, but legit. They've written us up for having the scale fixed, for not sweeping or blocking too much of the sidewalk; but they always gave us a paper where it said why they wrote us up and how much we was gonna pay so everything will be all set, but this time we don't know what's going on; we don't know what we did.

RAFAEL: They just forgot to put the reason in, that's all. What else could happen?

SABINA: No, that number was the reason.

RAFAEL: It wasn't right, old lady; don't be so hardheaded.

SABINA: So then why did they send us that other citation where it says that if we don't pay they're gonna put us in prison? We didn't refuse to pay; nobody wants to take our cash cuz we gotta wait to see how much more we gotta pay for not paying on time. They're laughing at us!

RAFAEL: No, that's the way these things work: if you don't pay on time, they charge with interest.

SABINA: But if they are saying there is no citation, what are they charging us? [*Pause.*] You . . . did you do something?

RAFAEL: What? You crazy?

SABINA: Sure, you musta done something! I know you, you musta been liquored up and outta line out there somewhere.

RAFAEL: No, *vieja,* no seriously. Damn, you're not gonna start with me now! If I had done something they would have taken me off to jail; they wouldn't be writing me up.

SABINA: But the thing is I haven't done nothing neither!

RAFAEL [*uneasily*]: Yeah, see, it's a strange thing . . . Well, by the fifteenth we'll know what the deal is in court, no need to make it so tough on ourselves. [*Moving* SABINA *away from him gently so that he can go toward the stove*] I'm gonna see bout this thing.

[RAFAEL *looks the stove over.*]

You took the spare part out again.

SABINA: All I did was make breakfast on that stupid thing.

RAFAEL: That's when you took it out then.

SABINA: No, I swear, I didn't take nothing out.

RAFAEL: Maybe it was the inspector then; maybe he's so nervy that he dropped in to have some tea.

SABINA: Forget about that!

RAFAEL: Exactly, that's right. Let's forget all about that nonsense.

SABINA [*getting a bag*]: Give me money to buy bread. With the story bout how you was gonna buy a wreath for the departed, you socked it all away in your pocket.

RAFAEL: You don't have no bread? And why didn't you say so on the way?

SABINA: And weren't you so pissed off?

RAFAEL: Nope, I was going along laughing. Didn't you see how I almost started throwing punches at the wake because of you?

SABINA: Out of plain-old nosiness you butt into the conversation. And right away you wanted to duke it out; you can use your words to work things out.

RAFAEL: That's for the ritzy; they're scared of wrinkling their clothes.

SABINA: Starting a ruckus right in the middle of a wake; that's too much. You don't even respect the dead . . .

RAFAEL: I wasn't no friend of the departed; he brought back memories. You know that I've never cared for the walleyed.

SABINA: And I've never cared for thiev—

RAFAEL [*quickly, drily*]: Go, go get the bread. I don't want to fight.

SABINA [*exiting*]: You like to dish it out, but you just can't take it, right?

[RAFAEL *begins to rummage around, looking for something he can use to repair the stove. He starts to work. He turns it on, puts on the teakettle. Then he takes out cigarettes and starts to smoke, standing by the side of the stove.* SABINA *enters with the bread.*]

SABINA: You fixed it?

RAFAEL: Of course. There's a reason I've got a degree in paraffin stoves.

SABINA [*taking out the bread*]: Carmen was on her way to the wake.

RAFAEL: Damn, that Wally was popular with the ladies.

SABINA: Don't be blasphemous. Can't you see he's dead?

RAFAEL: He may be dead, but he's still walleyed. [*Pause.*] Well, and what did he die of?

SABINA: Señora Julia says that the acids ate up his lungs. Don't know what he was working at now.

RAFAEL [*commiserating*]: Damn, he was more sucked out than a dog-catcher's bone . . . When I saw his face it made me wanna give him a sandwich.

SABINA [*setting the cups*]: Better watch out he don't come and suck your blood at night.

RAFAEL: How's he gonna suck my blood when he's walleyed? He'd spend the whole night sucking on either side of me.

SABINA [*holding back laughter*]: Cut it out, man.

RAFAEL [*going to sit on the makeshift bed*]: They say Manuel's not doing good neither.

SABINA: Maybe with all this rain he got a drop of water in his mouth.

RAFAEL: Did you notice how swollen he was?

SABINA: Course he's swollen; ya know, the cirrhosis has got him by the short and . . . Careful, honey, two already died this month.

RAFAEL [*interested*]: Two? Who's the other?

SABINA: Cacaraco, ya know.

RAFAEL: Yeah, but that guy got run over.

SABINA: Hmm, so if they run them over it don't count?

RAFAEL: Nope, that's different. [*Pause.*] When I worked at the mill . . .

SABINA: One guy died one week and the next week another one kicked off.

RAFAEL: Sure, that's kind of what I was gonna say: it was like death was drawing closer. That same sort of thing, but worse. I saw it once in an alley by where I lived; in just one month four people in four different houses died . . . Strange business, it sort of it spooked me a little bit . . . [*Pondering*] And now two have died here.

SABINA: And it's gonna be three, cuz Manuel don't have much more to go.

RAFAEL: All of a sudden we're gonna die . . .

SABINA: You ain't gonna die! A bad seed never dies; even poison wouldn't kill you.

RAFAEL: . . . We're gonna die, because we're old; we old folks have to die; there ain't no way out.

SABINA: Well, and did you want to stay on as fertilizer?

RAFAEL [*reflecting*]: Hadn't never thought bout that . . .

SABINA: Bout staying as fertilizer?

RAFAEL: No, bout how we gotta croak. [*Pause.*] I'm gonna miss you, as much of a pain as you is, I'm gonna miss you, even if I die first.

SABINA: You scared of death?

RAFAEL: Don't know; thing is I ain't never thought bout that. But now that everyone's dropping like flies . . .

[SABINA *stops doing chores.*]

SABINA: I ain't scared of death; I'm scared that they won't let me die in peace.

RAFAEL: Hmm, how's that?

SABINA [*uneasily*]: I don't know . . . It's this thing I saw when I was little; every time I get sick I remember.

RAFAEL [*worried*]: You sick now?

SABINA: No, but since we was talking about that . . .

RAFAEL: What did you see?

SABINA: A lady who was dying.

RAFAEL: Bah, I've seen that so many times.

SABINA: But they wouldn't let this lady die . . . I must have been about five or six years old. My mom had been a friend of hers so we went to have a look. I didn't want to go in cuz it was a real little house and it was real hot, but my mom didn't want me to stay outside . . .

RAFAEL: . . . So your mom was always good to you.

SABINA: . . . The lady who was dying was fat, like a pig, and her face was all red. She was drenched in sweat, completely drenched, and it seemed like she wanted to start screaming, but nothing but snores came out of her mouth. The whole bedroom was closed off with black curtains and there was about ten women on each side of the bed, crying and praying; they wanted her to grab hold of a bronze crucifix and the lady pawed around every which way and they held her and forced her to hold the crucifix . . .

RAFAEL: Oh, they were helping her die right.

SABINA: Yes, that's what they said. They were all sweating and they wouldn't stop talking or crying even for a little bit. The poor woman opened her eyes like saucers, she turned round and round, she pawed, she wanted to breathe. But they wouldn't leave her alone for even a second, because they said that she'd already been dying for about three days and that she shouldn't suffer no more. The lady would open her mouth like a fish outta water, but they'd push her down flat against the bed and rub the crucifix all over her chest, on her mouth, on her eyes, and they'd cry and pray nonstop . . . If you'd seen how they flattened her with the crucifix, how they'd put it in front of her face, "Ask him to take you, ask him to take you," they'd tell her and they'd hold her and hold her . . . I ain't never gonna forget about that.

RAFAEL: But that only happens in the sticks, you know, Sabina.

SABINA: No, cuz it wasn't in no sticks . . . Promise me that you won't let no one get near me when I'm dying. [*Startled*] Swear it to me by your daughter, by our Gloria. But hadn't I tole you this before?

RAFAEL [*passionately*]: No, never; I would remember, see! I swear, swear.

SABINA: But I've asked you the same thing a bunch of times. [*Hurt*] That's how much attention you pay to my stuff.

RAFAEL: Or maybe since you always talk the same kinds of things, you imagined it.

SABINA: I didn't imagine nothing.

RAFAEL [*emphatically*]: For real, *vieja,* you hadn't told me nothing.

SABINA [*disconcerted, to herself*]: And so what have we done then?

RAFAEL [*not understanding*]: What have we done, when?

SABINA: We've been married over thirty years!

RAFAEL: Well, but . . . Damn, explain yourself!

SABINA [*desolately*]: Thirty years!

RAFAEL: Yeah, well, and so what?

SABINA: Whaddaya mean, so what? Thirty years we've been talking every day, working together, sleeping together, and you don't know what we've talked about—don't you realize?

RAFAEL: Hey, don't get so carried away; it ain't such a big deal . . . With all that baloney we've talked you gotta forget a few things.

SABINA [*dejected*]: Bull. On top of all the garbage that's happened to me, I've been talking to myself, like a crazy person.

RAFAEL [*losing patience*]: Well, you know I've always had a bad memory. Whaddaya want from me? . . .

SABINA: If you was to die and someone was to ask me sometime what you was like, I would remember everything you liked, what you talked about, what you wanted. I'd even remember the way you walk, but you . . .

RAFAEL: Me too, yeah, me too.

SABINA: No, no one's gonna remember me. No one's gonna go see me or talk about me; I'm gonna die more than everyone else! I'm gonna die so much when I die!

RAFAEL: Whaddaya mean you gonna die so much? Don't be silly. We all die just once.

SABINA [*sadly*]: You remember the lilac dress?

RAFAEL [*defensively*]: What dress?

SABINA: A lilac dress with white polka dots . . . [*Sighing and still speaking to herself*] I never had one like that.

RAFAEL [*relieved*]: Well, then. And so how am I gonna remember?

SABINA: I'm the only one that knows about that dress . . . Like I had lived alone in the world; only I know . . . It was in a store window. I always took you to see it, and I would stand there looking at it . . . At that time we was gonna get married and you were earning good cash at the mill, but . . .

RAFAEL [*lively*]: Oh, of course! When I worked at the mill I was one of the ones that earned the biggest bucks, cuz . . .

SABINA [*mechanically, sadly*]: . . . Cuz when the wool arrived you would hide three bolts in a room to work it alone on the night shift.

RAFAEL [*happily*]: Smart, see; you hada be smart. Don't you know that when the supplies ran out they'd leave me alone upstairs with the mixer and then . . .

SABINA: . . . The supervisor Julián, the head of the looms, would say to Don Alberto, "Rafael is the only one we can hire for piecework because he always has mix for the carding."

RAFAEL: Exactly, and then I . . . [*Looking at her*] What's wrong? You're crying!

[RAFAEL *gets up and hugs* SABINA.]

Damn, don't be so difficult, Sabina; what's wrong with you now? [*Confused*] I didn't do nothing to you!

SABINA [*pushing him away as if he were a child*]: Sit down.

RAFAEL: For real, I don't remember that stuff you told me; but that don't mean nothing. Why did you start to cry?

SABINA [*pushing him brusquely*]: Sit down right now!

RAFAEL [*sitting, offended*]: The one I always remember is Wally. Him I really remember good.

[SABINA *doesn't answer. She serves the tea. They eat and drink, grimly silent.*]

SABINA [*resentfully*]: One time I dreamt myself; you never let me tell you that either.

RAFAEL: Aren't you talking now?

SABINA: . . . But I came to visit myself.

RAFAEL: You yourself? You cuckoo?

SABINA: It was a dream. I came to visit myself; I was young . . . All of a sudden I saw myself standing there.

[*She points out a spot in the room.*]

I was there [*gesturing*] putting a patch on your jacket.

RAFAEL [*amused*]: So, how is this now? You were there? [*Gestures.*] And you were there? [*Gestures.*]

SABINA: Sure, see; cuz I came to visit myself.

RAFAEL: And weren't you sleeping?

SABINA: Sleeping, yeah.

RAFAEL: And besides you were also there [*gestures*] and there [*gestures*]? In other words, you were in three places at the same time.

SABINA: Just in two.

RAFAEL: And who was sleeping then?

SABINA: Me!

RAFAEL [*certain*]: You were in three places then!

SABINA [*losing patience*]: Let me talk! Didn't I tell you it was a dream? I came and I watched myself for a good while.

RAFAEL: You yourself.

SABINA: Of course, me myself. But much younger. [*Pause.*] Like I was before I met you . . .

[SABINA *falls silent.*]

RAFAEL: And?

SABINA [*taciturn*]: And suddenly the two of us started crying . . . Out of pity, out of shame . . . If I'd had a gun I'd have killed myself . . .

RAFAEL [*gesturing to the teakettle*]: Is there water left?

SABINA [*desperately*]: Pay attention to me!

RAFAEL: I am listening to you; thing is, I don't understand you . . .

SABINA: If you suddenly appeared to yourself when you was young and you saw yourself, you would start to cry too and want to kill yourself. That's what happened to me. Say something!

RAFAEL [*detached*]: And whaddaya want me to say to you?

SABINA [*with desperation*]: Nothing, nothing; don't say nothing!

RAFAEL [*puzzled*]: Why would I wanna kill myself?

SABINA: Because you're nothing; because you're a poor loser, that's why!

RAFAEL: Hmm. And when have I been more of a winner?

SABINA: Never; but at least you could have wanted to have something sometime.

RAFAEL: Damn, like wanting was gonna get me anywhere.

SABINA: The thing with you is that laziness has always had you by the . . .

RAFAEL [*irritated*]: Know what else? I think I'm gonna hit the road, with all the stupid things you're talkin now.

SABINA [*to herself*]: Damn, I wish one of the kids would come now. Why the hell do you even have kids!

RAFAEL: And what do you want them to come for? Afterwards you'll say that they don't let us buy nothing.

SABINA: I wanna talk, ya know; I wanna talk!

RAFAEL: Talk something good then. When you're not nagging about the fine, you're raking me over. I don't know what's the matter with you.

SABINA [*violently*]: Don't bring up the fine! [*Putting aside her aggressiveness*] What are we gonna do if they take the stand away from us? It's the only thing we got!

RAFAEL [*playing it down*]: They ain't gonna finish us off. Well, any water left or not?

SABINA [*discouraged*]: Yeah, there's some left.

[SABINA *gets up mechanically and serves* RAFAEL.]

Sure they'll finish us off; they'll finish us off good . . . Where are they gonna give you a job? You don't know how to do nothing and you're old . . . I'm too old too for them to use me anywhere. We can't sell on the sly on the street. We ain't no spring chickens that can run away from the cops. They should let us die in peace. Why don't they screw with the ones that's got the fat wallets? That's what I say.

RAFAEL: Because we're the punching bags. If it wasn't for us there wouldn't be no inspectors or no judges or nothing.

SABINA: I ain't gonna let them take the stand away from me!

RAFAEL: And who you gonna complain to?

SABINA: To them, to whoever!

RAFAEL: To who? There ain't no one. The inspector says he's following orders, the policeman says he's following orders, their boss says he's following orders. And the boss's boss also comes out with how he's following orders. Who you gonna talk to? If they all say they're following orders, you'd have to talk to God himself; he must be the one that's giving them all their orders.

SABINA: God wouldn't want to take away the stand; don't be blasphemous.

RAFAEL: And how do you know? Maybe it's blocking his way.

SABINA: Don't make a joke out of everything!

RAFAEL: But you keep singing the same note. Nobody's gonna take nothing from us. The citation ain't wrote up right; it won't fly—they've already told us that in three places. When you gonna understand?

SABINA: Then why they send us more citations and tell us they wanna put us in jail?

RAFAEL: All the papers say that: "Notice of arrest." But you just go and pay.

SABINA: What are you gonna pay, then, what!

RAFAEL: The citation, what else we gonna pay.

SABINA: And how come you say it ain't wrote up right?

RAFAEL [*bewildered*]: I ain't said nothing; they told us over there!

SABINA [*fearfully*]: Then it might be wrote up legit?

RAFAEL: Over there in court they're gonna tell us for sure.

SABINA [*troubled*]: Don't you see that they're just gonna take the stand away from us?

RAFAEL: Nah, they ain't gonna take nothing.

SABINA: But, and if it is true? If it is true, Rafael?

RAFAEL [*confused*]: If it is true? . . . If it is true?

[*The same as the end of the first act,* RAFAEL *and* SABINA *suddenly remain silent and immobile. Footsteps can be heard approaching, now of two or three people.*]

ACT 3

[*The same set. The same entrance. But this time* RAFAEL *and* SABINA *arrive somber, demoralized.* SABINA *holds a large, plain purse in her hands. They look a little better dressed, but still shabby.*]

SABINA [*leaving the purse on the table, almost on the verge of tears*]: I knew it. I knew it . . .

RAFAEL [*sitting on the bed*]: They're crazy; they're all crazy.

SABINA: And what are they coming for, *viejo*?

RAFAEL: Coming? No, why would they come?

SABINA: Yes, I heard the guy yell at you that they was gonna come. What more do they wanna do to us? They have to help us; someone has to help us!

RAFAEL: Scream then; go out to the street and scream. See who will help you.

SABINA: So if they want to kill us, they just kill us? I can't believe it!

RAFAEL: They have the money, they have the power and on top of that, they say they have the right. What can we do?

SABINA: But we are people too!

RAFAEL: Who treated you like a person? Did they pay attention to you somewhere?

SABINA: The social worker! What if we went to see her?

RAFAEL: What for? She's gonna tell us the same thing: "I can't get involved in this matter, for that you have to go . . ." [*Enraged*] Who knows where?

SABINA: Maybe . . . if you hadn't gotten so bold . . .

RAFAEL: And what did you want? Did you want me to set to crying like you? They already had us up against the wall . . . Damn, and right now when the high season was coming . . .

SABINA [*stubbornly*]: Then if you don't want us to see the social worker, let's send another letter to the newspaper.

RAFAEL: And the one we sent?

SABINA: Yeah, why don't they put it in?

RAFAEL: Well, it's such a mixed-up thing; they probably didn't understand.

SABINA: But you put the right address on it?

RAFAEL: Bah, and didn't we go together to leave it?

SABINA: But maybe we were supposed to hand it in personally.

RAFAEL: That's what we did, see.

SABINA: No, we didn't hand it in personally at all. Remember how that guy at the counter said we should leave it there with him? Maybe he didn't hand it in.

[RAFAEL *is defeated and* SABINA *insistent.*]

There's got to be a way, they can't do this to us! It's worse than if they killed us!

[SABINA *sees that* RAFAEL *is getting ready to smoke.*]

Don't smoke no more!

RAFAEL: Hmm, great, oh: so now I'm not allowed to smoke?

SABINA: You have to do something!

RAFAEL: What? Hey, what?!

SABINA: Think! You're the man!

RAFAEL: I tole you we should try to sell the license.

SABINA: And what were we gonna work at?

RAFAEL: Now we're better off.

SABINA: And to top it off you gave Gloria two hundred pesos.

RAFAEL: One.

SABINA: Two, I was keeping an eye on you.

RAFAEL: For God's sake, isn't she your daughter too? You would think you had it in for her; you're always after me.

SABINA: If you go around giving away money, what are we gonna do when we start to go hungry? Watch what you do; you think I can live on air.

RAFAEL: What did I do to you?

SABINA [*exploding*]: I am your wife, shit; I am your wife. You have to take care of me!

RAFAEL: She's your daughter!

SABINA: But you should love me that way, me! [*Pause.*] If you had ever shown me all that tenderness, if you had took care of me the way you took care of her . . . Then I wouldn't feel so awful now . . . Seems like everyone and everything has gone away, like nobody but me was here . . . It's worse than if I had lived alone because I had to pull the weight of the kids and you, I've been nothing but an animal. So many things have died on me while I was sitting there in that stand . . . Damn, such a God-awful shame.

RAFAEL [*provoked*]: Why do you say that? So I'm nothing. Damn, you sure are sweet . . . Didn't you see how they were squeezing us little by little without ever showing their face. In the police station, at city hall, in court; they all said the same thing, "It's the law, we can't do nothing." And the law ain't nowhere: it don't have a face, it don't have eyes, it don't have a body. You can't fight that way! How the hell you gonna scrap with someone you can't see, that ain't nowhere. Get it through your head! . . . And you take it out on me. You are sweet.

SABINA: I gotta take it out on you, who else am I gonna complain to? Want me to ask the neighbor for help, is that what you want?

[SABINA *goes to the wall and knocks.*]

Pedro, Pedro! The law and the license.

RAFAEL [*alarmed*]: Don't be acting foolish!

SABINA: I gotta tell *him*, ya know—since you ain't to blame for nothing.

RAFAEL: But it ain't my fault that they gave us a citation! After a month, we realized it was cuz the license was expired. But it wasn't expired neither because the new ones hadn't come out yet at city hall. Then they made us take a paper that said that; but so that they would give us that paper they made us go to twenty different offices to get another paper first and by the time they gave us the paper they'd asked for, the licenses had already come out. So then we had to start to ask for another one that said that when we started doing the procedurings, it hadn't come out yet. And during all this time, the fine was going up and up, how could I not get mad: they were driving me crazy; that's why I lost it.

SABINA [*mimicking* RAFAEL]: That's why I lost it. Your whole life you've done nothing but mess up. Are you gonna feed me now?

RAFAEL [*exasperated*]: I'm gonna feed you! Or did you think Wally was gonna come and feed you?

SABINA [*puzzled*]: What did you say? . . . What did you say? . . .

RAFAEL [*going toward the stove*]: Better not make me talk.

SABINA [*not intimidated*]: Go ahead and talk, piece of garbage; go ahead and talk. What do you have to say to me?

RAFAEL: No, no, nothing. [*By the stove*] I'm gonna make some tea.

SABINA: I don't want any crap to drink! [*Grumbling*] See what he does remember, bout thirty years have gone by . . . You have to be a real [*makes an obscene gesture with her hands*] to bring these things up.

RAFAEL: Sure, you have to be a real [*repeats the gesture*] to take leftovers. [*Turning to work on the stove*] I ain't never gonna forget that thing.

SABINA [*playing it down*]: I didn't even know you.

RAFAEL: You told me a story bout how you was gonna go with your mama to buy fruit for the orchards . . . [*Reflecting*] Whaddaya mean you didn't know me?

SABINA: You were after me, but I didn't even pay you no attention.

RAFAEL: And all that talking we did? [*Pause.*] I'd give you gifts, I'd take you out . . . They'd ask us: "When are you gonna get married?" Then suddenly Wally turns up on the block, he smiles at you and you go sleep with him . . .

SABINA: . . . I didn't go sleep with him!

RAFAEL: . . . You put on lipstick and you fixed your hair a different way . . . The first day he spoke to you . . . [*With growing anger*] For God's sake, the first day!

[RAFAEL *bangs on the stove.*]

Why did you always treat me like a used rubber?

SABINA: I don't know what you're talking about.

RAFAEL [*violently*]: Why did you do that to me?

SABINA: How should I remember!

RAFAEL: I do remember. It was Wally's saint's day, the thirty-first of August . . . It was raining, I was all wet when I got there to look for you . . . You looked pretty; you'd never done yourself up like that to go out with me. To go out with me you didn't even put away the baskets . . . What I've never understood is how you could be so degenerate as to go to bed right away with some guy that you didn't even know . . . On the first date! . . . And me speaking to you formal, asking you out to eat, to dance . . . Maybe Rafael isn't even mine . . .

SABINA [*horrified*]: What did you say? . . .What did you say?

RAFAEL [*bitterly*]: If you was gonna bed down with someone, you should've bed down with me! [*Approaching her*] With me!

SABINA [*tortured*]: You're gonna pay a lot for this, a whole lot!

RAFAEL: I've already paid more than enough when I remember that I had to settle for leftovers. And you still look down on me.

SABINA: I look down on you for being a pimp.

RAFAEL: I don't pimp for you—not for you, not for no one.

SABINA: You are a pimp, you loser. Don't you live off of me? Why don't you get some other work?

RAFAEL [*turning to the stove*]: Go to hell!

SABINA: Because they threw you out for being a thief, that's why! You can't work anywhere.

RAFAEL [*vehemently*]: No, no, I didn't steal nothing!

SABINA: Sure you stole, and they didn't put you in prison just cuz they felt sorry for you.

RAFAEL: They set me up!

SABINA: They caught you.

RAFAEL: No, I was gonna . . .

SABINA [*implacable*]: Weren't you ashamed when they searched you and they found the wool rolled around your body?

RAFAEL: I didn't have nothing! Don Emilio was the one that slandered me because . . .

SABINA: . . . They locked you in the office and they called everyone to come and have a look at you . . .

RAFAEL: I hadn't done nothing! Don Emilio . . .

SABINA [*cruelly*]: So you don't remember when they had you locked up and they called over all your fellow workers so that they could have a look at you?

RAFAEL: Let me talk!

SABINA: Thief! A thief and a pimp, that's what you are!

RAFAEL: I caught him on top of the desk with Don Alberto's wife and that's why he slandered me!

SABINA: Yeah sure, and he wrapped the wool around your body. You are a thief and a pimp.

RAFAEL [*anguished*]: Seems like it makes you happy.

SABINA: It don't make me happy; it's the truth.

RAFAEL [*pained*]: You've got it in for me!

SABINA: Sure I've got it in for you! Because of you I don't have nothing; I've never had nothing cuz I married you! . . . And now since they took the stand away, they killed me.

RAFAEL [*humiliated*]: And all these years? All this time we've lived? [*Pause.*] It's not true; you would have said something to me . . . But . . . before the citation weren't we good? I thought.

SABINA: Good. What have you given me? I've never even been able to have a radio with a battery. Where is what we've lived, what you've given me?

RAFAEL [*obtusely*]: Are you angry about what happened with the stand? Is that why you say these things?

SABINA: The stand don't have nothing to do with this!

RAFAEL: Then is it because it's been a while since at night . . . Is that why you say I don't love you? Because nothing happens? [*Disconcerted*] It's that I . . . I don't know . . . Maybe the wine . . . But you know that before . . . You've got it in for me for everything.

SABINA: What are you talking bout?

RAFAEL: Bout the two of us, see; bout the two of us. We've had children . . .

SABINA: . . . Children? [*Looking all around*] If we'd had children they would come to see us, they would talk to us. We weren't lucky at all . . . And now we don't have no place nowhere . . .

RAFAEL [*furiously*]: It's all cuz of that damn citation . . . They tricked us. They massacred us . . . The law here, and the law there . . . And what did we do to the law? All we've done is try to live. And we ain't dead yet. We're still alive.

SABINA: We're dead, they killed us . . . Once people are dead they don't care about nothing no more; that's why we said all them things to each other.

RAFAEL: No, we ain't dead. Tomorrow I'm gonna go real early and . . .

SABINA: They're gonna come! I know they're gonna come now!

RAFAEL: For what?

SABINA: I don't know. How am I gonna know, if we don't even have a right to know why they killed us?

RAFAEL: No, they ain't gonna come. Tomorrow I'm gonna go first thing in the morning and I'm gonna tell them how it was. I'm gonna tell them everything from the beginning, without blowing my top. [*As if repeating a school lesson*] When they gave us the citation, we went to ask why that was, then they read the paper and they tole . . .

[RAFAEL *realizes that* SABINA *isn't paying attention.*]

SABINA [*emptily*]: If they don't respect us, they don't listen to us, we can't live . . . I've lived my whole life in a pipe dream; I couldn't never have nothing that was mine forever . . . They could come any day and take it all away . . . What world do we live in? What shitty world do we live in?

[SABINA *weeps.*]

[RAFAEL *and* SABINA *remain silent, still. The sound of footsteps grows closer, heavy and threatening.*]

THE BEASTS

Fernando Berríos (Javier), Graciela Navarro (Luciana), and Raquel
Toledo (Justa) in a 1983 production of *The Beasts* by Teatro El Farol
in Valparaiso, Chile. The play was directed by Arnaldo Berríos.

PRODUCTION HISTORY

The Beasts (*Las brutas*) opened August 1, 1980, at the Instituto Chileno-Norteamericano de Cultura, Teatro El Farol, in Valparaiso. It was directed by Arnaldo Berríos with the following cast:

Justa	Raquel Toledo
Lucía	Isabel Núñez and María Angélica Arcos alternated in the role
Luciana	Erika Olivares and Graciela Navarro alternated in the role
Javier	Fernando Berríos

Another significant early production, by Teatro el Rostro, opened in Concepción, Chile, on August 12, 1982, and toured the country for several months. Directed by Ricardo Montserrat, it featured the following cast:

Justa	Ximena Ramírez
Lucía	Berta Darritchon
Luciana	Odette Cortesi
Javier	Gustavo Sáez

The Beasts has subsequently been staged in Sweden (1987), France (1999), Uruguay (2002), and Slovenia (2003).

CHARACTERS

Justa
Luciana
Lucía
Javier

ACT 1

[*The house, if you can call it that, where the Quispe Cardozo sisters (*JUSTA*, fifty-six years old;* LUCÍA*, forty-eight;* LUCIANA*, forty-seven) live out their last few months of life—life is also a stretch—is located in a place called Puquio Lagoon, at the foot of the Andes, and the only geographical landmark is a very relative proximity to Inca de Oro and Potrerillos (some two days on muleback). It is an inhospitable, cold, and desolate site. It is October 1974. Large room with clay walls and a totora-reed roof, which serves as a dining room, bedroom, and kitchen. A dilapidated bed, two straw mattresses, a bench, a table, a floor. Shoved in a corner, a bunch of old, rusty mining tools, from which juts out a heavy sledgehammer. An old woodstove. Dirt floor, hard, uneven. The only entrance is a door that has been repeatedly reinforced with planks and cardboard; a window in the same shape: creaky, dilapidated. Various equipment: a drawer with wool to card, another three or four empty ones piled one on top of the other; besides these, a small, badly made table that* LUCIANA *uses to make breads and cheeses. Despite the crowdedness, there is a certain order, a certain cleanliness; the atmosphere is desolate, sad, squalid.* JUSTA*, the head of the household, stands, braiding a rope. The sound of* LUCIANA*'s voice, singing, wafts in from outside.* JUSTA *listens, surprised, disapproves with sadness. (Beat.)* LUCIANA *enters carrying some pieces of firewood.*]

JUSTA: Why you singing?

[LUCIANA *shrugs.*]

LUCIANA: Don't know. Just to sing.

JUSTA [*neutrally*]: We ain't never sung . . . Strange goins on here.

LUCIANA: What goins on?

JUSTA: We ain't for singin, we're for pulling up trees, for bringin up animals; songs is—

LUCIANA: For singin. We can all sing.

JUSTA: I don't like it.

LUCIANA [*arranging the wood under the stove*]: You're silly; you think we're changing. No, Lucía and me would rather herd and cut wood too, but we gotta stay here until the weather gets better; that's how we always done it. Well, and you're the one that don't wanna go.

JUSTA: I ain't saying that; I'm saying that you don't do the things we used to do no more. I went out yesterday in the wind and everything, and chopped four cords a wood.

LUCIANA: Four cords ain't nothing. And afterwards you slept all afternoon.

JUSTA [*violently*]: That ain't true!

[LUCIANA *stares at* JUSTA.]

LUCIANA [*puzzled*]: Why do you get sore when folks tell you you're tired? You're the one that's strange.

[LUCIANA *turns toward* JUSTA.]

Come on, why don't you tell me what it's like? Don't be mean.

JUSTA: What am I gonna tell you?

LUCIANA: What we was talking bout when you told me to go get more firewood: the business bout falling in love.

JUSTA: Did Lucía shut in the goats?

LUCIANA: Yes, but Shorty Tail went down toward the holler.

JUSTA: Go on and help her. The night will catch up to her.

LUCIANA: And then you'll tell me?

JUSTA: Go on and help her!

LUCIANA: Don't yell at me! You said we was gonna talk.

JUSTA [*as she stops working*]: What you wanna know that for?

LUCIANA: What for?

[*She shrugs.*]

Don't know.

[*She looks outdoors.*]

When the winter is endin, when the plants start growin again, especially the cabriosa, cuz it's so pretty, I get to wantin to know . . .

[*She shrugs.*]

Don't know.

JUSTA: Even when it ain't winter, don't no one never come by here.

LUCIANA: No, that's not what I mean. I'm getting on in years.

JUSTA: So then what you wanna know for?

LUCIANA: Just wonderin. [*Pause.*] It's this thing I get inside here [*touching her chest*], a thing like if a wind was blowing inside me; it's very strange, but it ain't nothing like a sickness.

JUSTA: Did you meet someone just now?

LUCIANA: No, who am I gonna meet here?

[*She sits.*]

You know? The Ole Girl got me sad. [*Thoughtfully*] No, not pure sad; jittery too, scared . . .

JUSTA: The Ole Girl? How many goats have you killed? And you're gonna get all sad bout one that died alone!

LUCIANA: Maybe it was because of that, because she died alone . . . She still had her eyes open, she was calling out, Justa.

JUSTA: If she had moaned, we woulda heard it; don't be silly. Now you're gonna go soft in your old age; you are a true ignoramus.

LUCIANA: But she didn't call out with bleats, she called out with her eyes; that's why we didn't hear her. It was getting light when I found her near the big rock, over there where the cold hits hardest . . . She was born old, she was born with the face of a martyr, no buck never touched her, and that's how she died, alone . . . Not even her mother loved her.

JUSTA: It ain't just her, lotsa times the mama goats won't care for one a their young; that's why we gotta nurse em.

LUCIANA: She never lived nothin . . .

JUSTA: And what was you wantin her to live?

[LUCIANA *shrugs.*]

LUCIANA: Don't know. What the other ones lived: so happy sometimes, they'd run, play, fight or try to get together with the bucks to make kids. Not for her. There wasn't nothing for her. She died of cold, but her eyes was the same like she'd been beat to death. It scared me to see her, seemed like suddenly everything got more quiet, like if everything was waiting to kill us, and there wasn't no escape routes; everywheres you looked there was pure black sky and empty land . . . I seen that we hada die, that we couldn't take off for nowheres; I seen death on top of us, Justa; I seen it the same as when . . .

JUSTA: Don't make crazy comparisons. Ole Girl was an animal.

LUCIANA [*to herself*]: She never knowed nothin . . . I know critters don't cry, but it seemed like she cried. She had so much sadness in her eyes. It was the same as a person, Justa, the same.

[*Distant shouts of* LUCÍA, *herding the goats.*]

JUSTA: Go along and help her then.

LUCIANA [*getting up, going to the stove*]: I'm goin; let me leave the stove on.

[LUCIANA *works at the stove.*]

God is for the animals too, ain't he? Specially for the does and the ewes . . .

[LUCIANA *looks at* JUSTA *disconcertedly.*]

But he didn't help her; he didn't help Ole Girl. Maybe he don't love us neither . . .

JUSTA [*annoyed*]: Don't talk to me all the time Luciana; can't you see I'm working?

LUCIANA: You sad? You worried?

JUSTA [*alarmed*]: Why do you say that?

LUCIANA: Cuz whenever you set to braiding that rope, it's cuz something happened to you. I know.

JUSTA: What could happen to me here; don't be silly. I just want to finish it sometime to take it to Daddy is all.

LUCIANA: It's been a while since he died; that was round the middle a winter.

JUSTA: The dead ain't concerned with anniversaries; I can take it to him whenever I want.

LUCIANA: And what for?

JUSTA: Don't you remember? . . .He said that the gold deposit could be at the bottom of the Cortadela Ravine, but we couldn't never go down there because we didn't have no rope, and by then he was too old to go down on his own: that's why I'm gonna take it to him.

LUCIANA: And what for? Flowers, OK—but what good is that to him? Besides, it's been years already since he died; his bones must have wore out. No, that ain't it. What it is, is you're worried bout something; that's why you're braiding. That rope is like an evil bird; it means nothing but calamities. You worried cuz they didn't buy our cheeses?

JUSTA: No, that don't have nothin to do with it; don't matter if they don't buy em, we'll eat em ourselves.

LUCIANA: But we've got to send for the sugar and tea . . . And also we're almost out of corn flour.

JUSTA: Don't worry, we didn't have enough to make the trip worthwhile, but we're gonna make two cratesful now and go sell them down by Inca de Oro.

LUCIANA: But that's more than two days away, Justa. And there ain't no money there neither: that's what our cousin said. He said folks don't have nowheres to work now.

JUSTA: Our cousin don't know nothing; don't fret. And we ain't just got the cheese to sell, we got animals too.

LUCIANA: I'm not no little kid that you gotta hush; you know that ain't it. What it is, is that the folks are gone.

JUSTA: Folks? What folks? We've always lived alone round here.

LUCIANA: Sure, but I remember that before there was some folks down by the Coipa Ravine, and when we went down by Tambería, by Salitral, or by Tola too, there was some that come to herd. How come we don't see them no more? Where'd they go?

JUSTA [*uneasily*]: Don't know. Maybe the same thing is happening now that happened years ago, when they all got it into their heads to go work as miners up at Dulcinea.

LUCIANA: No, that ain't it at all. You don't see people go by nowheres; it's something else.

JUSTA: What something? What do you know?

LUCIANA: No, I don't know nothin, but the air is dragging along the quiet of calamity. It's foretelling something and you know what it is . . . What is it Justa? Why don't you tell us?

JUSTA: Leave me alone, I don't know nothing. When Mr. Javier comes, we'll ask him. Go over by Lucía.

LUCIANA [*interested*]: Is he gonna come? You think he's gonna come?

JUSTA: Yeah, he's gonna come. He always comes at the end of the winter.

LUCIANA: And what do you think he's gonna bring this time?

JUSTA: Who can say. But he knows that what we need here is sweaters and thick pants.

LUCIANA [*daydreaming*]: What I'd like is a blouse, a blouse of that material they call silk.

JUSTA: Silk? You crazy? What you want a silk blouse for here?

LUCIANA: Another winter went by already and, well . . . and I ain't never had one.

[*New shouts from* LUCÍA.]

I'm gonna help her. Seems like Stubby Tail got stubborn again.

[LUCIANA *moves as if to leave.*]

JUSTA [*to herself, somberly*]: Winter ain't over; winter ain't never over here.

[LUCIANA *stares at her, surprised.* JUSTA *reacts, equally surprised.*]

Why you looking at me like that?

LUCIANA: You sounded just like Daddy . . . Remember how after he got sick and couldn't go out no more, he would stare out the window and complain bout the winter?

JUSTA: Yeah, I do remember. He wanted to keep looking for that good-for-nothin gold deposit.

LUCIANA: You sounded just like him. [*Distressed*] Don't die, Justa; don't leave us alone.

JUSTA: The three of us have always been together. Don't announce calamities, cuz that's evil. [*Crossing herself*] Cross yourself.

LUCIANA [*listening*]: Sounds like the wind started up. Damn, when's it gonna quit. I'm goin over there.

JUSTA [*quickly*]: Cross yourself first.

[LUCIANA *quickly crosses herself and exits.* JUSTA *keeps braiding for a brief moment. The furious barking of dogs can be heard.* JUSTA *pays attention. She opens the window, looks around, shouts out, "Saltpeter! Pallen!" . . .* LUCIANA *separates the dogs that are fighting with Alicanto again.*]

LUCÍA [*offstage*]: Hey, don't hit Pallen!

LUCIANA [*offstage*]: Let him go, Saltpeter; let him go!

[JUSTA *quickly picks up a stick and exits. Echoes of shouts, barking, interjections. Then the three return, arguing.*]

LUCIANA: You got to tell our cousin to take away that dog!

LUCÍA: Sure, he's the one that starts all the fights.

JUSTA: We can't return him. We've always had an Alicanto here.

[LUCÍA *sits down, drained.*]

LUCÍA: Those was the oddball ways of my mother's husband: he thought that would bring him good luck. But the real Alicanto got mad that he named a dog after him.

JUSTA: Let him stay mad. If he didn't find the deposit, then don't let no one find it.

LUCIANA: The old man wasn't even no good as a second-rate guide and he figured he'd find himself some gold.

JUSTA: What did you say?

LUCIANA: That he hadn't never been a miner, so he didn't know nothin. You can tell just by this: an *alicanto* is a bird that comes out at night— if he stops somewhere and his wings turn yellow, there is gold; if they turn white, there's silver. And how could a dog do that?

JUSTA: It wasn't so's he would find the gold at all: it was like when you like someone a lot and give their name to someone else; that's what it was.

LUCÍA: And he wasn't even close, cuz there ain't no *alicantos* round here; round here there's red foxes. Then when you find em and grab a rock to hit em, you realize the rock is made of gold. He didn't know nothing bout no mines; he shoulda just stayed a breeder. Bout that, bout goats, bout sheep, bout donkeys—bout that he knew a whole lot. But age turned him foolish.

JUSTA: He wasn't foolish. If someone had helped him to look and dig, he would have found something, but none of the men wanted to.

LUCÍA: Sure, and he started to sell animals just to buy those stupid tools, and you would help him while we wore ourselves out lookin after the animals.

LUCIANA: And we had to chop thirty cords of firewood per day so's he could keep buying good-for-nothin uselessness.

LUCÍA: I still get something like tired when I remember.

JUSTA: Yeah, you're a real weakling. Look how you got just from pulling a goat out of a holler.

LUCIANA: Well, they kick. It ain't nothing to yank them out. I'd like to see you try it.

JUSTA: Next time one gets stuck in there, I'm gonna get it out, so you can see how it's done.

LUCIANA: It ain't a matter of wanting, Justa: you've got to be strong and we're old already. You're old too; before you'd sling any old goat over your shoulder when they was sick, now you cut four cords of wood and your hands shake the whole day long.

JUSTA [*upset*]: That ain't true; I done got the same strength as before, that ain't true! [*Passionately*] I throwed over a bull. I grabbed him by the horns and I throwed him over!

LUCÍA: That happened a long time ago. And Luciana and I helped you; I jumped on top a him to push him to his side.

LUCIANA: And I didn't let him move his legs.

JUSTA: But I had him by the head! I twisted it so's he'd fall: you lie!

LUCÍA: Don't get mad, Justa, Luciana is right: ain't no way we can do the things we done before. [*Pause.*] I began to figure that out with the bucket, over there in the well. [*Gesturing*] Before, I could bring it up to the top of the water and I wouldn't feel nothing; now I bring it up halfway and my back starts to hurt.

LUCIANA [*pointing out the sledgehammer*]: Remember when you could lift that with one hand? Well, lift it now.

LUCÍA: Sure, lift it; see if you can.

[JUSTA *looks at the sledgehammer, hesitates, and starts to braid again.*]

JUSTA: Do it look like I ain't got nothing to do but play games?

LUCÍA: But it ain't no game; it's so's you can see we're all the same.

[LUCIANA *and* LUCÍA *approach* JUSTA *and egg her on.*]

LUCIANA: OK, ready?

LUCÍA: Do it the way you used to.

[JUSTA *continues to braid, uneasily.*]

LUCIANA: See how you can't no more? . . .

[*She sits, worried.*]

What are we gonna do when we don't even have the strength left to knead bread? [*Pause.*] The cousin said we should think about goin up toward that place called Copiapó . . . That's where Vicente is.

LUCÍA: And Raimunda too.

JUSTA [*hard*]: I don't know no Vicente nor no Raimunda neither.

LUCIANA: Don't be sac'erligious; Raimunda's your daughter.

JUSTA: I don't wanna see that cousin round here no more! He just comes to eat our food and fill your heads with stories.

LUCÍA: Not me. Her.

LUCIANA: They ain't lies; they're things that he's seen.

LUCÍA: No, Luciana; Justa is right about that; the cousin is a big liar. How you gonna have a box that talks by itself and a stove that gives off fire without you putting firewood in it? Same as the thing with the brooms he said sweep without straw.

LUCIANA: Course in Copiapó the brooms sweep without straws, cuz they're electic.

LUCÍA: Electic? What's that?

LUCIANA: Well, I don't know. That's what the cousin said.

JUSTA: The electicity is a thing that lights up by itself, that you just use at night. By day you can't see it.

LUCÍA: That lights itself? Now how's it gonna do that, Justa?

JUSTA: By doin it. It's like the sun, but at night. You hit something on the wall [*she does so*], and it turns on. But it's bad. It ain't natural; it ain't given from the Earth.

LUCIANA: And where did you see that?

JUSTA: I seen it a long time ago, one time that we went with my daddy to buy an auger up at Inca de Oro. They had them in the streets too, but I don't know how they turned those on; it was like having a piece of sun in a glass jar.

LUCÍA: And how do they keep em from goin out when it's windy or it's raining?

JUSTA: Well, cuz it's *like* it, but not exactly the same.

LUCIANA: And the box that talks on its own, you seen it?

JUSTA: No, I didn't see that nowhere; and I didn't see them spigots that our cousin told you opens and hot water comes out. That's a lie; everywhere I went and opened one, nothing but ice-cold water came out.

LUCIANA: They ain't lies; they're modern convinces they've got nowadays; you went a long time ago, that's how come you ain't seen nothin. But he went just a little while ago, cuz they hada take his wife to put some pieces of glass in her eyes so she could see things bigger.

LUCÍA [*laughing*]: Pieces of glass in her eyes . . . Damn, you sure do fib, Luciana; how could you get a crazy idea like somebody's gonna put glass in their eyes so they can see things bigger?

JUSTA: Them's bad things they got in the city. Let's not talk bout it no more.

LUCIANA: But Mr. Javier says the same thing too, Justa; ain't you heard him?

JUSTA: No, I ain't never heard him.

LUCÍA: I ain't neither.

LUCIANA: It scares you but it's true. In fact, he says that there's a box like this. [*To* LUCÍA] Look.

[LUCIANA *picks up the drawer of wool and puts it on top of the table.*]

See here?

LUCÍA: Well, that's the box that talks.

LUCIANA: No, this one does something more. It can be this big or bigger, but you put it there and you sit about this far [*backing away*] and you start to see things: that's what this box does, it lets you see things.

LUCÍA: What things?

LUCIANA: Well, whatever you want: folks, shacks, critters, water, rocks—whatever you want. And the folks talk and go everywhere! And if they want, they go on horseback or by truck.

LUCÍA: On the inside of the box?

LUCIANA: Sure, but they go around that city they got.

LUCÍA: How you gonna get a horse inside a box this size? You think I'm a birdbrain?

LUCIANA [*innocently*]: Well, that's what I tole the cousin too at first.

LUCÍA: And what did he tell you?

LUCIANA: That it wasn't for real.

LUCÍA: You see? What was I tellin you?

LUCIANA: No, that the city wasn't for real; you can see it, but it ain't for real at all and neither is the folks . . . But it's true . . . Damn, I don't know how to explain how they do it, but it's true; I believe him cuz he knows a lot. Don't you know that he's always goin from city to city and he sees all them things?

LUCÍA: And you believe him, Justa?

JUSTA: No, those are the devil's things.

[*She crosses herself.*]

It's bad to tempt him.

[*She takes the drawer from the table.*]

The city is evil: María went there and she died; Segundo went there and he died; and Clara too. Everybody that goes over there dies.

LUCIANA: Vicente is still alive there.

JUSTA: He's alive? You seen him?

LUCIANA: No, I ain't seen him, but . . .

JUSTA: He's dead: Everybody that leaves here is dead.

LUCÍA [*crossing herself*]: Cross yourself.

JUSTA [*ferociously*]: No, not for them!

LUCIANA: Raimunda is alive too. Our cousin says she's alive, that he seen her.

JUSTA: If they ain't buried in the earth, they're buried in here!

[*She thumps her breast.*]

Just the three of us is left.

[*Silence.*]

LUCÍA: When he used to stop by to see the critters he'd left us to watch, my mother's husband would say: "Just hang on, when I find that gold, then you're gonna see what life is: life is a beautiful thing, girls, a beautiful thing!

JUSTA: Why'd you remember that?

LUCÍA: Cuz life is ugly, cuz there is three of us left and we're old: that's why I remember when he went a laughing along the hills and would turn around to shout at us that life is beautiful . . .

LUCIANA: Not me, I don't never remember nothing cuz I start to get scared. First my mother died, then Clara Lú, then . . .

JUSTA: Don't talk no more bout the dead!

LUCIANA: . . . They all kept goin along dyin, like when you chop down a row of trees . . . And they all had the same things in their eyes that Ole Girl had when she died like trash, over there close to the big rock.

LUCÍA: Ole Girl was an animal; don't be blasphemisizing.

JUSTA: That's what I say, that she shouldn't take liberties with the dead.

LUCIANA [*listening*]: The wind is blowing . . .

[JUSTA, LUCIANA, *and* LUCÍA *pay attention.*]

JUSTA: Are the goats fenced in good?

LUCIANA: You bet.

JUSTA: And did you leave the jerky a ways from the dogs?

LUCÍA: Yep, it's hangin at the end.

JUSTA: Better go an see, Luciana. [*Listening*] Seems like the wind is gonna blow hard, better not let it blow down cuz the dogs'll get at it. But put another sweater on; must be cold outside.

LUCIANA: I'll just go like this. It ain't cold at all: summer's comin. [*To* LUCÍA] Put on water so's we can have some tea.

[LUCIANA *exits.*]

LUCÍA [*going toward the stove*]: Luciana's actin kind a strange.

JUSTA: It's the time of year . . . The spring.

LUCÍA: What's the time of year got to do with it? We ain't critters or plants.

JUSTA: It's the same thing; time puts strange things in everyone's blood. And more in Luciana, cuz she's always wanted to keep company with someone.

LUCÍA: Our cousin is the one who puts hogwash in her head.

JUSTA: No, our cousin only comes every once in a long while: it's life.

[*She goes to the window, opens it, looks out.*]

Time is the same as the wind: it pushes and pushes, and it don't care which way you go. How dare it make Luciana wait, when no one never comes round these parts?

LUCÍA: I remember when Segundo took to lookin off into the distance, the man-who-was-my-mother's-husband said: "Just stay here and help me look for the gold, don't do you no good to have strong legs, there ain't no paths to walk here." But he just up and went, he was young; and that supozed time of your youth; sometimes it's like a newborn colt that don't understand reason.

JUSTA: It was true what he told him, he couldn't find no path and he died of cold up there, of hunger and cold.

LUCÍA: You knew the footpaths. How come you didn't go with him, Justa?

JUSTA: If the men didn't wanna help my old man, it was up to me to help him. I couldn't move from here.

[*She slams the window shut.*]

But I forgot em; I got to an age where I forgot all the paths.

LUCÍA: I ain't blamin you. I never wanted to leave.

JUSTA: You was like all the rest: you wanted to go, but by the time the old man died, life had already passed you by.

LUCÍA: Life passed by all three of us.

JUSTA: But I ain't bitter. You and Luciana is.

LUCÍA: That's cuz you got to know other things, you had a daughter and you went along to Inca de Oro. But I don't wanna talk about that now; now that Luciana ain't here I wanna talk to you bout something else.

[*She looks outside.*]

The other day I heard that the Bordones had sold all their animals.

JUSTA [*worried*]: And so what?

LUCÍA: The Pastenes too. And the Lunas.

JUSTA [*evasively*]: Maybe they wanna work as miners; it's happened before.

LUCÍA: No, that ain't it at all.

JUSTA: So what then?

LUCÍA: You know. I know you know. When we go herdin you don't talk to no one, you stay away from folks; but you know everything that's goin on. I don't wanna leave here. We shoulda went when we was young; now there ain't nothin for us nowhere; we're too old.

If something happens that we gotta go, I'd rather kill myself: I ain't scared of that.

JUSTA: Don't say that! Nothin's happened!

LUCÍA: It is happening; you suddenly got older than what you is; and the grass has come up, but you don't talk bout takin the critters and goin. Luciana and I are hard as rocks, don't worry bout scarin us.

JUSTA: I don't know nothin; I really don't know nothin; leave me alone!

LUCÍA: So then why ain't we gone?

[LUCIANA *enters.*]

LUCIANA: We goin somewheres? When?

JUSTA: In a bit, once the weather settles in. Everything locked up good?

LUCIANA: Yep. What was you talkin bout? I heard you shoutin.

LUCÍA: We wasn't shouting; we was talking bout the time of year, bout what it does to folks.

LUCIANA: It don't do nothin bad; it's good. I didn't even get a little bit cold.

JUSTA: You musta, the wind's blowin.

LUCIANA: Well I didn't. It's such a big night. So pretty . . .

LUCÍA: Big? Whaddaya mean big? It's gotta be just the same as always; you ever hearda nights getting bigger or smaller? They're always the same, always freezin, long, and ugly.

LUCIANA: No, she ain't ugly, she's lovely; it's enough to make you wanna run, wanna sing.

LUCÍA: Truth is you're in heat, same as the animals. You should be ashamed of yourself: you're so old you're falling apart and you're in heat.

LUCIANA [*angrily*]: Just cuz you fought with Justa, don't come and take it out on me. I ain't nobody's slave.

JUSTA: Leave each other alone, we ain't never squabbled mongst our-selves! . . . What's wrong with you now?

[LUCIANA *shrugs.*]

LUCIANA: Don't know. I ain't squabblin; she is.

JUSTA: When we go to Inca de Oro I'm gonna tell the priest to throw holy water on you; you're possessed.

LUCIANA: Like heck we're gonna go; you don't never wanna go no-wheres.

JUSTA: We are gonna go.

LUCIANA: To look at it from afar or are we really gonna go all the way there?

JUSTA: We're gonna go right there.

LUCÍA: I'm staying here. I'm not moving from here. [*Going toward the stove*] I'm fixin to make bread; we only got enough for now.

JUSTA: You should start knitting instead. Mr. Javier asked us for caps last time; and he always comes when the weather changes.

LUCÍA: I just knit for us, not for no trading; he wants color and we ain't gonna set to dying wool just to make him happy. If he comes, let him take some critters, like he always done.

LUCIANA: He don't want no critters?

JUSTA: He do; he just asked if we could knit him some caps.

LUCIANA: He knows we ain't never been knitters; don't set to knitting, Lucía, let's eat instead; been awhile since it got dark, we should be in bed.

JUSTA: Yeah, that's better. Is the stew ready?

LUCIANA: No, I gotta heat it up; I was boiling the water.

[LUCIANA *takes out a pot, puts it on the stove.*]

LUCÍA: Is that rope to change for the one in the well or are you making it to take to . . . ?

LUCIANA: Neither one. It's to trade with Mr. Javier for a blouse for me.

LUCÍA [*to* JUSTA]: That true?

JUSTA: No, it's to take it to my daddy. But if I was wanting to trade it I'd trade it for a thick sweater, not for no nonsense.

[*Dog howls can be heard.* JUSTA, LUCIANA, *and* LUCÍA *pay attention, frightened.*]

LUCIANA: They're howling. What could it be?

JUSTA: Nothin. It ain't nothin. They always howl.

LUCÍA: We must be real old: we're even scared a dogs howlin.

LUCIANA: I ain't scared of what I can see, what you can't beat with a stick is what spooks me once in a while, but only once in a while.

[JUSTA *opens the window.*]

JUSTA: Can't see nothin; everything's quiet.

LUCIANA: Then it's worse.

LUCÍA: Sure, death might be goin round the goats again.

JUSTA [*closing the window*]: Don't talk no more bout that! It's cuz of you all that the dogs set to howlin; you ain't talked nothing but bad things all day.

[JUSTA *crosses herself.* LUCÍA *and* LUCIANA *do the same.*]

LUCÍA: They've stopped.

LUCIANA [*listening*]: Yeah, maybe the wind moved something and the dogs got scared.

LUCÍA: OK, give us some grub so's we can get to bed.

LUCIANA: I don't feel nothin at all like eating.

JUSTA: I do, and so does Lucía; come on.

LUCIANA [*stirring*]: Hold your horses. I just now put it on.

LUCÍA: Why don't you wanna eat? You sick?

LUCIANA: No, I ain't got no sickness.

[*More howling. Silence.*]

LUCÍA: Do you want a blouse, Luciana?

LUCIANA [*cheered up*]: Sure, a silk blouse, and instead of pants, a skirt.

LUCÍA: Oh, you want a fancy outfit.

LUCIANA [*happily*]: Sure, a fancy outfit.

JUSTA: And what for?

LUCIANA [*confused*]: What for? . . . Well, to put it on.

JUSTA: And what good is it gonna do you to go round here in a fancy outfit?

LUCÍA: If you want, trade La Changa to Mr. Javier for a fancy outfit.

LUCIANA: No, I won't trade La Changa! La Changa is my friend, you all are my sisters but she is my friend.

JUSTA: And you can't trade her for just a fancy outfit, it would have to be a lot more things. But you can't go round in a skirt and a blouse no more, ya know, Luciana.

LUCIANA: Summer's coming; I ain't gonna be cold.

JUSTA: It's not cuz of the cold; it's cuz of your age. You need to be more proper.

LUCIANA: And when was I the right age to wear a skirt and blouse?

[*Howls.*]

LUCÍA: Before . . . Same as me and Justa.

JUSTA: But that's all over now.

LUCIANA: We didn't never wear them! How could it be over?

JUSTA: Well it's over.

LUCÍA: Same as the age for goin to school that my mama talked about is over, the age for fallin in love and the age for havin children—all that's over.

LUCIANA: You done some of that?

LUCÍA: No, nothing; don't you know?

LUCIANA: So then how could it be over?

JUSTA: Life done her part; it ain't her fault that we ain't done nothin.

LUCIANA: That's the same as if I'd had La Changa penned in and tied up and then afterwards I said it wasn't my fault that she hadn't never bred, hadn't never run along the ravine, and hadn't never given milk.

LUCÍA: And who tied you up?

[LUCIANA *shrugs.*]

LUCIANA: Well, I don't rightly know . . . The age for running is over, the age for falling in love, the age for having kids, and the age for wearing skirts—what's left for us now, Justa?

[*More howls, long and prolonged.*]

JUSTA: Don't know. Don't know . . .

ACT 2

[*The same setting, days later.* LUCÍA *prepares wool to knit.* LUCIANA *tidies up, sweeps, cleans, moves things around, and so on.* JUSTA *patches an old pair of pants. The atmosphere is full of tension, of boredom. They work a moment in silence.*]

LUCÍA: Don't stir up the dust so much, Luciana.

LUCIANA: I gotta hurry. I gotta get to making the cheese.

JUSTA: How many you making?

LUCIANA: Bout twenty.

JUSTA: So little?

LUCIANA: Well there ain't nough for no more.

LUCÍA: We're running low on flour too.

JUSTA: Yep, saw that.

LUCIANA: The weather's settled in.

JUSTA: No it ain't.

LUCÍA: They ain't gonna come to us to buy the animals.

JUSTA: We'll let two more days go by, then we'll go.

LUCÍA: We have to sell them and then send for the things. By the time they bring them we'll be eating roots.

LUCIANA: She's waiting for Mr. Javier. [*To* JUSTA] Ain't that right?

JUSTA: Yep, we gotta wait for him.

LUCIANA: But you're waiting for him scared.

LUCÍA: Scared? How come?

JUSTA: She's making things up.

LUCIANA: No, I ain't makin up nothin. Two days ago when I fibbed and told you he was coming, you got scared.

JUSTA: I ain't scared of the pumas, and I'm gonna let some man scare me? You sure are silly. You ever seen me scared?

LUCÍA: None of us is scared of the things we can see. What scares us is what we can't see.

LUCIANA: How's that?

LUCÍA: You can see pumas, you can see condors, you can see folks; but you can't see calamities, you can't do nothing to stop em; that's what makes you scared . . . There ain't never no one round here, but now it seems like we're more alone.

LUCIANA: Sure, there's a strange thing in the air. I've noticed it too. And the air don't lie. If you look at it good and you feel it, you can figure out anything: if it's gonna rain, if it's gonna snow, if it's gonna quake; even the critters know that, they feel everything.

JUSTA: It's just the change in the weather, that's all . . . As soon as Mr. Javier comes we're gonna go up to Vaca Muerta.

LUCÍA: Why we gonna go so far?

JUSTA: It's for the best. That's where the better grass is at.

LUCIANA: And how long are we gonna wait for Mr. Javier? Maybe he won't even come.

JUSTA: He's gotta come; that's his living.

LUCÍA: He could be sick, or maybe he died.

JUSTA [*to* LUCIANA]: Wasn't you wanting a blouse so bad?

LUCIANA: Yeah, but I don't like being cooped up, we ain't never been cooped up for so long.

[JUSTA, LUCIANA, *and* LUCÍA *keep working in silence.*]

LUCÍA [*thoughtfully*]: And what good do it do you to know what's gonna happen if you can't do nothin bout it? If it's gotta rain, it rains. If it's gotta quake, it quakes . . . If we gotta die, we gotta die. We can't do nothing bout it.

[JUSTA *and* LUCIANA *remain silent. When* LUCIANA *gets to the door, sweeping, she stands looking out.*]

LUCIANA: Seems like it's Sunday.

LUCÍA: I lost myself in the days a long time ago. [*To* JUSTA] Is it Sunday now?

JUSTA: Seems like it.

LUCIANA [*always looking out*]: Sure, it's Sunday; I know because of the air, cuz of how the weather is so peaceful.

LUCÍA: And so what if it's Sunday?

LUCIANA: Nothin, I'm just saying . . . They say that in the city people don't work on Sundays.

LUCÍA: And what do they do?

[LUCIANA *shrugs.*]

LUCIANA: Don't know.

LUCÍA: One time Segundo told the old guy who was married to my mother: "Today is Sunday," he said. "Today we don't gotta work." And the old guy picks up a stick and almost kills him.

JUSTA: That's a lie. That didn't never happen.

LUCÍA: Course it happened. It was before he got sick in the head and started looking for gold.

LUCIANA: Oh, sure, when he would send us all over with the herds.

LUCÍA: Yeah, bout then, he sent me and Segundo over by Vega de Chinche, and when he came to look for the cheese and to see how the animals was, Segundo looked him right in the eye and said that to him. Then the man who was married to my mother said to him, "Maybe God can do that because he's got everything, but we're poor." And he got a stick and he beat him until he left him lying on the floor, so that he wouldn't never forget it.

JUSTA: Why do you always remember nothin but the bad things?

LUCÍA: And what good things am I gonna remember, huh? We've always been like beasts.

JUSTA: Seems like it's true that being cooped up is driving you all crazy.

LUCIANA: It ain't just being cooped up. Lucía is right, we're . . .

[JUSTA *tenses up, shushes her with gestures.*]

What's wrong with you?

JUSTA [*to* LUCÍA]: Who'd you put the cowbell on?

LUCÍA: On La Mancha's mama, why?

JUSTA: Then it ain't her at all. I felt something from over by Bolillo.

[JUSTA, LUCIANA, *and* LUCÍA *listen.*]

LUCIANA: I don't hear nothin.

LUCÍA: Me neither.

JUSTA: Yes, yes I felt it; I'm never wrong.

[*Distant barking.*]

You see?

LUCIANA: Sure, they're worked up. Let's hope it ain't a puma, we better go see.

LUCÍA: Could be our cousin.

LUCIANA: Nah, they know him. Let's go see.

[LUCIANA *moves as if to go out.*]

JUSTA: Wait! He must be very hungry if he's come up this way. Get a stick; you can't go like that.

LUCÍA [*handing* LUCIANA *a stick*]: Here, I'll hit him with the pickax I got outside. [*Exiting*] Come on Justa, fore he gets some critter.

[JUSTA *goes to the pile of tools and grabs the heavy sledgehammer with one hand. But it seems to be rooted in the floor; disconcerted, she takes it with both hands and pulls; she barely manages to move it from its location. Now the dogs' barking is mixed with* LUCÍA's *and* LUCIANA's *shouts.* JUSTA *gathers her strength and goes to make a new effort to lift it when* LUCIANA *appears, excited.*]

LUCIANA: Justa, Justa, it's Mr. Javier!

[JUSTA *doesn't move; she is deeply preoccupied by her failure.* LUCIANA *approaches her, troubled.*]

What's wrong with you?

JUSTA [*somberly*]: Nothing. Is it Mr. Javier?

[*She tries to smile.*]

Didn't I tell you he was gonna come?

LUCIANA: Sure, you knew; come on, let's go help him!

[LUCIANA *and* JUSTA *exit.*]

INTERMISSION

[*Shouts and exclamations until the dog barking dies down. Then they enter with* JAVIER, *who is any age over forty—cheerful, vital.* LUCÍA *and* LUCIANA *bring in a suitcase between them.*]

JAVIER: You don't have dogs; you have wild animals.

[*He looks for a seat with his glance.*]

Excuse me.

[*He sits.*]

LUCÍA: That's the only way we have to protect ourselves here, Mr. Javier.

[JAVIER *takes out a handkerchief and wipes his sweat.*]

JAVIER: And who are you gonna protect yourselves from when even the condors have a hard time getting to these here parts? The poor mule was almost down on her knees by the time we got here, any further and I woulda had to carry her on my shoulder. No wonder you've never been to Copiapó.

LUCIANA: No, we've went. One time we went to get ID cards.

JAVIER: But that was back when elephants had wings; see, I wasn't even born then.

[*He laughs.*]

Well, and how have you been round here, huh?

JUSTA: Just the same as ever.

LUCÍA [*to* LUCIANA]: Give him something for his tiredness.

LUCIANA [*to* JUSTA]: What can I give him?

JAVIER: Just water, cuz I gotta drive. If I get soused I might end up in Potrerillos with the mule.

LUCÍA: We was thinking that you wouldn't come no more. We was gonna leave with the animals already.

JAVIER: To turn em in or to graze?

LUCÍA: What do you mean to turn em in or to graze? Who would we turn em in to?

JAVIER [*puzzled*]: You don't know? You didn't sell them?

LUCIANA: Nope, we've been here. Justa didn't want us to leave.

JAVIER: Oh, that's good; I thought you had fallen for it too . . . No, but I says, "No, they ain't gonna pull the wool over their eyes that easy." Don't I know it, since I've been acquainted with you a whole bunch of years.

LUCÍA [*tensely*]: What happened? What you talkin bout?

JUSTA: Hurry up and give him his water, Luciana; can't you see he's thirsty!

JAVIER: Vicente wanted to warn you, but I said there wasn't no need. "They might not know how to read," I says, "but when it comes to business, they even outdance the gypsies." Don't I know it, after all they've held me up for.

[*He laughs.*]

JUSTA: Who's gonna hold you up, when for a knit cap you want a whole herd of sheep and then you keep eyeing a second herd.

LUCÍA [*confused*]: I don't understand nothing. Who wanted to make fools out of us?

JUSTA: Just some crazy notion he's got, you know how he is. Hurry up with that water, Luciana!

LUCIANA: Hang on, I was listening. [*Going to get it*] When you seen Vicente? Is he alright?

JAVIER: Yep, he's fine. He's working on a hacienda, the Gate . . . Well his health is OK, I mean, cuz you earn real little in those jobs. Since he's been there he ain't been able to buy nothing from me. He probably even goes hungry sometimes; things are real tough over there.

JUSTA: What did he tell you? Did he remember us?

LUCÍA: Why you ask bout him now? You never wanna know nothin bout nobody.

JAVIER: The only thing he said was not to even think bout goin over there.

JUSTA: We wasn't thinkin bout goin; we ain't never thought bout it.

JAVIER: Course, I know; it's just that with that lie and all, all the folks is goin over to the city . . .

[LUCIANA *hands* JAVIER *a cup of water.*]

Thanks. [*Gesturing toward the pile of tools*] How heavy is that sledgehammer? Over in Río Jorquera they asked me to bring one.

[*He gets up, takes it.*]

Let's see if we can make a deal.

JUSTA: No, the tools ain't for sale.

JAVIER: You all plannin to keep lookin for the gold?

JUSTA: No, but we don't want to sell our father's belongings.

LUCÍA: Justa, those things belong to all of us, ya know.

JUSTA: We said that the rest of it is yours: the tools is mine!

LUCIANA: And what do you want them for?

JUSTA: That's my business.

JAVIER: It ain't nothin to fight bout; it was just a thought.

LUCÍA: I remember that when I went to tell my mother's husband that she'd passed away, he stayed a while like he'd turned to stone. Then he said: "Then there ain't no more reason to look for the gold." And he came down from the hills just to get sick and die. [*Pause.*] He never looked for the gold to give us a better life, like he said, that was baloney; he didn't care bout us at all so we ain't got no reason to keep them things.

JUSTA: They're mine, I used them with him . . . That's all we got from that time, we ain't got nothin else!

JAVIER: But don't get mad; like I tole you, it was just a question; if we can't do it, we'll make a deal same as always and stay good friends.

[*He gestures toward the suitcase.*]

I've got some real nice things in there for you all.

LUCIANA: What things?

JAVIER: The very latest from the capital; a nephew went there and brung em to me.

JUSTA: Are they heavy clothes?

JAVIER [*going toward the suitcase*]: Hold your horses, hold your horses. I'm gonna show you now.

[*He puts the suitcase on the table.*]

In this weather you don't need heavy clothes, see; it's summer now; you need to wear lighter clothes. I've got some cashmere sweaters that . . .

LUCIANA: Cashmere? And what critter is that?

JAVIER: No, it ain't no animal.

LUCÍA: But all clothes comes from critters.

JAVIER: Course, but this must be an imported critter, cuz I don't know it.

LUCIANA: And skirts? You got skirts?

JAVIER [*taking out the sweaters*]: Yes, but look at this first. Look, there ain't no way you can't like these; see how soft they are, the colors; this is what you need to wear, see.

[*He hands one to each of them.* JUSTA *does not accept the sweater.*]

JUSTA: No, that ain't no good for us: we want heavy pants, heavy sweaters, that's what we want—it don't matter if they ain't pretty, just so long as they keep us warm.

LUCIANA [*caressing hers, a pink sweater*]: Look how soft it is Justa; it's like you're petting a little lamb, and the color is the same as the sky turns in the evenings when it's summer.

LUCÍA: But we'd have to wear bout three each to keep warm, Mr. Javier.

JAVIER: That's why you wear them when the sun is hot; they ain't for working.

LUCIANA: And what are they for then?

JAVIER: To go out, to have fun.

JUSTA: We don't do that.

LUCÍA: Yeah, where we gonna go to?

JAVIER [*mimicking* LUCÍA]: Where we gonna go to? Damn, you sure are good at putting yourselves down. If you was old and ugly, OK, but you've still got your charms. Thing of it is, is you don't know how to dress, you ain't got no taste, you ain't got no vanity. A woman's gotta have vanity, otherwise how's she gonna find a husband?

LUCÍA: Fat chance we're gonna find a husband.

JAVIER: And why not? Ain't you women? Women are for having a husband and having children. And they all like it; why, don't I know it. I bet you that at night . . .

JUSTA: Leave us alone. We live the way we want! God wanted us to be here; he knows.

JAVIER: No, that's where you went wrong; you're mistaken. Don't you see that God lives when folks lives? Cuz if no woman wanted to get married and have kids, the world would end and if the world ends God ends too: so that he and life don't end, woman has to give birth, that's the law.

JUSTA: We're like the fig tree, that's what my mother used to say: the fig tree is God's work too, even though he cursed it.

LUCÍA: We ain't bad women goin round looking for men. What do you want us to do since nobody never comes round here? They don't even come for you when you're dying. When that lady that lives near Salitral fell into the holler and broke her back, they said one of them gentlemen that cures all the sicknesses was gonna come, but she was screaming for two days and she died and no one never came: if they won't come for you when you're dying, how they gonna come for you when you're alive?

JAVIER: Yes, course, it's a little far off round here. But a woman can always find something. Don't you know that a single hair from a woman pulls more than a team of oxen? You just have to fix yourselves up a little bit and you'll find that there's plenty for everyone in God's bounty.

LUCIANA: You think?

JAVIER: Sure, don't I know it. Why, I had two sisters uglier than original sin and they married real good. Course the husbands ain't no knights in shining armor neither, but birds of a feather flock together.

JUSTA: This is our life; we're settled here. Didn't you say Vicente was goin hungry?

JAVIER: Yep, he don't earn much and he goes hungry; but I don't think wild horses could drive him back here again. Over there he got to know . . .

JUSTA: He didn't get to know nothing, we know! Over there the folks are bad, folks who leave here get treated worse than animals . . . One time Nicolás came by here . . .

LUCIANA: Nicolás, Justa? When?

JUSTA: Once when you all was out grazing. Then he came by here and he tole me he was runnin away.

LUCÍA: From who? What did he do? He was the steadiest one a the bunch!

JUSTA: That don't matter there. There it don't matter how steady or how honest you are. On the hacienda where he was working they had beat him cuz he tole em they had to pay him in money, not in food. And they wanted to cut him up; that's why he was running away. That's where you want us to go?

JAVIER: But that's not the whole story, that wasn't the only thing he done.

LUCIANA: You saying he stealed something? Nicolás don't steal from nobody. We don't do that!

JAVIER: Nope, he didn't steal nothing or kill nobody: he argued. And where he was working that was worse than stealing. But let's not talk no more bout that; when Vicente comes round here he'll tell you all.

JUSTA: He can't come; if he comes I'll run him off with a stick, same as I done Nicolás. God marked him for death too, cuz he let my father stay alone in the hills looking for that vein of gold: that's why he punished him and he's goin hungry; and he's gonna die on the run, with no one to help him. You just wait and see. One day they're gonna throw him off the hacienda and ain't nobody gonna pick him up, they're gonna do bad things to him and he's gonna do bad things; then they're gonna be after him to kill him and when he tries to hide the folks is gonna run him off with a stick same as me, cuz he can't have no shelter. That's what's gotta happen.

JAVIER: Damn, you sure are tough, Justa, I ain't never knowed no one like you.

LUCÍA: Don't get mad. We don't want you to tell us off; we wanna trade.

LUCIANA: Course, that's all we want: so if all you brung is harsh words, then you better be on your way.

JAVIER [to himself]: I tole you, Javier, a closed mouth catches no flies.

LUCIANA: What did he say? Does he wanna trade?

JAVIER: That's what I come for, see; that's why I'm on that damn mule all day.

LUCIANA: Did you bring skirts? Show em to us then, so's we can make fancy outfits with these sweaters.

JAVIER [relieved]: Skirts? Yeah, yeah I brung em.

[He looks in his suitcase, takes them out.]

Look, look!

[He hands one to LUCIANA and another to LUCÍA.]

What do you think?

LUCIANA [trying it on over her clothes]: Oh, how pretty! Look Lucía.

LUCÍA: That's too short on you. You can't go round in that; don't be a floozy. [Showing hers] Didn't you bring a longer one in this same color?

JUSTA: And what do you want that for? You can't go running after the goats dressed like that! [To JAVIER] Why you bring us this now? Why don't you bring heavy clothes?

JAVIER: There ain't any. Before I brung em cuz I buyed em used in Potrerillos and other parts, but now people use their clothes till they fall apart. We're in a crisis; got to settle for what comes.

LUCIANA: What's that, crisis?

JAVIER: That's when there ain't no money cuz there ain't no work; and there ain't no work cuz there ain't no money.

LUCÍA: How's that? I didn't get nothin.

JAVIER: No, I don't get it neither; nobody gets it, but we all suffer through it. In other words, to try to explain it better: can you pay me in money for these things?

LUCIANA: No, we ain't got none; we ain't sold nothin.

JAVIER: And why ain't you sold nothin?

LUCÍA: Why ain't we sold nothin Justa?

JUSTA: The owners of the herds don't buy cheeses; it's the Coya Indians that buys, but the herd owners say the Coyas don't buy their animals no more, so they've throwed out the Coyas: the Coyas don't have nothin to buy nothin with.

JAVIER: That's a crisis.

LUCIANA: And why ain't there work? The animals ain't died; the land ain't dried up.

JAVIER: Them's things that comes from the capital. When it rains there, we get wet.

LUCIANA: The capital is something like a big city?

JAVIER: Course, she's our stepmother.

JUSTA: Always the city; everything from the city is bad. Ain't that where Mr. Government is at?

JAVIER: Mr. Government?

[*He laughs.*]

JUSTA: Don't laugh, he's bad! [*Pause.*] He wants to kill us.

LUCÍA: He wants to kill us, Justa? Why?

JAVIER: No, not you.

LUCIANA: Then who? Who is it that guy called Government?

JAVIER: It ain't a person, and it ain't in Copiapó, it's far, real far . . . [*Recalling*] Oh, you're talking bout the erosion thing! Course, almost all the breeders got scared and started selling their animals for whatever they could get. That's why I asked you before if you had found a buyer. No, don't pay me no mind: it was a mistake, or a misunderstanding, but a lot of smartasses are trying to take advantage of this to scare folks and buy their animals by hook or by crook. Don't you know that while the kingfisher and the oyster struggle, the fisherman gets both? And don't I know how the waters is round these here parts?

LUCÍA: What's he talkin bout, Justa?

LUCIANA: What's this bout rosion? What's that got to do with us?

JUSTA: They say that the goats eat the rocks and the earth, that the earth can wear out . . . They say the sheriffs is gonna come and kill our goats and sheep.

JAVIER: No, don't believe that. Damn, how can I make you understand, that's just an idea that . . .

LUCÍA [*to* JUSTA]: Is that why we ain't gone out? Is that what you knew?

JUSTA: Yeah. But if they come they're gonna have to kill us first! I'm not gonna let them kill the animals!

LUCIANA: But we ain't done nothin to Government; we don't even know him! And he's lying bout us: the goats don't eat the rocks! That Government don't know nothing; he's a liar!

LUCÍA: If they kill the beasts, it's the same as if they killed us!

JAVIER: But they ain't gonna come; that was a lie!

JUSTA: I didn't wanna talk bout this. I didn't wanna!

LUCIANA: What are we gonna do? What are we gonna do, Justa? We gotta hide the animals!

JAVIER: But listen to me, I'm telling you the truth: that rumor ain't flying no more. It came to nothing!

LUCÍA: When did it come to nothin?

JAVIER: A long while ago, when they realized that the animals don't tear up the grass from its roots. It's true, Justa; I ain't lying to you. Damn, see what happens when you live all shut in?

LUCIANA: Maybe it really is a lie, Justa; he knows, he comes from the city.

JAVIER: Course, just trust me; don't sell the animals.

JUSTA: We gotta sell to be able to send for sugar and tea and cornmeal. And we're out of beans.

JAVIER: Oh, well, to buy things, sure, same as always.

LUCÍA: See, Justa? You was worried for nothin. If you had said somethin to us, we could have gone out to ask. But you never said a thing to us.

JAVIER: Well, well, don't set to squabbling; you have to calm down now. After the cloud comes the silver lining; so pick out your duds so you can pretty yourselves up for the fiesta of the Candelaria and get over the unpleasantness.

LUCIANA: What's that like? We ain't never gone. We've just heard it talked bout.

JAVIER: It's a real nice party; people come from all over. They dance, they sing, they visit . . . And they fall in love too. Why, love don't have no age, and you girls ain't so bad . . .

LUCIANA: What are you saying, Mr. Javier?

JAVIER: Well it's true. Thing is you don't fix yourselves up, but if you look with patience, the three of you is easy enough on the eyes. Ain't they never tole you that you're not ugly at all, huh? Ain't they never tole you?

LUCÍA: Hey, Justa; who's gonna tell us that?

JAVIER: Well, nobody, if you stay buried in here nobody's gonna say nothin to you. That's why you gotta go out, get together with other folks. God helps those who help themselves. And you bet that with these sweaters and these skirts, folks are gonna be fallin all over themselves to get to you . . . You ever danced?

LUCIANA: No, never; we don't know nothin bout that.

JAVIER: Can I show you a little? It's real easy. Look.

[*He takes* LUCIANA, *takes a few steps.*]

But don't be ashamed, see; look, it's like this . . .

JUSTA [*pushing* LUCIANA *away from* JAVIER]: No, leave her alone!

JAVIER: What's wrong with you? It ain't nothin bad!

JUSTA: Yes, it is bad! What you're doin is real bad . . . Over by the Coipa holler, there was an old man who'd been left with no one, but he had the memories of the folks that had died and he talked to them: cuz of that he wasn't alone. And then an evil, sick Coya Indian woman come to him and asked him did he wanna get together with her; and the old man believed her and started to love her. But after the Coya woman ate and slept good for a while, she got better; and then she up and went. The old man cried all day and all night. And afterwards he started to talk with the dead to console himself. But there wasn't no more dead in the house to visit with, it was all full of the evil Coya woman that had left, cuz she had touched all the things and had went in all the corners. And then the old man died of sadness, cuz then he was really alone forever. You're doin the same thing with us; you wanna make us forget what we've always loved; you wanna put other things in our heads. But those are bad things, same as the Coya. They ain't for real, they ain't for us, they go away.

JAVIER [*thoughtfully*]: Yep, maybe you're right. The devil you don't know could be worse than the devil you do know.

LUCIANA: But hey, I wanna keep these two things.

JAVIER: Did you knit caps for me?

LUCÍA: No, we ain't got many sheeps, we didn't get much wool; there was just enough to knit for us. And besides you want us to make them with colors . . .

JAVIER: Well, then for all this [*gesturing toward* LUCIANA] and for that [*to* LUCÍA], you gotta give me three sheeps.

LUCIANA: Three sheeps? That's too much, Mr. Javier.

JAVIER: But you gotta keep in mind that your sheeps are lower grade; they're Argentinean sheeps.

JUSTA: And that stuff you brung is real good? Nah, you brung it up here cuz there wasn't no one in the city that wanted to buy it. So for all they've got [*gesturing toward* LUCIANA *and* LUCÍA] and for sugar and tea besides, we could give you just one goat: [*looking at* LUCIANA] La Changa.

LUCIANA: No, I ain't trading La Changa for nothin!

JAVIER: I ain't got sugar or tea; others bring that. I work in clothes.

LUCÍA: Give us the money so we can order it ourselves then.

JAVIER: No, I can't. That won't work for me: one goat and one sheep for all the clothes, nothing less.

LUCIANA: I ain't trading La Changa.

[LUCIANA *hands* JAVIER *the clothes.* LUCÍA *does the same.*]

JUSTA: See how we like what's ours better than your outside things?

JAVIER: But that ain't fair: you can't love with an iron fist. You're bullying them.

JUSTA: Don't be scared. I just wanted you to see. Now we're gonna give you what you say; but if you don't bring what we want, better not come back round here no more.

LUCIANA: Are we gonna give her to him? Are we gonna give him La Changa?

JUSTA: No, not La Changa, others. If we don't give em to him, the craving to have that garbage [*pointing out the clothes*] is gonna stay stuck inside you like a sickness.

[LUCIANA *picks up the clothes again.* LUCÍA *does the same.*]

JAVIER [*closing the suitcase*]: Are you angry, Justa? Damn, there ain't no way to make you happy, but I ain't gonna say no more to you. Don't nobody know you like you know yourself.

JUSTA: Yep, we was born; the rest is up to God.

JAVIER: God's will? Careful with that. God is the same as the wind, he can't look back; once you've growed up you're all on your own: a stitch in time saves nine, don't leave it all to God, cuz later you'll be crying over spilt milk.

[*He laughs.*]

Damn, and I wasn't gonna butt in no more. When do you go out grazing again?

LUCÍA: Might be in a couple of days. Right, Justa?

JUSTA: Yep, we're gonna go soon.

[*She looks at the clothes.*]

You brung bad things . . . Very bad. [*To* LUCÍA *and* LUCIANA] Help him pick out the animals.

JAVIER: If I get my hands on some thick clothes, I'll come before the snows start.

[JUSTA *doesn't answer; they exit.* JUSTA *sits, lost in thought. Barking and exclamations can be heard from outside once again; they fade in the distance until they are quiet.* JUSTA's *glance falls upon the pile of tools; she stares at them an instant. She stands and looks out the door; then she goes to the tools; takes the sledgehammer by one hand, tries to lift it; pulls, anguished, desperate, but she can't lift it. Spent and terrified, she doesn't seem to notice the arrival of* LUCÍA.]

LUCÍA: Justa, we gave him the two old . . .

[*She stares, puzzled.*]

What are you doing? Let go of that!

[LUCÍA *takes* JUSTA *by the arms.*]

JUSTA [*slipping away*]: Leave me alone. I have to lift it!
LUCÍA: No Justa, don't do that. What for?!
JUSTA [*fiercely tugging*]: I threwed over a bull, one time I threwed over a bull: I have to pick this up!
LUCÍA [*holding on to* JUSTA]: Don't wear yourself out for nothin, Justa. Don't do it. I know you can't do it!
JUSTA: Let me go; let me go. I have to do it!
LUCÍA: Leave it, you could tear yourself up inside! Get up, get up!

[LUCÍA *helps up* JUSTA.]

It's the same as what happens to me with the water bucket. Don't be silly; it ain't your fault. It's just age. It's just age, Justa.

[*She hugs* JUSTA.]

What got into your head that you done this? Look how tired you are.

[JUSTA *doesn't respond to the hug.*]

JUSTA: Tomorrow I'm gonna lift it. I was tired now, but tomorrow I'm gonna lift it even if I bust myself. If you lose your strength here, you die; you know that.
LUCIANA [*offstage*]: Lucía, come help me pen up the goats!
LUCÍA [*letting go of* JUSTA]: Not yet, it's still light out!
LUCIANA [*peering in*]: Look, come see; suddenly the sky started to close and the wind is blowing.

[*She senses something strange.*]

What happened to you?

JUSTA: Nothin, ain't nothin happening to us. Did Mr. Javier go?

LUCIANA: Sure, Lucía and I gave him the two oldest goats, but he didn't have no chance to argue cuz if he hung round any longer the wind might catch up to him.

[*She looks outside.*]

Maybe he won't make it to Bolillo . . .

LUCÍA: Is it gonna be strong?

LUCIANA: Yep, and it was so pretty out before . . .

LUCÍA: That's the way it is at this hour though: It's getting to be bedtime.

LUCIANA: I don't feel like going to bed. You know? Feel like going out somewheres.

JUSTA [*looking for her materials to braid the rope*]: Where you goin to? You wouldn't even last an hour out there. I don't know how long you're gonna be stuck on that nonsense. Seems like you're goin crazy.

LUCÍA: A person's heart don't know where she's at, Justa; it's just in charge.

LUCIANA: Thing of it is since you already know everything you don't care bout nothin no more.

JUSTA: When they come a-killing the animals, ask them: you ask them to tell you what love is like.

LUCIANA: They ain't gonna come. Mr. Javier said they ain't gonna come!

LUCÍA: The sheriffs ain't never came up here.

JUSTA: I don't believe Mr. Javier.

LUCIANA: You don't believe him, Justa?

JUSTA: A lot of folks has went already, they couldn't have pulled the wool over all their eyes.

LUCÍA: But we ain't done nothing so's they'd kill our critters!

JUSTA: They're far away, they don't know that goats don't eat rocks, they don't know nothin bout animals.

LUCÍA: We gotta go tell em then!

LUCIANA: And how we gonna meet up with that there Government if we don't know where he's at? Didn't you hear how Mr. Javier said he ain't in Copiapó, that he's in some other place real far off? . . . What are we gonna do, Justa?

JUSTA: Don't know. Been thinking about it for a long time, but I don't know what we can do . . . They say that they come in a big bunch, that you can't do nothin against them.

LUCIANA: No, I don't believe you! They can't do that! You came up with that just so you don't gotta tell what you know.

JUSTA: What do I know? I don't know nothin; leave me alone with that nonsense.

LUCIANA: Yeah, you do know; you know everything Mr. Javier said we gotta do . . . Me and Lucía are like the *quisco* cactuses that come out of the earth, bloom for a while, then dry up and die, and nobody knows that they came out.

LUCÍA: That's the life that the man who was married to my mother gave us; it ain't got nothing to do with Justa.

LUCIANA: I ain't blaming her: I'm saying we're the same as the *quiscos*, but we ain't really *quiscos*. That's what makes me mad.

LUCÍA: We're old already and we don't need to know nothin. I get embarrassed when you ask those things like you was young.

JUSTA: I don't keep my mouth shut to be mean to you Luciana; I keep my mouth shut so's you'll think it's something nice . . .

LUCÍA: Don't say nothing; don't tell her nothin.

JUSTA: Don't know why you're so stubborn. Don't know how you can still expect, at your age . . . But since no one never comes here, I'm gonna tell you how it is: it's bad, it makes you hurt forever like it was a curse . . .

LUCÍA: Don't say nothin, Justa; what you gonna remember for?

JUSTA: . . . I was seventeen years old then and we was lookin for the vein of gold over near the boundary line. He turned up all of a sudden, he said he was after a cave where there was some gold coins; my father made room for him round the fire and we offered him some coffee. He knew more things than Mr. Javier, prettier things . . . He had a look like the color of water when it's all clear and you don't know if it's green or blue, and his face wasn't all burnt like ours: it was golden. He said he came from a place where it was always sunny, where it didn't never rain; maybe that's why he was like that. He said that since we knew those parts good, we should help him look and that afterwards he'd help us. The three of us began to go out, and I would stand next to him so's I could hear him talk and so's he'd look at me. At night we'd make a big fire and talk and talk; he'd tell us what them parts he was from was like, bout the folks, bout the things, and I liked to look into his eyes when the fire lighted them up. I was happy, I was very happy to be alive . . . And one night he came by my side, and he started talking to me, and he took my hand; I got scared cuz my father might wake up, I tole him to go away, but he didn't pay me no mind. He kissed me, it was the first time in my life that anyone had kissed me and I liked it and I was ashamed; after a while he started to breathe like he was tired, like he'd run a long time, and he tole me to let him look at me under my clothes, that there wasn't nothin bad bout that. But I knew it was bad, and I tole him that if he kept it up I'd wake up my father and tell on him. I started to shake, I had this fear like animals get when they know there's gonna be an earthquake. "Don't be scared, nothin is gonna happen to you," he tole me. And he came and covered my mouth with one hand and with the other he opened my clothes, then he clumb on top a me with his whole weight; the rocks dug into my back like knives, and it felt like I was gonna smother; I started to claw at him and scratch him with all my strength. But it didn't hurt him none; he didn't feel nothing. His face had turned ugly, all sweaty, all twisted out of shape. And suddenly I felt like I was being split in two, like I was being killed, and in the middle of the pain I saw my mother, the house, the animals: I saw everything spinning round in my head, and I cried and cried and tried to scream, but he pushed down harder and harder on my mouth and hurt me worse . . . Afterwards he got scared and started banging my head against the ground until I passed out . . . When I woke up, he was gone and my father had me in his arms. "What are we gonna do now, Justa. What are we gonna tell your mother?" he says to me, and his face was full of tears, same as mine . . . [*Spitefully*] It was their fault; if they had come along with my father, nothing would have happened . . .

LUCÍA: Our brothers, you mean? No, Justa, they wasn't to blame for nothing: it's the life we lead; if me and Luciana had met somebody he would have done the same thing to us; who would want to get together with someone in this godforsaken place, who would wanna respect us . . . This is the life that the man that married my mother gave us.

JUSTA: . . . She just stared with her mouth shut. Didn't say nothin; didn't say one single word.

LUCÍA: She was sad, Justa; she was very sad.

JUSTA: If she had been sad, she would have cried, she would have hugged me; but she just stared at us without sayin nothin: her heart was closed.

LUCIANA [*frightened*]: You saying my mama didn't believe you?

LUCÍA: Let's not talk no more bout that; let's not talk no more! We're gonna pen up the goats. I'm tired of being awake.

LUCIANA [*discouraged*]: I knew that, I knew everything that happened to you . . . You should have said something else. You should have at least lied! But you never say nothin good, you've got a hatred for life.

JUSTA: I ain't got no hatred; I'm just telling it to you straight.

LUCIANA: Yes you are growin a hatred, that's why you don't never talk to nobody. You know the paths good; when the old folks died you could have taken us to some other parts.

JUSTA: To where? We don't know how to live in a city, we wasn't born for that.

LUCIANA: And what was we born for then?!

LUCÍA: It's dark already; come on, let's pen up the goats!

LUCIANA [*angrily*]: Well, fine, let's go!

[LUCÍA *and* LUCIANA *exit reluctantly.* JUSTA *keeps watch on them from the door, grim, desolate.*]

[*Two or three hours later. The stage is dark.*]

LUCIANA [*softly*]: Lucía, Lucía . . . Can you hear it? It's raining; it's raining and it's windy.

[*Silence.*]

Lucía, Lucía, listen . . .

LUCÍA: Be still, will you? Let me sleep.

LUCIANA: But do you feel it?

LUCÍA: Yes, yes, I feel it; it's the last rains.

LUCIANA: Seems like the weather wants to leave us here forever, Lucía.

JUSTA: Tomorrow it will be fine at dawn; these rains is short. And I already tole you we're gonna leave soon. Go to sleep.

LUCIANA: Were you awake too?

JUSTA: Yeah, well, you're waking me up.

LUCIANA: We only just now started talking; you were awake. Why were you awake?

JUSTA: Sleep, the point of goin to bed is to sleep.

LUCÍA: But you were thinkin, Justa: what were you thinkin bout? Why can't we sleep?

LUCIANA: I ain't angry at you; we ain't never been angry at each other . . . I didn't wanna make you talk bout that; don't think no more, Justa.

JUSTA: I ain't thinkin bout that; calm down, sleep.

LUCÍA: My mother wasn't mad at you; something else was goin on with her.

LUCIANA: Sure, Justa, since she wasn't born here she missed her land; that's why she was quiet.

LUCÍA: She was always inside, she didn't want to be with us or with the man who went to the city to be her husband; that's why loneliness swallowed her. And the same thing is happening to us, so now that we know that it's not true that they're gonna come and kill the goats on us, we gotta go; when you're locked up you can't fend for yourself.

LUCIANA: Listen . . . isn't the Candelaria a virgin? And if we was to tell her that we're in trouble, that we've got . . .

JUSTA [angrily]: Sleep, right now!

LUCÍA: Don't get mad, Justa, you can't sleep neither . . . Loneliness is talkin to us and when loneliness starts to talk to you it's cuz she's swallowing you. We ain't gonna be human no more; she's started to swallow us.

LUCIANA: That's a lie! . . . Ain't it so that that's a lie, Justa? . . .

[Silence.]

Why don't you answer? . . . Why don't you answer? . . .

ACT 3

[*The same setting, the morning of a cold, gray day.* LUCIANA, *who has been ill, is half sitting up in a rough bed. She looks carefully at her surroundings, tries to listen. She calls* JUSTA *and* LUCÍA. *Waits. As* LUCÍA *enters,* LUCIANA *is about to get up. She looks tired, deathly pale.*]

LUCÍA: You up? Me and Justa thought you wasn't gonna wake up no more. You all right?
LUCIANA: Yeah, just beat.

[LUCÍA *touches* LUCIANA.]

LUCÍA: You don't got fever no more; yesterday it started to pass.
LUCIANA: Is Justa mad?
LUCÍA: Nope.

[LUCÍA *sits at* LUCIANA's *side.*]

Dint nothin but your body grow up, Luciana; nothin but your body got old. What did you do that for? Why did you go up to the big rock when it was so cold?

[LUCIANA *shrugs.*]

LUCIANA: Don't know, fool headed.
LUCÍA: We was easy. We was happy cuz we was gonna go out with the animals, and then all of a sudden, you went off your rocker.
LUCIANA: Them's things that the air brings, that life brings, you can't do nothin . . . We was outside, talkin bout what we had a take with us, when all of a sudden Justa says: "Don't forget the water can, last time we had a come back to get it." I was gonna answer her when you said from a ways off: "Look at that there mountain, Luciana: it's turning colors." And I looked and I got this strange thing in my heart, a thing like I'd been smacked, like this. Because exactly that: the evening, the hill turning colors, and you all sayin that it had already happened a few times before . . . with even the same wind blowin and the same color in the sky . . . You get me? We had already lived that . . . Then I got real, real scared cuz I saw how all the days is just the same for us: it's like we ain't alive. That's why I put on the new clothes and I went

over by the big rock to wait, to wait for something to happen that wasn't the same; but nothing happened, the sun went down, the cold came, and nothin happened . . .

LUCÍA: Justa was right. We had no business puttin on them clothes.

LUCIANA: So why'd we buy em?

LUCÍA: Out of sheer muleheadedness, sheer muleheadedness.

LUCIANA: Our hearts is muleheaded, Lucía, not us.

[LUCÍA *looks outside.*]

LUCÍA: Don't matter. Don't matter no more.

LUCIANA [*surprised*]: Don't matter. Why not?

LUCÍA: When you was sick, me and Justa got real scared, we couldn't figure out what to give you, cuz the herbs didn't wanna bring down your fever. Then Justa went out to see if she could find someone to help us, but she walked all night and all day and didn't meet up with no one . . . And it was rainin, and the wind was blowin, rainin and blowin . . . When she got back we got to talking; we was talkin for a long time . . .

LUCIANA: What about? Bout me?

LUCÍA: No, not just bout you. Bout the three of us . . . There ain't nobody, Luciana.

LUCIANA [*tensely*]: Where? Where ain't there nobody?

LUCÍA: Nowheres, there ain't nobody nowheres: they all left. We're the only ones still here.

LUCIANA: They can't be gone, they musta moved up by Pantanosa or by Río Figueroa.

LUCÍA: They ain't; the worry musta run em far off. Sold their animals before they could be killed and then they left.

LUCIANA: That wasn't true! The sheriffs woulda come this way too!

LUCÍA: It's only just lately that you can come up this far, before they couldn't get through.

LUCIANA: It ain't true, it wasn't true. Mr. Javier done tole us he wasn't gonna hornswoggle us!

LUCÍA: He wasn't gonna be spreading rumors! And even if it wasn't true, all the folks believed it: we're alone, that's why we wanna go . . .

LUCIANA: Which way?

LUCÍA: Which way all the folks gone; which way all them that leaves goes. We're old. We're wore out.

LUCIANA: Justa says we wasn't born to live nowheres else!

LUCÍA: Listen, time passed through us and left us all dried up, left us same as the desert wildflower! . . . We don't have no life to take nowhere else, we wanna die: that's which way we wanna go.

LUCIANA: Kill ourselves? That's bad, we could end up wanderin in circles round here forever! You ain't supposed to kill yourself; you're supposed to die on your own, or else it's bad.

LUCÍA: No, it ain't bad, Justa knows. When you ain't got no strength no more and you ain't got nothin, it ain't bad. We're dead Luciana; loneliness killed us a long time ago, but they ain't buried us yet, that's all.

LUCIANA: But I don't wanna die, I don't!

LUCÍA: You can't stay on alone!

[LUCIANA *clings to* LUCÍA.]

LUCIANA: No, not alone, don't leave me alone!

[LUCIANA *weeps.*]

LUCÍA: Don't cry! We ain't never cried!

LUCIANA: It scares me! It scares me! I wanna get out a here too, but not by dying, not by dying!

LUCÍA: There ain't no other way to go. But don't be scared, we're gonna go together; we ain't never been apart.

LUCIANA: If we die we ain't gonna be together.

LUCÍA: Yes, cuz we're gonna tie ourselves round the waist, so's no one can separate us; that's why we waited for you to get better.

LUCIANA [*separating from* LUCÍA]: What's it like? What's it like to die, Lucía?

LUCÍA: It's good. You get to rest from everything, from winter, from hunger, from wind, from everything; and you don't have to think no more; you don't have to miss what you ain't never had no more; it's good to go, it's good to rest.

LUCIANA: But are you sure we ain't gonna be condemned to go round in circles here forever?

LUCÍA: That can't happen to us; God is in charge of everything you do. He musta helped Justa think, cuz he knows we ain't got no strength left to live without animals and with nothin in our hearts. He is good and he knows everything. How could we keep goin round in circles, when he himself takes away the terror so's we can go? He can't get burnt up about something he himself done.

LUCIANA: Yeah, that's for sure . . . Must be nice not to have this tightness in here no more.

[LUCIANA *touches her own breast.*]

But you're sad, Lucía.

[LUCÍA *turns her face away.*]

LUCÍA: No, I ain't sad at all.

LUCIANA [*sitting up in bed*]: And Justa? Where's Justa at?

LUCÍA: She's at the big rock . . . tying up the ropes.

LUCIANA [*fearfully*]: So's . . . so's we can hang ourselves?

LUCÍA: Don't be scared, Luciana. Dyin is the same as sleepin, but you wake up somewheres else.

LUCIANA [*disheartened*]: Course . . . Why do we have to kill ourselves, Lucía? Why can't we live?

LUCÍA: There ain't nothin . . . Living is like goin on up a mountain, goin on up thinkin your gonna find something, believin things. But if you get up to the top and there ain't nothin there, what are you gonna do? There ain't no more to go up; you can't go no farther. You ain't gonna go back down to climb back on up when you know there ain't nothin at the top, right?

LUCIANA: Ain't you scared? Ain't you even a little bit scared?

LUCÍA: No, when Justa tole me, I was; but now I wanna go.

LUCIANA: Death is sad, it's not good; remember Ole Girl.

LUCÍA: Ole Girl was an animal.

LUCIANA: Seems like we was born accursed. For us life ain't no good and death ain't no good neither . . . Ain't there more? Ain't there nothin more?

LUCÍA: Nope, there's just life and death.

[JUSTA *enters, hard, somber.*]

LUCIANA: Is it true what Lucía says?

JUSTA: Yep, it's true, we gotta go. [*Pause.*] You over your sickness now?

LUCÍA: Yeah, she's fine; she's all better now.

JUSTA [*to* LUCIANA]: Can you get up?

LUCIANA: Yes . . . but I'm scared.

JUSTA: We washed in ice-cold water, we throwed over animals, we clumb mountains, and nothin happened to us, now you got sick cuz of a handful of wind; age is takin our lives little by little. We aren't gonna beg it not to make us hurt; we ain't never begged nobody.

LUCIANA: Is it true that everybody left?

JUSTA: Yes, they was scared.

LUCÍA: We can't wait no more. So what if it ain't true? They ain't gonna come back; they done sold their animals. Not even Mr. Javier is gonna come back up here no more; he ain't gonna come just to do business with us; the folks that come to buy cheese and animals neither . . . But that don't matter, what matters is that all the tiredness buried me; I don't wanna keep goin no more. What for?

JUSTA: You scared?

[*She approaches* LUCIANA.]

You wanna stay here?

LUCIANA: No, no!

[*She hugs* JUSTA *impulsively.*]

Not by myself!

JUSTA: Ain't you seen what happens to those folks that dies of cold when they gets lost up there? They look for a cave or a big rock and they curl up there; but they can't do nothing, cuz the cold gets into them from every which way, they shrink up, they wrap themselves tight in the blanket, they warm their hands with their mouth, they rub themselves; but they keep losin strength little by little and they have to be still: then the cold starts to kill em real slow, like an evil animal, that's why their eyes stay open . . . Age works the same way, it comes up on you little by little and you can't do nothin to defend yourself but the dying takes a lot longer. I ain't gonna wait for that; nobody mocks me.

LUCIANA: And . . . and the animals?

[JUSTA *moves away from* LUCIANA.]

JUSTA: The animals come with us; they're even more helpless. We can't leave em to suffer.

LUCIANA: La Changa too?

JUSTA: La Changa too.

LUCIANA: I can't do it! I can't do nothin to em!

JUSTA: I'm gonna do it.

LUCÍA: You need help?

JUSTA: No, you help Luciana. I got em penned up already.

[JUSTA *starts to put on a kind of overcoat.*]

LUCIANA: La Changa first, Justa; so she don't see nothin.

[JUSTA *nods in agreement, takes out a long knife from a drawer.*]

JUSTA: We gotta leave it real clean in here.

[JUSTA *exits.* LUCIANA *starts to get dressed.*]

LUCIANA: Is it cloudy out?

[LUCÍA *is doing things with her back turned to* LUCIANA.]

LUCÍA: Why does that matter?

LUCIANA [*looking*]: Yep, it's cloudy. Why has winter dragged on so long?

[*She sits again.*]

It's not that you kill yourself cuz of loneliness; they kill you.

LUCÍA: Who?

LUCIANA: Everyone.

LUCÍA: Everyone?

LUCIANA: Yeah, everyone.

LUCÍA: How's that? Ain't nobody here.

LUCIANA: That's why: cuz they left us throwed out here like animals.

LUCÍA: The man that was my mother's husband . . .

LUCIANA: It wasn't just his fault; I don't know how to put it, but it's like loneliness was a stick and everybody hit us with it.

LUCÍA: Stop thinkin; if you get to thinkin you're gonna find your hate and you're gonna tighten up all over. You gotta go there easy, you gotta . . .

LUCIANA: What are we gonna do with the new clothes?

LUCÍA: Wear them. [*Looking at* LUCIANA] Don't dress like that. Justa says we gotta go in the best clothes, and we gotta leave it real clean here too, cuz . . .

[*The sound of blows, bleats, moans, and so on.*]

LUCIANA: La Changa, that's La Changa!

[LUCIANA *runs toward the door.* LUCÍA *intercepts her.*]

LUCÍA: No, stay here, don't look!

LUCIANA [*struggling*]: Changa! Changa!

LUCÍA: Stay here, I tell you. She's gotta kill em all so's they don't suffer.

LUCIANA: We're gonna go in sin!

LUCÍA: No, if we abandon em, then we're gonna go in sin!

[LUCÍA *and* LUCIANA *remain in each other's arms, listening to the commotion. It stops.*]

LUCIANA: Now we're really alone . . .

[LUCÍA *releases herself from* LUCIANA.]

LUCÍA: Help me, we have to leave things fixed up in here, if we leave it dirty the spirits could move in here.

LUCIANA: What spirits?

LUCÍA: The ones that's round here.

LUCIANA: There's spirits round here? See, I tole you: we're gonna be left roamin around.

LUCÍA: No, not us. The ones that's roamin is the ones that did somethin wrong; the ones that's killed, the ones that's . . . But come help me; don't look outside no more!

LUCIANA [*listening*]: See how quiet everything got . . .

LUCÍA [*listening*]: Yeah, there ain't nothin no more.

LUCIANA: Is that how it is over there?

LUCÍA: Don't know, don't know. You see Justa?

LUCIANA: Yeah, she's washing off . . . And what if it's worse lonely and quiet over there than it is here?

LUCÍA: That's where everybody that dies is; it can't be lonely.

[LUCIANA *shrinks, trembling.*]

What's wrong with you?

LUCIANA: I'm cold. I'm gettin cold again.

LUCÍA: It's cuz you ain't dressed warm enough, come here.

[*She takes* LUCIANA *to the bed.*]

Sit here. I'm gonna help you dress.

[LUCÍA *helps* LUCIANA.]

LUCIANA: Why did this happen to us, Lucía? Why did we have to kill ourselves?

LUCÍA: Be quiet. I don't know those things.

LUCIANA: Death is forever, everything ends with it . . . And it can be so quiet and so black . . .

LUCÍA [*uneasily*]: No, it ain't like that at all: God is there, it can't be bad.

LUCIANA: He's here too.

LUCÍA: Yeah, but it ain't the same.

LUCIANA: It's gotta be the same; it's the same God . . . Instead of givin us the strength to go, why don't he give us the strength to stay?

LUCÍA: Don't ask me no more; we don't know a lot of stuff about God here, we ain't in no city: all we know is that he exists. But if Justa says we gotta wash up, that we're goin in our best clothes, that's cuz it's good over there, she knows. Haven't you noticed that they put the best clothes on everybody that dies?

LUCIANA: Yeah . . .

LUCÍA: You see?

LUCIANA [*impulsively*]: Let's pray; let's pray, Lucía, so the fear passes!

LUCÍA: No, not yet, when we're ready to go. But don't make me talk no more; I ain't Justa, she's the one that knows everything.

[LUCÍA *and* LUCIANA *work a moment in silence, dressing and tidying up the hut.*]

LUCIANA: What would you do if you clumb to the top a the big rock and you seen folks far off? What if it ain't true that they's all gone?

LUCÍA: Nothin.

LUCIANA: Nothin?

LUCÍA [*firmly*]: No, nothin; I get more mad at life all the time. Seems like I been doin the same foolishness for a hundred years . . . And that I'd have to live another hundred years. Don't you feel nothing? Don't you realize?

[LUCIANA *looks outside a moment.*]

LUCIANA: If I own up, I'm mad at life too . . . But it's not cuz of what Mr. Javier said, cuz this happened to us: it was cuz of being cooped up; it's cuz we stayed here, Lucía . . . It's like when you hit yourself on the arm or the leg while you're herding the animals, with the heat of the hurry you don't notice nothin and you could go the whole day without feelin nothing; but when you take off your clothes at night and you see the wound, then all the pain and the fear gets inside you; that's what happened to us for staying cooped up, we saw our wound . . .

[LUCÍA *and* LUCIANA *continue doing their chores.* JUSTA *enters; she has taken off the overcoat and washed up. She starts to change her clothes in silence.*]

LUCÍA: Did you ? . . . Did you ? . . .

JUSTA: Yeah, all of them, except Saltpeter and Pallen; they're gonna come with us.

LUCÍA: And not Alicanto?

JUSTA: Nah, he was from here; there ain't no gold for him to look for over there.

[LUCÍA *gestures toward the clothes she is putting on.*]

LUCÍA: Ain't you got nothin new to put on?

JUSTA: Just one thing is enough; did you make the caps?

LUCÍA: Yeah, here they are.

[*She takes out the caps.*]

Luciana says are we gonna pray?

JUSTA: Pray?

[*She sits on the bed.*]

Why would we pray? We was put at the start of a path that killed us little by little; why we gonna pray?

LUCIANA: Don't say those things now!

JUSTA: The beasts I was killing up against the stone wall had a lot of things in their eyes, but none of them looked like prayer: why should they pray to me, since I was killing them?

LUCIANA: We ain't no beasts!

JUSTA: To time, we're beasts. Or did he treat you like something else?

LUCÍA: Time ain't no god.

JUSTA [to LUCIANA]: Why are you all shrunken up? You cold? I tole you them sweaters are too thin.

[She hands LUCIANA another sweater.]

Here, put this on a top a that one.

LUCIANA: No, I wanna go with this one.

JUSTA: Then move out the way a the door.

LUCIANA: Leave me alone!

LUCÍA: What you think so much for?

[LUCIANA doesn't answer. JUSTA takes out the rope that she's been braiding.]

That's the rope you was makin for . . .

JUSTA: He knows. I tole him already. We have to use it; we don't wanna get separated: we've always been together.

[She goes toward LUCIANA, ties the rope around her waist and calls to LUCÍA.]

Come here, I got everythin ready outside.

[JUSTA continues to tie up LUCIANA.]

LUCIANA [looking outside]: Who's gonna find us? . . . Are we gonna stay out there alone forever?

[JUSTA begins to tie herself. The lights go down.]

Are we gonna stay out there forever? . . . Answer me, answer me! . . .

[It would be ideal to be able to show the rock with the three nooses. And it would be best if the rock has the vague shape of a scaffold.]

FUNERAL DRUMS FOR LAMBS AND WOLVES

Berioska Ipinza (younger Isabel, left) and Valerie Cihylik (older Isabel, right) in a 2003 LaMicro Theater production of *Isabel Banished in Isabel* at the Workshop Theater in New York City. The play was directed by Martín Balmaceda.

PRODUCTION HISTORY

The *Funeral Drums* trilogy was the first production of El Telón theater company, founded by Radrigán. The trilogy was first staged in a community center, the Centro Eucarístico de Maipú, on the outskirts of Santiago on November 1, 1980, and opened in the Teatro Bulnes in Santiago on January 31, 1981. Under the Spanish-language title *Redoble fúnebre para lobos y corderos,* it toured the Santiago area for about a year. All three plays were directed by Nelson Brodt with the following casts:

ISABEL BANISHED IN ISABEL

Isabel ..... Gloria Barrera and Miriam Pérez alternated in the role

WITHOUT APPARENT MOTIVE

Pedro . . . . Nelson Brodt

THE GUEST, OR TRANQUILITY IS PRICELESS

Sara. . . . . .Mariela Roi

Pedro . . . . José Herrera

Isabel has been performed in Argentina, Uruguay, Belgium, Sweden, Australia, and the United States. The professional U.S. premiere of *Isabel* was produced by LaMicro Theater at the Workshop Theater in New York City on June 17, 2003. Directed by Martín Balmaceda, the role of Isabel was divided between Valerie Cihylik and Berioska Ipinza. The set was designed by Carlos Doria.

CHARACTERS

ISABEL BANISHED IN ISABEL
Isabel

WITHOUT APPARENT MOTIVE
Pedro García

THE GUEST
Sara
Pedro

ISABEL BANISHED IN ISABEL

[*The action takes place on any street anywhere. The set is limited to a gar-bage can, half of an oil drum. A white, saddish light illuminates the scene. The woman* (ISABEL), *shabby, any age over forty, enters limping. From one of her hands hangs, half dragging, a flour sack that constant use has turned an indefinite color. In it she keeps some of her belongings. She quickly looks around. She returns to the drum, leaves the sack on the ground, and sits on the curb.* ISABEL *takes off a shoe.*]

ISABEL: Damn, a flat, just what I needed.

[*She examines it.*]

Oh well, it's just a nail.

[*She searches with her glance.*]

There ain't even a rock. Sheesh, we're messed up Isabel. [*To the can*] You got somethin you can borrow me to hammer with? I'll give it back right away.

[*She stands, looks, takes out a piece of metal.*]

Here it is. Thanks man, you're the only good guy I've met today. All the others take off when I get close; they take off like I had the plague.

[*She shrugs.*]

Well, whaddaya gonna do? That's life. OK, ready Isabel, with this piece of metal we're all set. One tiny tap in case dust comes up when we hit it, and we get down to work. [*To the can*] Yeah, ya gotta take good care of your throat: doncha know that smog makes ya hoarse?

[*She sits down again, rummages in the jacket, takes out a bottle and drinks. She closes it, puts it away. She picks up the shoe and begins to bang it. She examines the result.*]

Know what else, Isabel?

If you keep smashing it, it's gonna break in two, better fix it right at home. [*To the can*] Yeah, I got a home. [*Pause.*] But it's not like me to be cooped up; I like to be in the middle of life: see houses, people, dogs, trees, birds, all those things that let you know you're not dead, though your heart has fallen in a hole where there ain't no light. It's true, I'm alone every day, but Sunday it's like I'm twice abandoned. Dunno why that happens to me, dunno why on days off the loneliness hurts me deeper inside. That's why I go out to walk.

[*She pays attention to a passerby who is not visible.*]

[*As he goes past*] Hey, gotta smoke you can give me? It's been so many days . . .

[*The passerby seems to go on without stopping.* ISABEL *shrugs.*]

[*To the can*] What was we saying? Ah, the house. Of course, I do got one. I'm not going to tell you that it's a terrific house; no, not gonna tell you no story. It's just a good little one that Aliro and I put up at the end of Santa Rosa . . . You know, we was doin real good, but suddenly they decided to build one of them pretty buildings where the people with the big bucks live, and they came and they took all of us off to other places. They dint even give Aliro and me the time of day cuz we wasn't married at all and dint have no kids. I loved him and he loved me, but they asked us for a signed paper where it said that. [*To the audience*] Listen, I said to the man that was writing, that paper could only be signed by God. And where we gonna find him? And I started to ask. [*Gesturing*] Do you know where he's at? Do you know where he's at? Do you know where he's at? [*To the can*] Folks would shrug, they'd look away, or they'd start laughing, like I'd asked about someone who'd died a long time ago. [*Pensively*] But he hasn't died, right? Cuz if he'd died, life would have died too . . . Well, the thing was that they took em all, and they left us throwed out until the machines come to knock everything down. It's the same as living in a cemetery: that's where the pure elements live, the day, and the night, and the moon and the wind. All things that don't answer when you talk to em and I like to talk, ya know, that's why I go out . . . I've been walking since my mother died; go figure how long that's been . . . No, better not think bout nothin. Cakehead was right. He always use to say to me: "Don't think Chabela, cuz thinking is the same as if they was to slash hope's throat right in front of your eyes." [*To the can*] Cakehead was a guy who always wanted to take me home with him but I never believed it, cuz the poor guy was crazy. When he didn't have enough to drink, or when he fell in love with some girl who didn't pay him no mind, he'd go and stick his head in some oven to kill himself: that's why they called him that . . . One time death got fed up that she had to come for nothing, and she didn't let him shut off the gas . . . I think he should have fallen in love with life and not with people. Whadda you think?

[*She bangs the can happily.*]

Damn, I wish I could be with Aliro, now that I found you to talk to. Course he's a little jealous, yeah? But since you talk so little . . . Still, there's gonna be plenty of chances for him to get jealous, right? We used to go all over together, he was even gonna take me to Lota one time, so's I'd get to know his family: my mother-in-law and my brothers- and sisters-in-law.* We couldn't go cuz the sale of bones and papers got bad and he wanted me to go real sharp. "Cuz since they ain't in love with you, they're only going to look at your clothes," he'd tell me . . . Now who knows when we'll be able to go cuz he's doin time. He's been inside a long while . . . What's he thinking? Does he remember me? He wasn't mad at all, he was laughing as he left. He stared at me and said, "Nice, the way you show you like me, good thing I didn't kill no horse." And he laughed and laughed. [*Pause.*] Maybe that's why I talk so much. Loneliness sucks, huh? It's like a dog after you; it follows you wherever you go. But the hardest thing is the night. That's when the troubles suddenly hit you all at once. Memories is the worse executioners there is, cuz they scream on the inside and you can't make em shut up with nothing. I don't know why things you done before have to bother you so much. Damn, I'd be OK with it if bad things hurt, but it turns out that what bugs you the most are the good things! So, what really gets to you is the days when you was young and pretty, the time when a guy grabbed you and kissed you down at the park on Independence Day; the time when you had

---

* Lota is a mining town in southern Chile.

a mother and father and everybody talked to you: that's what makes you wanna cry when you find yourself throwed out. [*Pause.*] They say that you can go crazy thinking, that you don't even notice when you start talking to yourself: that's the scariest . . . But I say: how can you go crazy just from loneliness when there are so many people all around? It can't be. That's how I stand it. Hmm, imagine if I went crazy, who'd wait for Aliro? [*Nostalgically*] Good ole Aliro . . .

[*She cheers up.*]

One day, I'm gonna introduce him to you, ya know? He's really great . . . Do you know how I met him? I was eating this real good thing that a lady had given me, it was over by a plaza that's down by San Diego. I was bent over like this, eating, when suddenly, I hear someone singing . . . I'm going to remember it as long as I live, that song that goes . . .

[*She sings a bit of one of those weepy boleros by Lucho Barrios or Ramón Aguilera.*]

Pretty, huh? It was him, ya know; it was him that was singing down the middle of the plaza, drunk up to his eyeballs. When he got to where I was, he stopped and stared:
"Hey honey," he said. "Where am I?"
"Right there," I said. "Can't you see yourself?"
It was one of those cloudy and humid days, one of those days when it seems like they're crying on top of you. But when I told him that, he busted out laughing and it was like the sun had suddenly come out all over. He said he'd come the other day from Lota, and he'd hit the bottle cuz he dint even have one friend. "So when you finish lunching, I'll treat you to a *digestif*," he says to me and busted out laughing again. He didn't want to talk no more bout himself, and he didn't want me to tell him stuff about me, cuz he said that people are born when they meet, that the rest don't matter at all. And me, that had never loved nobody, and that nobody had ever loved, began to feel like I wanted to thank life for things, like I wanted to hug it . . . That's how we got to know each other and we started to . . .

[*She falls silent, looks around, listens.*]

Maybe this guy has a smoke, the night is so long . . .

[*She smoothes her dress, fixes her hair, smiles. The man, who is not seen, passes by her.*]

Sir, might you have a cigarette that you could give me?

[*She stops, follows him a few steps with her shoe in her hand.*]

It's been about a week since . . . Damn, how can he not have . . .

[*She turns, discouraged.*]

With that fancy getup and he's not gonna have cigarettes . . .

[*She sits again.*]

[*To the can*] No, I do got some, it's just that I've only got two left, and I'm so scared of the night . . . Damn, I'm just like a blind woman that can't get away from biting dogs. I'm so calm and all of a sudden I get a big bite from out of nowhere . . . In fact, this morning I got up real happy. [*To the can*] I dunno, I dunno why.

[*She shrugs.*]

The summer, the sky, the people in short sleeves, I don't know. Thing is I found out there was a party in a house over by San Paulo and I went to look for the leftovers. I told the housekeeper there I could help her clean and she went to ask the boss and then she told me OK. Damn, there was stuff there! Chicken, potatoes, sandwiches, everything.

[ISABEL *gestures as if drinking.*]

And this stuff, what can I say, anything you'd want. Course I don't do none of those strange labels. I'm not gonna put you on. Aliro would. Aliro goes crazy when he sees them colored bottles. Not me, cuz I take a swig and fall flat on my face. Can't you see I'm not used to it? Rotgut is safer. Well, the thing was that the sly girl had me bustin my butt for her all morning; she even had me mop the bathrooms for her and when she was making up the bag lunch for me, in comes the old man, the boss that is, and he tells her: "No, no. These people aren't used to eating. Give her a bottle of wine and she'll appreciate it a lot more. But give her the bad one, because that's what these people drink." And he came and gave me this bottle.

[*She shows it.*]

That was when I felt a jerking inside cuz I remembered one time when we went with my dad to ask a neighbor to borrow us a few bucks and he said he didn't have it . . . My dad begged him, cuz hunger was making us see everything black. Then the neighbor invited us to drink a bottle of wine, and we went with him, hoping he'd borrow us some cash, but he had us drinking all afternoon and then the neighbor got mad: "Snotty bastard," he said to him. "Even after I give ya enough to get ya shit faced, you still want me to borrow you money" . . . When we got home, my dad started to cry. [*To the can*] Have you seen a man cry? They don't say nothing, they don't whine, they don't yell; they stare off like into the distance, and suddenly you see the tears start running down their face, and when you catch them, they try to smile, and then it's like they was crying twice . . . I was about six, but I remember real good . . . That's why I started to cry when the old man passed me the bottle; he laughed and told the girl: "Didn't I tell you that these people will go so far as to cry with happiness when they see a bottle of wine? Don't I know them." [*Pause.*] What was I gonna say to him? I came back, got to walking . . . We was always hungry, hungry for food, for clothes, for happiness and for everything, and that hunger we had since we was born got even bigger when my mom had a fight with my daddy cuz he couldn't find work and she told him to hit the road. "And the kids?" he said. "They stay with me, I'm gonna work to feed em," she told him. [*To the can*] I don't know much, but if one person forgets another all of a sudden, it's cuz they've got something new in their heart, right? [*Pause.*] Why does your mom stay with you always? I got to know hopelessness looking at my daddy's eyes, looking at his eyes you got to a dark courtyard, a courtyard where everything was dead; my mother had sorrow in her face, but my father had sorrow in his heart; he had sorrow there where it don't come out no more, where the stain stays forever . . . Why does your mother stay with you your whole life?

[ISABEL *takes out the bottle.*]

That's when things got worse for us, cuz after all he'd get some job here or there, but my mom hardly ever got work. [*Pause.*] Hunger, my friend, is long and black, like a hole you never stop falling into. But you don't fall down the middle, free like this, no, you fall hitting yourself against the sides, tearing off bigger and bigger pieces of yourself. That's life for us, to fall and hit yourself inside and out, but especially inside. In the afternoon I went to look for banged-up fruit at the market; at about six the garbage trucks arrive, and then they begin to take the cans from the stalls. Before, that was a real good scoop, but now lots of people get there and they crowd in behind the dump trucks. Old people, young people, children, everybody, even pregnant women and women with babies come to feed . . . They get like wild animals: they scream, they shove, they fight; and since they all get in up to their elbows looking for the least rotten, right away the fruit gets crushed, it ends up a mush the color of earth, and they start eating it right there or they put it in a nylon bag to divvy up at home . . . I couldn't grab nothing. Actually, I had caught an apple, caught it in the air, just as it was falling from the can into the truck. But this kid turns up, bout eight years old; she hadn't been able to get into the dump truck and she started to look at me: she was long and skinny, her bones stuck out all over the place . . . But the worst thing was the eyes she had, the eyes of an animal that's been run over, the eyes of a sick kid. She just stared at me; didn't say nothing to me. And what did she need to talk for, cuz her eyes was screaming everything that was happening to her . . . When I gived her the apple, she took it with both hands, and she bit it so eager that I got to wanting to cry . . . She didn't even realize she was eating the rotten part, that soft part, coffee colored, that turns to mud inside your mouth; I knew she was gonna start to throw up, so I left . . . Poor kid. How much longer will she last? [*Pause.*] Damn, if I was God's wife, I'd say: "Listen up, my old man, you're so into the miracle thing, open the eyes of the dopes down there. They're making a mess of the life you gave them. They dished out the laughter and bucks to a few, and to the others they gave silence and kicks in the ass. I know you don't want to get involved in nothing, that you want them to learn on their own, but they don't learn man, and you can't just stand there with your hands in your pockets. How do you expect them to warm up to you when they eat in garbage dumps and sleep thrown out on the streets? That's a lot to ask, ya know. And it's also a lot to ask the other ones to remember you because they're very busy having fun and dining out; it's a serious problem man: if you don't send a little miracle soon we're going to end up more alone than loneliness; and to top it all off, they killed the son. Wake up, wake up, my old man, we're dying down there."

[*She laughs.*]

The wife of God, the things that pop into your head when you don't have no one to talk to . . .

[*She takes out the bottle, drinks, sadly.*]

Yeah, well, the only one who talked to me was Aliro; but now he's in prison . . .Want me to tell you the truth? I put him in prison; I didn't know that without him this was gonna happen to me . . . Know why I put him in prison? Cuz he squeezed the birds. See, we sold birds. When they stopped buying bones and papers at San Camilo, Aliro got the idea of selling birds; it went good for us. See, it didn't cost us nothing, ya know? But I hadn't never got it that when he handed em to the people, he'd give em a little squeeze. Then they'd die in two or three weeks; they'd be dying little by little. He'd say that that's how the business had to be so's the sales wouldn't stop; but I couldn't stand that, it made me very sad, cuz it's like killing children. Now no one talks, no one laughs, no one says hello; the birds are the only ones that sing. If they're quiet, all of life will be quiet, and us that don't have nothin, we's gonna die crushed by the silence . . . I begged him, I cried, but there was no way: "That's how life is, Isabel," he said to me. "If we don't kill the birds, you're gonna die of hunger. I do it so's you don't die." He said a lot of things, but I couldn't stand it, and I went and turned him in. Fair is fair . . . What else could I do? How much time do they give you for killing birds? He must have been in there more than a year by now and I haven't been able to see him, cuz first they took him one place, then another. I've asked, but no one knows. [*To the audience*] Where could he be? Where could he be? Where could he be? [*Discouraged*] No one knows where God is or where the people are . . . [*To the can*] What's going on with everyone? What's going on that they don't talk? What's wrong with them that they don't kiss, that they don't laugh? What's wrong with them that it seems like they're dead? [*As if someone were going by*] Hey, listen, don't you have a . . . [*Discouraged*] Damn, I missed him cuz I was talking.

[*She looks all around.*]

Wonder what time is it? Must be real late . . . But there's no one in the room, what's the point of going? Where I live, there's not much traffic, so you don't even get to hear the hustle of the buses. Shit, it's a crime what they're doing with me; they're killing me, and I ain't done nothin to nobody, just be poor, go round like this. But that's not a crime, ain't no reason to leave me alone, no reason not to talk to me . . .

[*She picks up the bottle, drinks. She rummages through the jacket, takes out a pack of Liberty cigarettes, shows it to the can.*]

Can't you see, I got some. But it's just two and the night don't never end when you live missing someone, cuz it's not just him that's gone. See, with Aliro we'd have tea, we'd make a tomato salad, and we'd get to chatting: that disappeared too. When he was drunk, he'd sing, he'd laugh at everything and chase me round the room . . . And he was so funny when he talked; see, I'm the queen of shut-eye, so every night I'd bundle up good and cuddle up by his side and tell God, "Dear God, make it so that the night will last forever, so that it don't never end." And then he'd come and tell me, "Get with it, girl, one day he's gonna pay attention to you and it's gonna be your fault that we kick the bucket. He always talked to me like that, with some smart remark . . . But there ain't nothin like that nowhere now; there ain't nothin but silence, nothin but darkness. No, I can't be in the bedroom: what with all his eyes saw, all his hands touched, it throws me into sadness. Sometimes I look at a chair and I feel like I've been stabbed from head to toe: that's why I go out.

[*She drinks.*]

But that don't get me nothin neither cuz when its daytime and there's lots of people in the street nobody even looks at me cuz they're scared

I might ask em for somethin. What can I do then? I'm not gonna start talkin to myself cuz that's what scares me, goin crazy . . . Damn, if Aliro don't get out soon, my daddy could at least turn up around here. [*To the can*] Don't laugh. You think cuz I'm old I've never had a father? I remember that when I was little and I went out with him, he always used to say to me: "If you ever get lost, just sit and wait for me right there. Don't get to walking round, cuz that's worse. You sit and wait for me." I don't know where I lost him, don't remember; but sometimes when I go out to walk, I sit an hour or two out there in case he comes to look for me . . . But he hasn't never turned up. And how's he gonna turn up, since he's lost too . . . [*To the can*] Are you tired of talking to me? Well don't get tired. Can't you see that I don't wanna go yet? After all, there's a nice breeze here and we're comfy. Ain't it true that we're comfy? Sure, see, we're fine; it's not like you're just OK when you've got bucks, no: you're fine when you've got somebody to listen, to pay attention, just like you. Cuz if you're not gonna talk to nobody, you're better off dead, see; no point in goin through the motions. [*Thoughtfully*] But people are real strange, huh? Like yesterday I was sittin in a park, fixin this piece of crap [*showing the shoe*]. When some guy comes and sits next to me. Made me happy, ya know. "Now you're gonna talk and talk, Isabel," I tole myself. But I didn't even look at the guy, cuz you can't be so bold neither. Don't you know that right away they think something else? And just cuz you're poor it's not like you don't have no dignity, ya know. So I kept fixin the shoe like nothin was goin on. And suddenly I hear him talk. But since he talked on this side [*gesturing to her left*] and I'm kinda deaf in that ear; I didn't understand nothin. Then I turns around and I says with all due respect: "Excuse me sir, but I didn't understand nothing you said to me." The guy kept blabbering without paying me no mind, so I told him again to forgive me, but that I couldn't hear nothin on that side cuz once I'd been smacked there with a bat in a fuss we had with some neighbors who wanted to hit Aliro over there in a bar in San Rafael. Listen, and when I finished explaining the matter good, the guy turns round to me madder than if I had cussed him out, he looked at me with these crazy-man eyes and says to me, "So get it through your head, busybody bitch, I'm not talkin to you; I'm talking to myself!" And he got up and he went off swearing at me. [*To the* can] What do you make of that? [*Wondering*] By himself. Talking to himself . . . Damn, that's gotta be sad. Don't I tell you that people is goin crazy little by little? Listen, the worst is that nobody gets it, like in everything, when it's too late we are just going to stare [*she looks at the audience*] and we're gonna say: "How could we let this happen? How could we let it happen?"

[*She is quiet. She keeps thinking. She turns her head slowly toward the can and looks at it fixedly.*]

Listen, well, damn, I've been talking to myself for a while now, ya know. So ain't you my friend? Didn't you lend me a piece of metal? Didn't you listen to me for about an hour? [*Aggressively*] Or you think you're hot shit too?

[*She hits the can.*]

Talk then. Ain't I a person? [*Anguished*] Ain't I a person?

[*She shakes the can.*]

Talk, talk, talk! [*Weepy*] There ain't nobody in the room. There ain't nobody nowhere . . .

[ISABEL *shakes the can desperately.*]

Please, talk to me, talk to me, talk to me . . .

WITHOUT APPARENT MOTIVE

[*The present. The action occurs at dusk on September 17 in a deserted site in the center of which can be seen a deep hole.* A shovel has been thrown down at random.* PEDRO GARCÍA, *any age over forty, enters restless, uneasy. He is a man who returns to a place of horror, attracted by a blind, nameless force.*]

PEDRO: So I came back sir . . . Know why I came back? Don't know, see. I swear . . . I mean, I remembered that I hadn't told you nothin. I just left. I thought that's the way it was, that there wasn't no more to say, no more to do. Same as when you go out to do a job or a chore, you finish and you go . . . But I started to feel weird, like I was hungry or thirsty, but not hunger for food or thirst for wine, for something else: it was hunger for crying . . . But how am I gonna set to crying, sir, for God's sake! . . . Ain't you never felt like a caged animal? Ain't you never felt like you don't know what you want, like the only thing you know is that you can't get a grip? Well that's what's happening to me. That's why I had to come and explain things to you; the bad news is that I don't know what I have to explain to you. [*With a certain pride*] But don't think that I'm afraid of you or that I've come to beg you: I ain't never begged nobody . . . Damn, sure, I'd like it if you wasn't mad at me, same as I'm not mad at you, it's real simple. Don't you know that tomorrow is Independence Day and I'm gonna take the old lady to the fair? Then over there I'm gonna get to drinkin and for sure with the hangover I'm gonna start remembering you, so we better talk. I understood the thing real good, you should understand it too . . . Did I understand?

[*He shrugs.*]

Know what else? Let's not talk at all. I just came to pick up my shovel.

[*He goes to pick it up.*]

[*With it in his hands*] So . . . so you're married and have two kids?

[*A police siren is heard passing and fading away.*]

---

* The day before Chile's national holiday celebrating independence from Spain.

It was a strange thing, huh? It started little by little, same as when a person gets a cold in one house and then afterwards goes round giving the cold to the neighbors and the neighbors to the neighborhood, and before you know it, the whole city's got a cold; epidemic is what they call that, I think. What kind of epidemic could we call it? . . .

[*He takes a few steps toward the audience and talks above it.*]

[*Recalling*] My buddy was better than a whole lot of tomato with onion and hot pepper. Even when he was hammered, you'd look into his eyes and it was like you went into a place where everything was different, where everything was good; he had a laugh that would stay balanced in the air . . . And he always had such lousy luck, ever since he was born they started to beat up on him . . . "He would throw me in a pit," he'd say. "He would throw me in a pit and I hadn't done nothin to him; I had been born and I wanted to live, wanted to live because the days are for living and the paths are for walking" . . . For walking? No, now they're for being left flat out, for grabbing your guts and starting to rattle, for calling and nobody coming, for going and never being able to come back no more . . . that's what paths are for now, buddy. [*Pause.*] I know you wouldn't have liked this business: you was different. But I'm a common guy. I don't know them pretty things that you knew. Where'd you learn them? Who got them into your head? [*Brief pause.*] Goddamn . . . and what good did they do you? [*Gloomily*] Goin over all that, I decided to come here to think. Rosa used to say:

"So whaddaya doin here?"

"Thinkin, can't you see?"

"And why do you come over here to think when the house is over there?"

"Cuz you can't be cooped up to think, ya know.

"Ah," she'd say. "And what are you thinking bout?"

"Bout the thing with my buddy."

"The older you get, the sillier you get," she said. And she went off fussin.

Least in those days she was happy, cuz I'd promised to take her to the fair, otherwise for sure we'd have had a fight, cuz I wasn't bout to put up with no crap, and she couldn't stand him. Ya know? She said he was too much of a boozer. Course it was true, huh? Cool as he was, when he got the urge to hit the bottle he wouldn't stop drinking until he could see movies without going to the movies. Then she'd say it was his fault that I didn't give her no money for groceries; you know how women are bout naggin. If my buddy had been married, his wife woulda been on my case; the point is to make trouble . . . Damn, and to go and pester him, when he was more quiet than a wake for a mute.

[*He brightens up, gets closer to the pit.*]

When I met him, I had gone out to see if there was some day job I could get. I work in the terminal for buses that come from outside Santiago, I find taxis for the passengers; but cuz that day there wasn't none gonna come, I stayed home, and I was more bored than a cart horse: that's why I went out for a walk. I found him propped up against a tree, already half wasted. His royal highness was admiring the view! When I passed by his side, he says:

"Damn, how beautiful life is, pal!"

"Beautiful?" I says.

"Course, pal. Can't you see?" he says. And he shows me like this, to both sides, so's I would appreciate it.

"Hey, where you from?" I says.

"From all over, like life," he says.

And later he asked me where he could find a dive.

"Damn, but you're already plastered," I says.

"Hey, don't make problems for yourself, old man," he says. And he started to look in his pockets; he took out some wrinkled bills and showed em to me. "Looky here, I've still got some . . . Whaddaya say we go get a drink? I'll treat."

He didn't have to ask me twice; so we left, see. He told me he had come up from the south cuz he had started to fall in love with a girl and he didn't wanna be tied down. "I'm used to getting my stuff and goin off whichever way I'm turned. Was born like that, ya know, can't do nothin bout it: I ride life bareback and go wherever it takes me. Bottoms up, ole buddy!"

Life had taken him so many places that I spent the whole afternoon with my jaw dropped listening to him talk. Damn, the man had stories! He told me about the celebration for the Virgin Carmen and the procession for the patron saint of fishermen and the festival of the rock; he jabbered on about threshing, and grape harvests, and even about *machitunes,* this thing that the Araucano Indians do.* For sure, he was kind of a strange talker, cuz he'd be right in the middle of telling one thing, when suddenly he'd go off on something that dint have nothin to do with it, and he'd stare at you; later he'd go on, like nothing had happened. Like this one time, I remember he was telling me bout a place that he called ghost town San Gregorio up north, when suddenly he looks me in the eye and says, "Know what? When you say you don't wanna fight with nobody, you have to defend yourself from both the good guys and the bad guys."

"Hmm, how's that?" I asked him. "Think, man, think," he says, then he picks up his glass right away, drains it and keeps talking about San Gregorio. When they was bout to close the dive, he got round to the childhood memories:

"Know what my daddy would do when I'd run away from home? He'd throw me in a pit, buddy!"

"In a pit?"

"Sure, in a dry well . . . I'd be screaming so hard all night that I'd even wet myself, but he wouldn't get me out . . . Goddamn, in a pit, buddy; me, the best guy for wandering around that ever was! That's authority, the law they want to teach us; but once you've been on the road, once you've tasted freedom, they have to slaughter you to make you stay still."

[*To the pit*] Course, sometimes I didn't understand him. [*Confused*] Well, the truth is that it's always been tough for me to understand things, cuz I had to figure everything out for myself from when I was real young. The first job I had was straightening out nails on a construction site, then they had me stir up the mortar, but I couldn't handle it; I was too puny, right away I started sanding furniture in a . . . Hey, didn't you tell me you made furniture? I thought I heard you say something like that. What's that gig like? Is it shitty too?

---

* The Araucanos are an indigenous people of Chile and Argentina, also known as Mapuches. The Mapuche language is still spoken by about three hundred thousand people in the two countries. *Machitunes* are ritual prayers for rain and good harvests.

[*A fire truck is heard.*]

A fire . . . Where could it be?

[PEDRO *looks around, tries to see.*]

What could be burning now? [*To the pit*] Have you ever been in a fire? I have, it was about thirty houses, some big shots was burnin em cuz they said the people hadn't paid the rent. [*To the pit*] Damn, nice the way the big shots send the eviction notice, huh?

[*He shrugs.*]

Well, what was I telling you? Oh, bout the time I met my buddy. Course I liked the guy right off, so the next day I took him to the bus terminal and I started to train him:

"Look, I says, the gig here is real sweet, all you gotta do is wait till the buses come in and offer the passengers a car; if you get ten good tips in a day, you're doin great.

"Go find them a car? That's all?"

"Sure, that's all. Later, after you're trained, you'll figure it out right off when the passenger is a hick, I mean green, like you; then you'll let the taxi driver know, so that he can take a few wrong turns fore he takes them where they're goin: you make some more that way."

"So they con them. Is what you mean?"

"Well, you gotta make a living," I says to him.

"No, I don't do that," he says, offended.

"And why not? Don't be a dope, you gotta wise up."

"No buddy, I don't do none of that stuff; I fight with life above the belt."

Damn, and it was true. He didn't do none of the things we did; he was more wholesome than a bottle of aspirin. In the stories he told there wasn't no slashing or robbing or fights. There was other stuff: pure friendship, pure joy. They'd never caught him at nothing underhanded; trying to accuse him of somethin was like trying to grab hold of a handful of wind. You stared at him as he talked and this thing started to flow inside you, a strange thing, like it could . . . Damn, like it could be good to live.

"That's the only way to be free," he'd say. "Don't you see that bad things tie you down? They tie you down to prison or to regrets. And a man with regrets is stuck in a cell with no bars. No, to die at the right moment, what you gotta do is live fighting, but fighting a clean fight."

"How's that?" I'd say.

"Think, man; think," he'd say. [*Pause.*] The only time I saw him sad was after the troubles, when we found a guy's body. "Know why they killed this boy?" he says. "Cuz he said he was fighting for peace and justice. And know who killed him? Someone else who said he was fightin for peace and justice."

I hadn't never known nobody that wasn't a scammer, so he had me hooked. I didn't get how different he was; I started to love him like a brother or a son; I don't have no sons or brothers, maybe it was cuz of that . . . No, no, it wasn't cuz of that neither, it was cuz I would have liked to have been like him, to feel that peace and happiness that I dint know how you could feel . . . I've always lost things on the roads of drinking or fighting.

"To understand life you have to have a bit of sorrow," he would say. But I dint never understand that neither, though I liked everything he said. The only thing I didn't like about him is that he dint never bathe; he was stinkier than a pig's belly. Oh, and also that he suddenly started to butt into my private life. The first time was after we was drinkin together nonstop for bout a week.

"You know?" he told me. "You're messin up. How come you don't never stay with your woman?"

"Don't know really . . . What am I gonna stay for?"

"People are important," he told me.

"The old lady, important?"

"Sure, see, if she wasn't important to you, you wouldn't have married her. Why do you leave her all by herself?"

It got to me, but I didn't say nothing to him. [*Pause. Directly to the pit*] Your woman is important to you, friend? You love her and all that good stuff? I hadn't never thought about that. Don't you see that when you get married, you got her for sure? So by giving her enough to feed Mr. Hunger everything's fine, see; what else can you do? But my buddy would say that it don't do women no good to be loved quietly, that you gotta tell them or show them every once in a while. I mean take them out for a walk, or stare at them all of a sudden and tell them they're beautiful . . . Damn, but my woman is real ugly, how am I gonna tell her that? [*Pause.*] Well, now she's ugly, before . . . What happened? What happened that she got ugly? Where was I when her face got wrinkled? When she got skinny on me and her eyes sank? Strange, suddenly I felt like goin and hugging her. My buddy was right. Goddamn, the old lady is important! You should have seen how happy she got when I told her I was gonna take her to the fair . . . But, what if they kill her on me? What do I do if they kill her on me? Don't you see that these days you can go walking peacefully down the street and suddenly you're down on the ground with the blood pouring out all over your body? And the worst thing is there ain't nobody to pin it on! [*Pause.*] Damn, a mother of a thing came down on us . . . Who would've thunk . . . Thing is, you know? When bad things don't happen to *you* it seems like they happen way far away; and there's the fear too, nobody wants to get stuck in a hornet's nest. And standing up for someone now is a real big hornet's nest. Haven't you noticed that when something happens in the street, people turn their heads away and start walking like they was glued to the wall? Some people seem like they turned into hunchbacks all of a sudden, they walk so bent over. It's screwed up, huh? And there ain't nowhere to go, cuz what we lost here, we lost everywhere. My buddy got it. He always said: "Damn, how beautiful life is! He said the same thing whether there was sun or it was one of those winter days when its screaming rain and all the doors is closed. Beautiful life here, beautiful life there. And suddenly, he stopped, he didn't say that no more; his lips stopped moving, his look turned black.

"I'm a leftover here," he'd say. "I'm a leftover, cuz I can't get myself to feel hate." [*Pause.*] I think that's why he didn't even try to get better. Cuz he got sick, you know?

One day we had to take him to the clinic with Rola and Lobito.

"I screwed up buddy," he said when we left.

"Screwed up? What did they say you have?"

"I've got the Rosy."

"You're kidding!"

"Hey, what did you want me to get? I wasn't gonna come down with a cold; all us boozers gotta die of cirrhosis, you act like you was a hayseed. Well, what's wrong with you?"

I dint know what to tell him. I looked inside myself but I dint have even a single word: it was like I had been swept clean.

"You gotta take care of yourself," Rola told him. "You're gonna have to put away more food and less booze."

"Get out of here!" my buddy says to him. "No way I'm gonna start taking care of myself now. I'll drink just the same. I'm already up to my eyebrows."

"Ain't you scared?" I asked him.

"Of what? Of dying? You crazy?"

"For real, buddy?"

"Damn sure," he says, offended. "The questions you ask. It's up to me to die the way I want. I got a little sun rising inside me, a sun that's sweeping away all my dark spots, how could I be afraid, pal?"

Right there we passed the hat and we went off to hit the bottle, what the hell!

And between one drink and the next, I got the idea: Of course! It was only right that my buddy should have a home and a wife before dying. But there wasn't no point in saying nothing to him, in case it didn't work out; why get his hopes up?

Judging by his gut, we figured he had about two months before he'd croak, so we started to ask the girls around there if they'd do him as a favor.

But none of them went for it: some of them claimed they already had a man, and others wanted him to take a bath first.

But even if we washed him for a week, the stench wasn't gonna come off. And besides, he might get water poisoning and croak on us right there. The only one who didn't have . . .

[*In the distance, a police siren passes and is lost.*]

The only one who didn't have nobody to pimp for her was Tricky Step. We called her that cuz she had a leg that was half crooked and she never stepped where you thought she was gonna step. But she backed out of it too.

"No way, I ain't goin with that guy," she said.

"But you're not gonna sleep with him," we told her. "You just have to pretend to marry him."

"No, I can't stand lies. Later he might get to wanting some and he might even asphyxiate me."

"Goddamn you're mean," Coriza says to her. "Don't you remember all those times he gave you a place to sleep when you wasn't earning nothin? Nope, you just have to marry him or we won't let you work round here no more."

But there was no way. And we was bout to get into it when something pops into Peter's head and he takes me aside. "Let's not tell her nothin. Let's just get her loaded; once she's got a buzz on, she'll run to all the bases," he says to me. Fine then, we had the bride for sure. And we started to work on the wedding. A wedding with a bachelor party and everything. Stinky Meat was in charge of getting together the bucks for the wine. Peter and Lobito were gonna get the music and Coriza was gonna take charge of the peaches for the punch; the rest of us just had to get cash for the chow and the room rental. I was so happy cuz I was doing something for him that I didn't have time to feel sad that he was gonna die. The thing was that we even had the car ready—the car from Four Eyes Letelier, so you can see how much everyone loved my buddy—when I find out that Tricky Step has gone on the wagon, that she don't wanna drink no more.

"Well, and what's up with you?" I says.

"I'm on the wagon."

"Till when?"

"No, I don't drink no more. I went to Yamile the Healer and she cured me.

"Don't be silly, fit and healthy you ain't gonna get no action," I says. "You need to drink with the guys so's they go with you, otherwise you gonna die of hunger."

But there was no way. Luckily, when I told Peter, his lightbulb went on again. "Don't make trouble for yourself," he says. "Give her a couple of kicks in the good leg and she'll start hitting the bottle right off."

"Ah, for real?"

"Sure, that's how Paila would manage when she got snooty on him. Don't you see that she takes better care of that leg than a gold watch? But you need to smack her a day earlier, so the sadness gets to her."

Fine. Thursday night I worked up some hatred for Tricky and I gave her two kicks in the good leg: one sidekick and a forward punt, to be sure. Right away I had a couple of drinks and I went to give the good news to my buddy . . . He got spooked. I swear it seemed like he'd got an electric shock. He said he'd never wanted to be tied down to nobody or nothing, and that he wanted to die that way, cuz he was happy. "I don't have much time left, don't mess me up now . . . don't mess me up now buddy for God's sake!" he says. And it seemed that he was suffocating, that he wanted to cry . . . And suddenly I got it: course, ya know, he wanted to die by his own law, he wanted to die like he'd lived: alone, free, upright; and even more now that everything was all out of whack . . . That night we drank till we couldn't get up off the floor. And the next day I washed a few cars, so we kept goin until Friday night. [*Pause.*] Damn, we was flyin high . . .

[*Loud ambulance siren passes and fades.*]

. . . We was flying high at Pete's place when Coriza comes in with a bagful of peaches. She hands it to me and says, "Here, this is for the punch, the other guys are right behind me . . . Where's the thing gonna be at?" Damn, and suddenly I realize that we hadn't told nobody that we'd called off the wedding! We'd stepped in it big time. They said my buddy was a crook, that he couldn't get it up and all kinds of crap, so I got steamed and we went out to the street to discuss it. Lobito, who'd ripped off a boom box to brighten up the party, got to arguin that we'd run off with the money for the wine . . . And that's when my buddy messed up totally, cuz in the middle of his drunkness he puts his hand in his pocket and says, "You pay up . . . you pay up. If you've ordered something, you pay . . ." And then, then some guy in fatigues goin by pulls out a shooter this big and pops him twice . . . Damn, you get it? Just like that, without havin nothin to do with it, not knowing him or nothin; he went and killed him, left him lying there, like a dog. And afterwards, he just left. What was they gonna do to him? What was they gonna do, since he claimed that my buddy was armed and that he'd threatened him? [*Pause.*] What do you say to that? What do you say? Dint I tell you that's how things is now?

[*Pause.*] Sure, I know you weren't even near the fuss, you never met my buddy and you never even heard of me; but you gotta face up to it, see, cuz we're all in the same boat here. You don't get nothin by running away, by being good or being innocent: when it rains, we all get wet . . . Damn, sure, it would be real nice if there was a law against killing people, or that would punish the ones that kills, but there ain't, so what can we do. And don't think I'm telling stories, no: I'm talking with the dead on my hands; but you know that too, so why do you play dumb? Too bad you're married and have kids, too bad they're gonna be waiting for you forever! I have a debt to collect, and might makes right! . . . But, you know? I wanna tell you something: when I hit you with the rock and I dragged you to this pit, I felt a real big pain inside, I felt like my heart had been slashed forever, cuz I don't have nothing gainst you, how could I have something gainst you, since I don't know you: I didn't even get to see your face, that says it all. So don't be mad at me, it's nothin personal . . . Goddamn, how could it be anything personal when all I want is for you to come back to life and forgive me, sir, for you to come back to life and tell me you understand me! . . . What it is . . . What it is, is that the thing is like this, see: they did in my buddy and so I rubbed you out, now we are even. An eye for an eye and we're all goin to hell. But don't think that I'm home free; no, tomorrow or later, it might be my turn . . . Who can know now when they're gonna kill you and why?

[*Pause. He looks up.*]

It's gettin to be night . . . You know? I'd thought I would cover you over, but I ain't gonna cover you over neither; these damned days, who the hell is gonna bother to get you out of there?

THE GUEST, OR TRANQUILITY IS PRICELESS

After the tranquil night
gives way to the tranquil day,
tranquilly I get up.
I put on my tranquil pants,
glance sidelong at your tranquil sadness
and tranquilly go wash.
Afterwards I go into the tranquil kitchen;
tranquilly you tell me the same as yesterday:
Don't look, there's nothing.
Tranquilly I go out and sink
into the tranquil city.
Tranquil dogs piss on tranquil trees
under a sky with a tender rhythm,
while the tranquil unemployed, like me,
envy the tranquil beggars
who dig through the tranquil trash.
Tranquilly the morning passes,
tranquilly the beautiful afternoon;
(tranquil I want to find you Sara,
when I arrive empty-handed).
Tranquilly I keep looking
until the warm night arrives;
tranquilly I return home,
tranquilly I sit on the bench
and I hear you tranquilly say: "I didn't find nothing neither."
Tranquilly we go to sleep
and dream with tranquility.
Tranquilly we wake up,
you begin to cry tranquilly
and tranquilly I go out walking.
What great happiness
to be dying in tranquility!

[*The present. The only thing on the stage is a black bench.* SARA *enters, looks at the audience. She goes back.*]

SARA [*calling*]: All right then, come in.

[PEDRO *enters, unwillingly, not at all tranquil.*]

Speak. [*Gesturing toward the audience*] There they are.

PEDRO [*trying to see*]: What are they doin?

SARA: Nothin, they're sittin. They did their stuff and now they're sittin.

PEDRO [*trying to stall*]: I don't see em good.

SARA: It don't matter. Speak up so's they can hear you and that's that.

PEDRO: How come I can't see em and you can?

[SARA *shrugs.*]

SARA: Maybe I've got more light on my side. Or maybe men have always seen less than women. And what do you want to see more for if all you do is look down and carry on straight ahead, since you isn't the ones who foot the bill . . .

PEDRO: Howdya figure? So we get the bed of roses?

SARA: You always start the fights and us women and kids lose em; it's always been like that. But I don't want to talk no more bout that; ask how they did it and we're outta here.

PEDRO: First we have to tell them who we are and all that, just like when you go to the doctor. [*Looking around*] How do they look?

SARA: Like always: tranquil.

PEDRO: Then they must be in debt up to their elbows, cuz tranquility is priceless; haven't you heard?

SARA: Don't talk bout elbows, listen, cuz our hands is tied.

PEDRO: Don't worry, we'll always have the comfort of the good: we did the best we could. [*Pause.*] Did we?

SARA: I tole you I don't wanna talk no more bout that. It's over; talkin bout it just makes the words like knives. What we gotta do now is forget—forget, so we can begin to live.

PEDRO: Like slaves?

SARA: To begin to live.

PEDRO: Like animals?

SARA: To begin to live.

PEDRO: Like idiots?

SARA: To begin to live!

PEDRO [*after a pause*]: To begin to live . . . Sometimes I'm glad when they don't answer us; there's somethin in me that don't want to crumble. I've never wanted to die.

SARA: Me neither; that's why we're here.

PEDRO: No, well, you don't understand me: we came here to kill ourselves, we came to kill all the good that's left inside us, I mean, to murder it.

SARA: Well, you go then.

PEDRO: And you?

SARA: I'm staying. I gotta know; I've got life left and I have to live it like everybody else; it's the only way . . . Don't be silly; I don't understand and neither do you but we gotta do it. We agreed, you can't go back!

PEDRO: Ya think they're gonna tell us?

SARA: Yeah, I'm sure.

PEDRO: Why?

SARA: A hunch.

PEDRO: So far, don't nobody wanna tell us; they all deny it. "No, not me. I'm just the same as before," they say. Why do they deny what they are?

SARA: Nah, what it is, is we've had bad luck. We've only asked people who are new to the thing. But this morning a green fly came in the bedroom and started to buzz around. That means good news.

PEDRO: Green flies mean you gonna get a letter.

SARA: It's good news. You don't know nothin about those things. OK, don't play dumb no more and ask.

PEDRO: But like I say, with a running start; I mean, since the beginning, since we was born.

SARA: If we're here, it's cuz we was born. Whatcha gonna say that for? Just since the Guest arrived, that's when it all started.

PEDRO: They know that better than we do.

SARA [*bored*]: Well, do what you want.

PEDRO [*stubbornly*]: From the beginning.

[PEDRO *strikes a pose and addresses the audience.*]

One day a man that worked on construction met a woman that worked in a factory: that's when I was born. My name is Pedro, like my father; but if I go passing by anywhere and someone says José, Mario, Guillermo, Pancho, Tito, or Antonio, I turn my head and look, because it's me they're calling. I'm the one who never went to school, the one who only got up to sixth grade, cuz he had to go out and earn a living; the one who falls from the top of the scaffolding and the one who picks him up, the one they run over in the street cuz he's going along thinking about how the old lady at home is gonna manage to make dinner, the one who spends what he doesn't have, the one full of doubts, the one who's sometimes happy and the one who's almost always sad. I'm a dent fixer, house painter, furniture maker, mechanic, market loader, shoe shiner, press operator, and everything you can do to make sure you got a place for living, a piece of bread for your hunger, and a woman for your heart. [*To* SARA] Now you, from the beginning.

SARA: My name is Sara, but it's the same as if it was Carmen, Rosa, or María, and it's the same as if I was smaller or bigger, more black or more white; it's just the same, cuz inside my bones is stuck the same laughter and the same troubles. I won't say nothin bout the beginning cuz that's already dead. But for years I've been crying and missing the time when I was poor, not cuz I'm doin so good now, but cuz now I'm flat-out broke. I ended up this way after a miracle, an economic miracle, I've heard em call it. Since then I'm not a dressmaker, cook, factory worker, or maid no more; since then I beg on the radio and TV shows. I don't talk about things of the heart, cuz it gets me to crying; it's not that I've stopped loving or that Pedro doesn't love me anymore: it's that the love got stuck between one sign that says NO OPENINGS and another one that says NO CREDIT . . . Let's just leave it like that; I don't talk about things of the heart, cuz I get to crying.

PEDRO: What did you say?

SARA: That I made boiled potatoes so much, I forgot how to cook; and I saw troubled people so much, I forgot where your mouth goes when you laugh, so that when I laugh I feel like an evil wind has twisted my face and people ask me: "What's wrong? Gotta toothache?"

PEDRO: But before we wasn't like that; everything started when the Guest arrived.

SARA: Guest, no. Guest is when you invite someone; and that one I didn't invite.

PEDRO: Neither did I. He arrived on his own.

SARA: Not even the wind arrives on its own, but we'll suppose so.

PEDRO: Whaddaya mean *suppose*? You startin somethin? You blamin me?

SARA: I already tole you that I don't wanna talk no more bout that. [*Narrating*] The thing is, is that he arrived, and we have everything together.

PEDRO [*narrating*]: We mean that now we live in just one room. We have the dining room and the bedroom in there.

SARA: And the kitchen too.

PEDRO: Of course, the kitchen too. I always forget it, since there ain't nothin to do in there . . .

SARA [*moving around and gesturing*]: Here on this side we have our bed and the Guest's is over there on that other end. [*Gesturing*] At the head of his bed there's a poster of Colo Colo,* at the head of ours there's one with three bread rolls.

PEDRO: In other words, we're the height of fashion: bread and circus.

SARA: I can't stand Colo Colo, they started to bug me cuz they're a cover-up. Cuz of it, you can't know none of the things that really happen.

PEDRO: Sure, if Colo Colo didn't exist, the newspapers would have to come out with half their pages blank. And they're cocky from head to toe. I remember that time an earthquake killed five hundred people and all the newspapers came out the next day with the front page: "Colo Colo's heroic deed: won with five hundred fewer fans."

---

* Colo Colo is a wildly popular Chilean soccer team and sports club. During the dictatorship, Pinochet was named its honorary president. Colo Colo's rival, the University of Chile, was considered symbolic of opposition to the dictatorship.

SARA: At least they started the team after the war, otherwise we wouldn't have known nothing bout Arturo Prá neither.*

PEDRO: No, see, before the thing wasn't never like that; it ain't such a big deal. You shouldn't never forget the good, cuz you can get used to the bad.

SARA: Are you startin somethin with me?

PEDRO: [*After a brief pause*] Damn . . . if you'd wanted to have a child, everything would have been different for us.

SARA: The only thing that would have happened is you would have wanted him to be what you wasn't.

PEDRO: No, seriously Sara, why didn't you never want to have even one kid?

SARA: I wasn't blind or deaf; I saw and heard. Those days were sick with rage, it was like an animal that's scratchin the floor before it jumps, and I . . .

PEDRO: Thing is you were never a good trooper.

SARA: A woman without children may be pathetic but a woman with a dead child or goin door-to-door beggin for food is a hundred times more pathetic.

PEDRO: Us poor people can't give ourselves the luxury of security; we have to make do however we can. If you was wantin to spend your days eatin cakes you should have married a baker, not me; you women are real uppity, when things get tough, you always put the blame on us. How do you eat?

SARA: I open my mouth, see.

PEDRO: Don't be beatin round the bush. I'm asking how you make ends meet.

SARA: I enter radio and TV contests: don't ya know?

PEDRO [*as a television announcer*]: And now, the moment we've all been waiting for: *Cheer Up, Ms. Dying-of-Hunger!*† And don't forget, you

---

* Arturo Prat Chacón is a Chilean national hero, a naval captain who fought against Peru in the War of the Pacific (1879–83), during which Chile consolidated its control of the rich nitrate-producing regions to the north.

† A parody of a segment, "Buck Up, Buddy!," of an actual Chilean television program that ran from the late seventies to the early eighties. The show was called *The One O'Clock Festival.*

folks out there in TV land, to use the key phrase for this week: "Happiness comes to us from Taiwan," with which you too can win fabulous prizes. Take heart and write!

[SARA *moves up, fainting.*]

Very well, here we have the first contestant!

[PEDRO *holds* SARA *so that she doesn't fall.*]

[*Holding her up*] Married or single?
SARA [*barely audible*]: Married.
PEDRO: Profession?
SARA: Unemploy—
PEDRO: Out!

[PEDRO *lets* SARA *go.*]

SARA: But I ain't sung yet, sir.
PEDRO: The next cont—

[*He looks up.*]

Flash. Last-minute flash.
SARA [*as a smiling society news announcer, reading*]: This afternoon José Herrera de las Mercedes Irigorreb was married to Miss Mariela la Roi. There is no doubt that the news of the marriage of Mariela and José will leave an indelible mark on our society as one of the most elegant affairs of the year. The mothers-of-honor: Maria Teresa Stuven wore a suit of chiffon *pervachais* brought from Paris especially for this wedding in which she looked so beautiful that it was hard to believe she was the grandmother of the bride; Nancy Correa de Arratia wore a smoke-colored dress with brown trim, a superchic and modern combination, so distinguished and elegant that she clearly stood out. Winzlia Lage de Webwe, stupendous in lilac with white flowers; Chepita Tolosa, sensational as usual in a striped print; Margot Arraigada, in jersey with colored flowers; Marisol de Huneeus, in a butter shade; and Virginia Sotomayor, in turquoise. This was an up-to-the-minute flash brought to you by national broadcasting; television and radio stations may now return to their regularly scheduled programming.

[SARA *steps back.*]

PEDRO [*euphorically*]: Very well, my dear television viewers, after this sensational news, we return to our program, *Cheer Up, Ms. Dying-of-Hunger!* Hurry, hurry, the next contestant!

SARA [*even weaker than before*]: I . . . I . . .

PEDRO: Faster, faster! What do you do? Sing? Dance? Recite? What do you think you do?

SARA: Sing . . . I sing.

PEDRO [*holding* SARA *up with difficulty*]: Name? Are you registered? When was the last time you had a me——You participated? Answer, answer!

SARA: What?

PEDRO: Your name, your name!

SARA: Sara Moreno.

PEDRO: Profession?

SARA: Room owner.

PEDRO: What's this, room owner?

SARA: The thing is that Pedro and I don't have a house, we live in just a single room. The Guest . . .

PEDRO: Since you're the last contestant of the afternoon, you have the right to say hello to someone. Who would you like to say hello to?

SARA: Would you have a little bit of water you might give me?

PEDRO: Who do you want to say hello to?

SARA: Would you have a little bit of water . . .

[PEDRO *struggles to extract a card from his pocket as he holds* SARA *up.*]

PEDRO: Very well, the lady will perform on the subject, "Smile at life!"

[SARA's *expression changes.*]

SARA: Smile though your heart is breaking
    Smile, what's the use of crying,
    Though there are tears in your eyes . . .

PEDRO: Out!

[*He throws* SARA *to the side.*]

But anyway, the lady has won a beautiful windshield wiper for her personal vehicle.

SARA [*desolately*]: A child . . . Wouldya have liked to have a child, Pedro?

PEDRO [*confused*]: Well . . . it's that . . . Damn, now things are like this, but before . . .

SARA: And outside a bunch a guys with a car are waitin for you; they jump at you and tell you they represent performers and that you sing so good that they wanna give you an audition. The problem is they wanna give it to you in some dark place, at night, and in the car.

PEDRO: But you didn't never go . . .

SARA: No, course not. But the humiliation stays scrapin inside you and piles on others.

PEDRO: What others? It's just now that things are goin bad for us. When I was a dent fixer we had everything; our house was a house full of food and friends. And before that, before we got married, I took you everywhere: to the theater, to dances, to the shop picnics . . .

SARA [*forward, talking above the audience*]: I remember that everybody at home knew when you was gonna come and see me, cuz I'd spend the whole morning singing while I did my chores.

PEDRO [*relieved*]: Sure, see, we was in love.

SARA: We was young and happy . . . We loved each other so much . . .

PEDRO: You'd come to wait for me at the job.

SARA [*to* PEDRO]: You think I woulda sung if I'd a known what was gonna happen to me?

PEDRO [*angrily*]: What's happened to you? Nothin terrible has happened to you; why lay it on so thick? I still love you just the same. For me, love don't have nothin to do with being poor.

SARA: For me neither, but love don't know that: love just comes and dies of hunger.

PEDRO: But whaddaya want me to do! There ain't nothin else I can do. Didn't ya see how last time they slapped me round the ring. When did I ever fight?

SARA [*as a secretary for a boxing promoter*]: Where are you coming from?

PEDRO: From work, miss.

SARA [*smiling*]: No, I mean, where have you fought before.

PEDRO: Ah, well, wherever they insult me, I fight right there.

SARA [*surprised*]: Do you know what this is about?

PEDRO: Sure, it's about punching each other out. Yeah, it's goin great for me; I've fought lots of places. I've even been in the papers; that says it all.

SARA [*interested*]: In the newspapers? That's very good. How is it that I don't know you?

PEDRO: I was real beat up in the photo; the other joker was real big. Damn, but he groped Sara, so how could I hold myself back? You should have seen the slugfest: jabbin and kickin, with spit in the eye and everything. See, I don't give in: If I can't stay up, I get down on the ground, but I don't back down.

SARA [*laughing*]: No, no. I thought you were a boxer. We're not interested in that sort of fight here: this is a different kind of fight, with gloves and inside a ring.

PEDRO: Ah, with gloves? Great, that way the punches hurt less. How much do they pay?

SARA: No, I'm very sorry, but you would have to be a boxer for me to hire you; we're not flexible about that, without a medical certificate and a permit from the federation, it's impossible to hire you.

PEDRO: Well, since I don't have that, then just pay me half. How much is it?

SARA: Well, not much, but you would have the opportunity to appear on television. And with that wonderfully foreign look you have about you, maybe they'd hire you for some soap opera, because that's how things are now.

PEDRO: Ah, is this about going out to fight on that carpeted space, where the snooty people go to have tea while they bash in your head? That thing like the Roman circuses they have in the movies? No, I'd have to make big bucks, cuz it's true that getting slugged doesn't kill nobody; but how are you gonna erase from inside you the mark left by those rich girls and boys who laugh and eat while inside the ring they're kicking your ass? No, it would have to be big bucks. How much do you pay?

SARA: It depends, if they get you out in the first round, three hundred pesos.

PEDRO: And if they get me in the second?

SARA: Four hundred.

PEDRO: And if . . .

SARA: Look, it's one hundred more pesos for every round you last.

PEDRO: And if I win, miss?

SARA: Then they're going to wait for you outside afterwards and they're going to beat you up, because it's the other one who has to win, he's the one we're promoting; or haven't you read in the newspapers that he's the best athlete in recent times?

PEDRO [*recounting*]: And what was I gonna do then, see; I faced up to it. Shit, the guy hit me like he was swinging a ham. The first whap he gave me made me do about three full turns round the ring. And right away he just set to waiting for me to pass by him and from there he'd take the next swipe, and you just started spinning again, Pedro . . .

SARA [*as* SARA *again*]: Wonder how it went for Pedro? He's real skinny; maybe they didn't let him fight. He didn't want me to go with him. He was embarrassed . . . And what would I have done if I'd seen them hitting him?

PEDRO: Damn, if I bring home four hundred pesos that's enough for four days, I thought, maybe this guy will mess up a punch so that I can last until the next round. At least my saint was lookin out for me, cuz in one of those turns I ended up on the ropes and I hung on to them like crazy.

SARA [*as a referee*]: OK, sir, let go of that: fight.

PEDRO: Hah, maybe if you tie up that bastard, I'll let go. Can't you see what he's doin to me?

SARA: Fight! Fight!

PEDRO: Yeah, sure, ya think I just picked up this face at a sidewalk sale? No way I'm gonna let go.

SARA [*pulling at* PEDRO]: If you don't let go, I'll disqualify you. Let go and fight!

PEDRO: And if you disqualify me you don't pay me?

SARA: No, how are we going to pay for you to hug the ropes: you have to put on a show!

PEDRO: Damn, and if that guy kills me or leaves me all stupid?

SARA: That's your problem. The people here came to see you fight and you have to fight!

PEDRO [*narrating*]: Then I got scared. "OK," I told him, "I'm gonna let go, but tell that guy that I want to tell him something before we keep fighting." And then he calls him and the other one gets close to me; the truth is I wanted to give him a kick in the balls, to preserve my dignity.

SARA [*as* SARA]: Hope things went well for Pedro, so's we could at least pay the grocery store guy. Gosh, we owe so many people that I'm ashamed to go out on the streets. If this keeps up, we're gonna have to walk on the rooftops so they don't see us . . .

PEDRO: Damn, and so don't I go and notice that he's sort of crying? "Goddamn, aren't you a good guy," I told him. "After you beat me to a pulp, you start to cry." "Sorry buddy," he says. "I know you're broke, but whaddaya want me to do; if I don't go at it hard they'll end my career, and I got three kids and they wanna throw us out of our place." "But aren't you the champ?" I says. "Yeah, but I ain't hardly seen none of the dough yet. They say that when I'm South American champion they're gonna start to pay me more. And I gotta put up with everything cuz I'd been looking for work for more than a year when they offered me this. I used to work as a loader in the market.

SARA: So then to preserve your dignity you started to insult all the people at the tables.

PEDRO: If I didn't, I might have had an attack. Don't you know that it's bad for you to keep your anger inside?

SARA [*narrating*]: And because His Majesty had to let it all out, we had to eat dignity the whole week; in the morning we made it without nothin; and in the afternoon we had it plain.

PEDRO: But for Sunday we mixed it with a little water.

SARA: That's how love got thin as a knife; it was goin blind, like when they cover the wind's eyes.

PEDRO: Love conquers all. And God's will be done. But he didn't will much.

SARA: How was we gonna defend love, when the one who came into our house wouldn't let us do nothin?

PEDRO: The Guest wasn't just in the house: he was everywhere, wherever you were, there he was. It was like having a spy stuck between skin and bone.

SARA: And we didn't even have the hope of waiting cuz the whole city was burnin up with hunger on all sides; there was sorrow on one corner and fear on the other.

PEDRO: He took our bread.

SARA: He took our house and our happiness. He didn't let us have a child.

PEDRO: But the worse thing was that he did it little by little, like he'd been feeding a hatred for us for years and years . . . and you used to be so happy Sara!

SARA: Not just me; all of life was like a song giving birth to another song.

PEDRO: Goddamn, how I loved her!

SARA: Goddamn, how I loved him!

PEDRO: We'd been struggling for a long time, but together; then she suddenly began to get weird on me. She'd run away from me.

SARA: What it is, is that you don't have no delicacy. You're a pig.

PEDRO: Pure lies. [*Narrating*] I'd come back from the stupid employment office . . . cuz now I work at the welfare job; the Guest got me in there.

[SARA *and* PEDRO *stand in line.*]

SARA [*rubbing her hands*]: Gosh, it's cold. Don't you have a cigarette you could give me?

PEDRO: No, I don't have nothin. Been two years since I worked. It's been goin good for me in the ditches, but since it rained last night, the butts fell apart.

SARA: Sure, same thing happened to me, I didn't even find one dry butt. [*Pause.*] What did you used to do before?

PEDRO: Bang out dents. And you?

SARA: Everything, but my job was sewing.

PEDRO: You got kids?

SARA: Sure, three.

PEDRO: And you stopped?

SARA: Yeah, we was real down and out.

PEDRO: Nothin is goin on with my wife neither.

SARA: It's the same everywhere: these days the only time you get between the sheets is when you're hangin em up to dry.

PEDRO: Yeah, I'm in a slump. I close my eyes and right away I see myself doin it. Like yesterday, I was reading an old newspaper when suddenly I fall asleep and dream that they've called me to do some work. Know who'd called me? The blonde woman who does the ad for martinis on the TV. She comes and says to me: "I want you to wallpaper the living room." "OK," I says. "We'll make up an estimate for you right away. How much did the paper cost you?" [*To* SARA] Course, don't you know you gotta charge based on the price of the paper? But she didn't understand much about the science of charging, so she started to argue and treat me like a thief. Then I step back, I give her a look, like this, from the side, and I slap her twice.

SARA: That's OK; cuz you wasn't saying nothin to her bout how she had to do her crappy ad, so she didn't have no business telling you how to do your job. Everybody should mind his own beeswax. That's what I think.

PEDRO: That would be nice, if nobody got into where they wasn't wanted, but you know that's not how it works . . .Well, as I was saying, I slap her and get my things to go, when she stands up and tells me: "That's how I like my men." And she gives me a big wet one; listen: we start to do it right there. [*Pause.*] Damn, dreams are nice, huh? You can do whatever you want . . . Damn. Would you believe that it had been about three months that I'd been wantin to nail that blonde . . . Well.

[PEDRO *looks around.*]

What time do they open here? Don't they start seeing people at eight?

SARA: Sure, at eight. But it's just eight thirty, so there's still about an hour before they start seeing people.

PEDRO: Wonder what this job is like? They say it's about sweeping plazas and fixing up the roads.

SARA: It's real strange; I gotta brother-in-law who started last month and he told me how it works: here at the welfare job, you don't work nothin, but they don't pay you nothin neither. They just give you enough for the bus, cuz if you come in late, they fire you right off.

PEDRO: Hey, what's this about? Are you laughing at me?

SARA: No, buddy: we're the ones being laughed at.

PEDRO [*narrating*]: So there I am, breaking my balls at the welfare job. I get home bored to tears and I cuddle up to her, and she says. . .

SARA [*uneasily*]: Watch out; be careful.

[SARA *shrinks from* PEDRO.]

PEDRO: Hey, what's wrong with you?

SARA [*gesturing*]: He can see us.

PEDRO: How's he gonna see us if it's dark and besides he's sleeping with his face to the wall?

SARA: And if he wakes up and turns this way? No, let go of me.

[PEDRO *lets go of* SARA.]

PEDRO [*narrating*]: Then we decided to put the bureau in front of his bed.

SARA: Chest of drawers. Bureaus have mirrors.

PEDRO: Fine, chest of drawers.

[PEDRO *and* SARA *move the chest of drawers.*]

That's great now.

SARA [*looking carefully*]: Yeah, but it don't cover everything.

PEDRO: Damn, but what do it matter if it don't cover that side? He's not gonna see us with his feet.

SARA: No, if it ain't completely covered, it's the same as if it ain't covered. The thing is you're dirty and you don't care if they see you.

PEDRO: What do we do then?

SARA: Let's put the table in front too; we put a long tablecloth on it and it covers all the rest.

PEDRO: And where are we gonna get a long tablecloth? Everything shows through the plastic one.

SARA: I don't know then; we'll put a sheet there then.

PEDRO: He'll take offense.

SARA: Good.

PEDRO: Really, maybe he'll get the hint and go.

[PEDRO *and* SARA *simulate putting on the sheet.*]

SARA: Pull it more on that side.

PEDRO: Let go. There. How's it look?

SARA [*looking appreciative*]: Yeah, now its fine.

[*She goes toward the place where the bed would be.* PEDRO *hugs her.* SARA *rejects him again.*]

Let go, I can't.

PEDRO: Now what's wrong?

SARA: I don't know. I'm embarrassed.

PEDRO: But now he can't spy on us even if he wanted to!

SARA: He can't see, but he can hear.

PEDRO [*bored*]: So we're stuck. We can't put the pillow over his head. What do we do?

SARA [*gesturing, narrating*]: On this side, we had a bench like this one, but unpainted.

[*She picks up the bench, changes its position, and sits.*]

I sat and I said to him: "I don't know! What do you want me to do! This has to be private, not with some guy in the room!"

PEDRO: I didn't bring him here.

SARA: Neither did I.

PEDRO: Then who did?

SARA [*cranky*]: How should I know . . .

PEDRO: Well, but don't get mad at me.

SARA: I'm not mad; I'm bored.

PEDRO: Cuz we don't have no private life?

SARA: Or the other kind either. Or you call this garbage life?

[PEDRO *keeps quiet.*]

Answer. You call it life?

PEDRO: It's not life that's bad; it's the human race that's ignorant.

SARA: Same difference.

PEDRO: No, no it's not the same.

SARA: It is the same.

PEDRO: Didn't I tell you no? Don't be stubborn.

SARA: Are you gonna get mad at me?

PEDRO: Careful, little girl, don't be playing with me cuz it might backfire.

SARA: It might backfire on you; listen, you got me real fed up.

PEDRO: What do I got you fed up with?

SARA: Everything.

PEDRO: What everything?

SARA: Just everything. You don't do nothing. You're just hanging around for decoration.

PEDRO: Go to hell.

SARA: Sure, that fixes everything.

PEDRO: What do you want me to do?

SARA: I don't know!

PEDRO: Then keep your big mouth shut!

SARA: Big mouth is what your old bag of a mother has!

PEDRO: She's dead: the one who still has it open is your mother. It's so big that when she smiles she bites her ears.

SARA: And since you know what's good for you, you smile so that she feeds you; if it weren't for her you would have died of hunger, you good-for-nothing.

PEDRO: What are those raggedy asses going to have to give; they only eat when the supermarkets throw out the trash. [*Pause.*] I hope you don't got no crush on one a those jerks that wait for you outside the TV place, and that that's why you're so high and mighty, that's all . . .

SARA: That's all what? [*Scornfully*] What are you gonna do? [*Gesturing*] The Guest almost has you walking on all fours and . . .

PEDRO: Not just me, you too.

SARA: You should be ashamed to say that, being the kind of man you are. And you was the one that was gonna defend me? That was gonna take care of me?

PEDRO [*broken*]: Yes, well, that was . . .That was all of us; we was the ones that was gonna defend what we loved, that was . . .What happened? It's just that we only have one life, it could have been that, the fear, or also . . . But what do it matter now?

SARA: It don't even matter? It don't matter to you no more?

PEDRO: It ain't never gonna be the same again. You changed little by little into a handkerchief waving in the distance, waving goodbye . . . We can't do today what we didn't do yesterday, now that love's dead; who you gonna conquer the world for? To go for a walk, to sit and have a smoke?

SARA: I haven't gone.

PEDRO: Neither have I. But we're far apart; to stay together I had to beg you, and when you beg, what you get isn't worth it. It's just living to live.

SARA: I ain't said that I don't love you; thing is, we have time for hunger, for shame, and for despair, but we don't have time for love. It would be nice if I could go wait for you at work, or if you would kiss me when you get home, but where am I gonna go wait if you're unemployed? And how are you gonna kiss me when I always have the face of someone who's going to the cemetery; it's not your fault or mine. Better not think no more bout this.

PEDRO: How long was it before this happened?

SARA: Years already.

PEDRO: Do you remember that we met on a bench? You was sittin—you always went to sit there—and I'd say: how is this girl gonna love me when I'm so skinny and ugly? But afterwards I thought that sometimes women love men not because of what they see but because of what they can't see: I mean, the heart and all them things. And then one day I made up my mind and I got close.

[*He approaches, circles.*]

Who you waiting for?

SARA [*flirting*]: What do you care, sir?

PEDRO: No, it's just that if you're waiting for someone, I won't sit down there. [*Gesturing*] You have a ladybug on your shoulder.

SARA: Leave it there.

PEDRO: But it might sting you.

SARA: Ladybugs don't sting. Where do you come from?

PEDRO: From work. I work over there on the other block.

SARA: I mean where do you come from since you don't know that ladybugs don't sting.

PEDRO: From work. Aren't I telling you? I work on the other block. I'm a dent fixer. Actually, an assistant, but I almost learned the whole job already. And you?

SARA: No. I've never fixed a dent.

[SARA *and* PEDRO *laugh.* PEDRO *sits by her side.*]

PEDRO: No, I'm asking if you work.

SARA: Yes, I do work.

PEDRO: Where?

SARA: And whaddaya wanna know for?

PEDRO: To go wait for you.

SARA: No, I don't like for people to come and wait for me at work, cuz right away they start to talk.

PEDRO: And what's wrong with that?

SARA: I don't like it.

PEDRO: Then I'm gonna wait for you by your house.

SARA: That's worse, cuz there my dad don't like it.

PEDRO: But I'm not gonna wait for him; I'm gonna wait for you. [*Pause.*] Could it be someone else who gets mad?

SARA: What do you think?

PEDRO: I don't know. I ain't never seen you with nobody, just with me.

SARA: With you? When?

PEDRO: In my dreams.

SARA: How you gonna dream bout me. You don't even know my name.

PEDRO: Your name is Rosa.

SARA: No.

PEDRO: Carmen.

SARA: No. I have an old-lady name; my name is Sara.

PEDRO: And I'm Pedro. Sara and Pedro.

[PEDRO *gets up.*]

Good ole Sara and Pedro.

[SARA *gets up.*]

SARA [*narrating*]: That was ten years ago. Then I lived in a house that had a separate dining room and bedroom; in that house . . .

PEDRO: Afterwards too you had all that, it's when the Guest arrived that we started to go downhill. With what I earned as a dent fixer we did good. [*Pause.*] Do you remember those Fridays when you'd come to wait for me at work and we'd go off to the movies or the diner? We also used to go exchange magazines to read at night: Harlequin romances for you and cowboy novels for me . . . There are no magazine exchanges no more, huh?

SARA: No neighborhood movie theaters neither.

PEDRO: And the soda fountains are dying out too.

SARA: Everything's dying out.

PEDRO: Us too?

SARA [*gesturing*]: Wonder when he's gonna go?

PEDRO: Later.

SARA: Later?

PEDRO: Sure, when they tell us what we came to ask: that's what you was saying; forget in order to begin to live.

SARA: You gonna start again? If you hadn't spent your time talking with the neighbors, we could have seen him coming and closed the door on him.

PEDRO: And where were you that you didn't close it?

SARA: Asking you what you was talking about, don't you remember? But you'd never tell me nothin. "Don't butt in, you don't know nothin about these things," is all you'd say. There you have it.

PEDRO: So it's just my fault? If you saw that I was screwin up you should have butt in; you should have faced up to things.

SARA [*angrily*]: Don't talk no more about that; ain't no point. Go on, ask now!

PEDRO: You got mad again . . . You think that if they tell us what we wanna know here that we're going to be saved, I mean, be together and all that?

SARA: I don't know. [*Gesturing at the audience*] They're all together.

PEDRO [*gesturing*]: Wonder what this bench is for?

SARA: For people to sit, not for waiting for the bus. Come on, cut out the drama and ask.

PEDRO: I get this thing like fear or sadness. Don't you feel nothin?

SARA: Ask.

PEDRO: No, misery loves company, let's ask together. [*To the audience*] Damn, he threw us out of everywhere: first it was the job, then the great house we had when I was a dent fixer, from the clothes we wore, from the street, from the foo—

SARA: But that wasn't the last or the worst: the worst was that he also threw us out of ourselves.

PEDRO: What's gonna happen? What's gonna happen to us Sara?

SARA: Happen? It already happened. He left us like if we suddenly found ourselves in God's tomb. Ask.

PEDRO: I'm asking you what's gonna happen with you and me; what the hell is gonna happen with love?! Are we gonna get it back?

SARA: I don't know, don't know: they're together! The only thing I know is that we can't go on like this, we can't: we have to get used to it to be able to live. Ask, ask!

PEDRO: The hell with everything! Yes, that's what we came for: we want you to tell us how you got used to living with the Guest. We want to be like you!

SARA: We can't be different: tell us, tell us!

PEDRO: Tell us, tell us!

SARA: Tell us.

PEDRO: Tell us . . .

FINISHED FROM THE START

Mariela Roi (Aurelio), Pepe Herrera (Emilio), Nelson Brodt (Miguel), and Silvia Marín (Marta) in the 1981 original production of *Finished from the Start* by Teatro Popular El Telón in Santiago, Chile. The play was directed by Nelson Brodt.

PRODUCTION HISTORY

Finished from the Start was first produced under the Spanish title *Hechos consumados* in 1981 at the Teatro Bulnes in Santiago, by El Telón. It opened on September 26, 1981, ran for two years, and toured the country for about three more years with the following cast and production team:

Director	Nelson Brodt
Emilio	Pepe Herrera
Marta	Silvia Marín
Miguel	Nelson Brodt
Aurelio	Jaime Wilson
Set and Costumes	Francisca Rosa
Lights	Mario Suazo

Among the play's most significant restagings was the production by the Chilean National Theater (1999), under the direction of Alfredo Castro, with José Soza, Amparo Noguera, Pepe Herrera, and Benjamín Vicuña.

Finished premiered in the United States in a workshop production by Northwestern University in conjunction with LaMicro Theater, directed by Martín Balmaceda, at the university's Struble Theatre, April 16 to 18, 2004. It was staged by LaMicro at the Centro Cultural Julia de Burgos in New York City in November 2004.

The play has also been produced in many countries in Latin America and Europe.

CHARACTERS

Emilio
Marta
Aurelio
Miguel

[*An empty lot on the outskirts of the city. Rocks, weeds, some papers, and so on. On one side—left—can be seen the figure of a sleeping person* (MARTA), *covered by an old overcoat. By her side, sitting on a rock, a man heats water over a small fire. Close to them, on a clothesline improvised between two stakes, hang a blouse, a skirt, a sweater, and a pair of stockings; one can also see a flour sack and a potato sack, both half full. It is a cold, gray afternoon. The woman turns restlessly, murmurs things; the man gets up, leans toward her, keenly interested. He listens for a moment. He soon grows tense, as if he had heard or perceived something in his vicinity. He rises, startled, peers around. He takes a few steps, trying to get a better look. The woman wakes up startled. She stares at him without understanding and searches with her gaze.*]

MARTA: And . . . and Mario?

EMILIO [*without looking at* MARTA]: Good thing you're up; you was starting to worry me.

MARTA: What happened?

EMILIO: I thought I heard footsteps, [*peering around*] but I don't see anyone.

MARTA: No, I mean, what happened? Where's Mario?

EMILIO: What Mario? You were alone.

[EMILIO *sits again.*]

MARTA: . . . Yeah right. [*Smiling, apologizing*] I was dreaming. [*Pause.*] And you?

EMILIO: No, I don't dream no more.

MARTA: I'm askin who you are; where you from?

EMILIO [*vaguely gesturing*]: From over there.

MARTA [*looking around*]: Where we at?

EMILIO [*indifferent*]: Don't know.

MARTA: What do you mean you don't know?

EMILIO: I don't know, see; there ain't no signs round here.

MARTA [*looking*]: Wonder what time it is?

EMILIO: The afternoon. Of who knows what day.

MARTA: Hey, how can you not even know that?

EMILIO: Not knowing.

MARTA: You mad?

EMILIO: Nope.

[EMILIO *stirs the fire.*]

Thing is, I don't like to talk.

MARTA: And why don't you like to talk? What else you got going on? . . .

[MARTA *points excitedly toward a spot in front of her.*]

Hey, look; look at the bunch of people going along there! . . . Who are they? Where they goin to?

[EMILIO *looks without answering.*]

You goin with em?

EMILIO [*smiling*]: How am I gonna be going with em when I'm sittin here?

MARTA: No, well, I meant to ask if you was goin with em and then sat down to have some tea.

EMILIO: Nope, got no idea who they are or where they're goin to.

MARTA: I don't like it; it scares me . . . Maybe something happened.

EMILIO: You sayin you don't know what happened?

MARTA: I mean now.

EMILIO: I ain't heard nothing, [*looking*] but they don't look scared.

MARTA: Or happy neither.

EMILIO: Hey, don't ask cats to bark. If there was somebody happy out there they'd take him away to the funny farm.

[EMILIO *takes out cigarettes.*]

You smoke?

MARTA: No, just once in a while. [*Wrapping herself in the overcoat*] Damn it's cold.

[EMILIO *lights the cigarette on the embers.*]

EMILIO: Freezin.

MARTA: You live close by?

EMILIO: No.

MARTA: What you put on your face so it don't hurt?

EMILIO: On my face?

MARTA: Sure, see, your jaws must be dislocated from all your jabberin.

[EMILIO *laughs.*]

EMILIO: What you want me to talk bout?

MARTA: Well, I wanna know what I'm doin here.

EMILIO: You're sittin here askin foolishness.

MARTA: But how'd I get here?! I don't remember.

EMILIO: You were drownin. I fished you out of the canal; later you fell asleep. [*Pause.*] Did you jump or did you fall?

[MARTA *remains quiet, shrugs.*]

Ah, you jumped.

[EMILIO *empties water from a tin can into another can that serves as a mug and hands it to* MARTA.]

Here, nice and hot.

[MARTA *blows and takes a few sips in silence.*]

MARTA [*to herself*]: Course, I'm confused cuz the thing was at night . . . You say it's afternoon now?

EMILIO [*gesturing*]: Have a look.

MARTA: Then how much time did I sleep?

EMILIO: I found you bout one in the morning and you're just now wakin up: figure it out.

MARTA: And you was watchin over me all that time?

EMILIO [*standing up*]: Well what was I gonna do? Least it didn't rain. The night was real ugly.

MARTA [*looking*]: But it's nice now, huh?

EMILIO: Nice? Can't you see it's a crappy day? It's really gonna pour now. Seems like some water soaked into your brain.

MARTA: I don't pay you no mind; I already got it figured out that you're bitter. [*Looking*] It's nice.

EMILIO [*abruptly*]: Whaddya see? What could ya see?

MARTA [*surprised, wary*]: When?

EMILIO: Before I fished you out.

MARTA [*cornered*]: Nothin.

EMILIO: Whaddaya mean, nothin? You bout passed over to the other side. Think: were you afraid?

MARTA: No.

EMILIO: OK with it?

MARTA: No.

EMILIO: Happy? Did you feel like you were gonna rest?

MARTA: No, I didn't feel nothin!

EMILIO [*impassioned*]: You hada felt somethin! You hada see somethin!

MARTA: Go ask *them* then!

EMILIO [*taken aback*]: Who?

MARTA [*surprised*]: Why you askin me?

EMILIO: Cuz you peeked into a place where we all gotta go. Who you sayin I should ask?

MARTA [*evasively*]: No, never mind.

EMILIO: Seems like we're talkin bout two different things.

MARTA [*spirited*]: No, bout the same thing; we're talkin bout the same thing. It's just that I ain't seen nothin; it's true, I dint see or feel nothin. You was wantin me to do some thinking in the water?

EMILIO: They say you see; they say that first all the moments that you lived pass before your eyes, and that afterwards you see somethin.

MARTA [*resolutely*]: I already tole you. If you're so interested, you throw yourself in the water.

EMILIO [*going to stir the fire*]: If only that was possible . . . Cuz it's such a strange thing: when there ain't nothin to live for there ain't nothin to die for neither. [*Pause.*] Besides, if we bother em so much, let em finish what they started.

MARTA [*cutting him off, as she walks around trying to get to know the place*]: I don't like talkin bout them things. I like life.

EMILIO: So then why you try to kill yourself? Cuz you was so happy bout winning the lottery?

[MARTA *turns violently toward* EMILIO.]

MARTA: I dint . . . [*Taking it back*] You got no business asking me nothin. I don't even know your name.

EMILIO: My name is Emilio. And you?

MARTA: And what you work at?

EMILIO: You think that even if there was work, someone would give it to me looking like this?

MARTA: And where you live at?

EMILIO: Where they let me.

MARTA: And what was you before?

EMILIO: I thought I was a person. Why you ask me so much? Don't you trust me?

MARTA: It's that now . . .

[*She approaches* EMILIO, *looks at him.*]

Nah, you ain't bad, you got the eyes of an animal that was throwed out.

EMILIO: How's that?

MARTA: It's like a two-time loser, cuz of animal and throwed out.

EMILIO: Ah, thank you very much.

MARTA: No, it ain't an insult; it's the truth.

[*She walks around again.*]

All right then, tell me where we're at.

EMILIO: Where you like to be, in life. But not in the middle of it, on the side.

MARTA: I'm talking serious to you, ya know. Can't you see I don't know nothing round here?

EMILIO: I can't tell you more. I don't pay no attention to where I am no more. What for?

MARTA: Damn you sure are cheerful. Did you used to tell jokes on the radio?

EMILIO: For real, you're that into life?

MARTA: Sure, the problem is that she can't stand me.

EMILIO: For me it's the opposite: she loves me and I don't love her. [*Pause.*] Damn, we'd be happy if it didn't take two to love, right?

[*Brief pause.*]

MARTA: I don't talk bout love. It could make me . . . sad.
[*Walking around*] And this ain't no time to get sad . . . Seems like Sunday. Nope, don't seem nothing like Sunday. Seems like dawn . . .

EMILIO: Now we're in real good shape: old, stubborn, and crazy.

MARTA: Hey, back off, Romeo; sweet talk me first, before you get mean.

EMILIO: I ain't sayin nothin to you; I'm sayin it cuz of life. Imagine, trying to act all happy when you ain't even got a pot to piss in.

MARTA: You gonna keep it up?

EMILIO: No, it ain't no insult; it's the truth.

MARTA: Well, if it bothers you so much that I'm happy, I could poke my eye out with a stick or put my head under the wheels of a bus, ya know.

[MARTA *laughs. The distant sound of cans.*]

EMILIO: What was that?

MARTA [*gesturing upstage*]: It's coming from over there . . .

[AURELIO *emerges from the night. He is a strange being. The rags he wears are unclassifiable; actually, they aren't rags—there is a subtle difference between what is worn by time and what is destroyed through friction, through daily use: his clothes are worn by time. Strings of empty cans, not many, hang on his body.*]

MARTA [*softly*]: It's a psycho!

EMILIO: No, it's a man.

[AURELIO *looks at them from far away.*]

MARTA: Hey, don't you see how he's dressed?

EMILIO: He must think the same bout us . . . To think different . . . that's what we all call craziness. [*To* AURELIO] What's up, pal?

AURELIO: Hunger.

MARTA [*in a show of solidarity; to* EMILIO]: Got any bread?

AURELIO: No, not for bread.

[AURELIO *comes closer, points to the fire.*]

May I?

MARTA: Sure, come right up. [*To* EMILIO] Give him some room, huh.

AURELIO [*making himself comfortable*]: No, I'm fine over here.

EMILIO: But take off the armor, so's you'll be more comfortable.

[AURELIO *draws back, frightened. He hugs himself violently, safeguarding the cans.*]

AURELIO: I can't! They saved me!

EMILIO: From what?

MARTA: That don't make no difference. [*To* AURELIO] If you don't wanna take em off, don't take em off; he thought they was bothering you. You come from far away?

[AURELIO *draws close to the fire again.*]

AURELIO: Yes, from very far, from nowhere.
MARTA: How's that?
AURELIO: Freezing and leaden.
EMILIO: No, she means, how can you come from nowhere?
AURELIO [*abruptly*]: What are you doing here?
MARTA: Here?

[*She shrugs.*]

Nothin.
AURELIO: How did you come to this place?
EMILIO: She came swimmin; I came more or less from the same place you did, sir. Why?
AURELIO [*almost to himself*]: You had to have found something: no one lingers where there is nothing awaiting him . . . What did you find?
MARTA: Nothin. We ain't found nothin. Ain't that right, Emilio?

[AURELIO *stands, sniffs around.*]

AURELIO: If you have lingered here you must have found something. Is it true that you do not know it?
EMILIO: True, yep, so true; what could we find here? This ain't nothin but an empty lot.
AURELIO: Something must be awaiting you. [*Indicating the cans*] They ring. An announcement.
MARTA: Can you tell fortunes?
AURELIO: There are no fortunes, ma'am: there are men, rivers, stars, wind, flowers, and knives . . . Everything has a name and an inescapable destiny.
MARTA: And what's my destiny?
AURELIO: To live, ma'am.
MARTA: Yeah, OK, but how?
AURELIO [*roughly*]: I want to know what you found here. Tell me, it's important: say it.

EMILIO: Don't lose your cool, man; I already . . .

[AURELIO *jangles the cans and listens. He stares at* EMILIO *and* MARTA *compassionately.*]

AURELIO: All you have left fits in a fist or in a scream . . . Empty vessels and a cry rings inside them, that they stay, that they are still staying . . . The old dream of the peaceful place, an internal river that can't overflow onto the world, that they stay, that they are still staying . . .

MARTA [*to* EMILIO]: I don't understand nothin.

EMILIO: That we're stayin; that we're still stayin.

[AURELIO *jangles the cans and listens.*]

AURELIO [*somberly*]: The water . . . the broken bones against the sky. The black water of death . . . [*Restlessly*] The night falls; I will go.

[AURELIO *gestures.*]

MARTA: What did you see? What did you see in the cans?

AURELIO: Nothing . . . They didn't tell me anything. [*To the ancient labyrinths of knowledge*] Why here? Why here?

MARTA: Here, what? What did you see?

AURELIO: Does one build just the same by lighting flares or by snuffing them out?

EMILIO: Listen, Tinkerbell, if you seen somethin, cut out the guessing game and tell it straight. Don't be scared.

MARTA: Yeah, ya know. If you seen somethin, say so.

AURELIO [*gesturing*]: This man is approaching the measure of death!

[*He jangles the cans with a growing rhythm, as if refusing to believe, and listens.*]

[*Taken aback*] The wind of injustice blows again . . . Until when? Why? [*Pause.*] It blows and blows again . . . What is it looking for now? Until when? [*Pause.*] Where is the bread and the wheat? What happened to the cosmic joy of having a child? Was the sweat we sweat in vain? So much death and nothing, so much death and nothing! [*Burdened*] Never again shall I enter the city . . . Never again will I be able to enter . . .

[*A can sounds against his body as if by chance. He remains still, listening; his expression changes, turns happy. He makes the cans jangle.*]

She wears white and smiles: death comes smiling! Of course, what falls is reborn purified! . . . God, you finally decided to elevate human beings! . . . Could it be here? Could it be only here? I have to go see, I have to go see!

[AURELIO *springs away.* MARTA *follows him a short distance.*]

MARTA: Hey, listen!
EMILIO: Let him go.
MARTA: Was he a psycho?
EMILIO: What do you think?
MARTA: Yeah, for sure.
EMILIO: Then whaddaya askin me for?
MARTA: Don't you care?
EMILIO: If what he said was true, there ain't nowhere I can escape to, and if it's a lie, ain't no point in worrying.
MARTA: Hey listen, and what was he hungry for if it wasn't for food?
EMILIO: Now there he was really screwed, cuz the only bread that cures all hungers is justice, and that thing is more lost than the city of Atlantis.
MARTA: Damn, and he went off that way: maybe to top it all off the poor psycho-boy is gonna fall into the canal.
EMILIO: No, the canal is over there; it goes this way, not across.
MARTA [*surprised*]: That way? And why are we so far?
EMILIO: It ain't so cold here.
MARTA: And how'd you bring me from so far off?
EMILIO: On my shoulder.
MARTA: Hey listen . . . was I . . . was I dressed?
EMILIO: Sure enough. Or did you think I brought them in a suitcase? I took them off you. Since I fished you out of the canal, I wasn't gonna let you die of pneumonia.

[*He points out the clothes.*]

Put them on.
MARTA: They must still be wet.

EMILIO: I dried them for you; I dried them on the fire.

MARTA: Why did you dry them for me?

EMILIO: Cuz they was wet.

MARTA: No, I mean . . . That is, nobody never done nothin for me before. People always just pass right by . . . And you took care of me and you dried my clothes . . . Thank you.

EMILIO [*after a brief pause*]: Welcome. Next time you throw yourself in the water, you come by here and I'll dry your clothes. You live far?

MARTA: I don't have no house . . . Ever since Mario beat it I been alone.

EMILIO: That's why you wanted to wash your clothes with you in em?

MARTA: No, something else happened.

EMILIO: What else?

MARTA: Somethin else. [*Pause.*] Mario left a while ago; left a long while ago: it's been three months . . .

EMILIO: Where'd he go to?

MARTA: Who knows? He died.

[*She goes to the clothes, feels them.*]

They really are dry. I'm gonna put em on. Go on, turn round. Be a gentleman.

EMILIO [*pointing*]: They're gonna see you. And there's little kids too.

MARTA [*looking*]: Yeah, OK. Get in front then.

[EMILIO *gets up, stands facing her.*]

But turn around that way, smartass.

EMILIO: I can make jokes too, see?

[*He turns around.*]

Was Mario your man?

MARTA: My boyfriend.

EMILIO: Did he die on his own or did they kill him?

MARTA [*getting dressed*]: No, you see . . . the thing is, he's only dead to me: he dumped me. [*Pause.*] Did he die or did they kill him? I hadn't never thought bout that. One day he picked up his tools, he stood there looking straight at me, and he says: "Know what else? You do absolutely nothing for me." And he left . . . we'd been together more than six years.

EMILIO: And you didn't say nothin to him?

MARTA: No, see, what was I gonna say? When it comes to bed and food, you can't beg nobody . . . And besides, you can't fix things of the heart with words, cuz you can't win love like a fight.

EMILIO: The street kid is proud too.

MARTA: No, it ain't that I'm proud; it's that you need real love, not fake love. Cuz you're living for real, see?

[MARTA *is finished getting dressed.*]

OK, if you wanna turn round, you can look now.

[EMILIO *turns, stares at her fixedly;* MARTA *is embarrassed.*]

All right, already, just a quick look.

EMILIO: You're fixed up real nice. The only thing is you look like your clothes was run over by a truck . . .

[EMILIO *becomes still, as if listening.*]

MARTA: What's wrong?

EMILIO: You feel kind of like we're being spied on? Like there's someone round here?

[EMILIO *looks around.*]

MARTA [*frightened, following him*]: The psycho!

EMILIO: No.

MARTA [*gesturing*]: Them!

EMILIO [*searching, sniffing around*]: It's somethin else . . . I felt it since before too . . .

MARTA: Can't see no one; there ain't no trees or big rocks. Ain't nowhere for someone to hide.

EMILIO [*darkly*]: There's someone . . . Someone's snoopin round here.

MARTA: Did you do something wrong?

EMILIO: Don't think so. But you never know . . . And you?

MARTA: I don't know. I talk. I laugh. Is that bad?

EMILIO: Could be.

MARTA: Why don't they tell us what we can do and what we can't do?

EMILIO: They can't.

[*Pause.*]

MARTA: We should get out of here.

EMILIO: To where?

MARTA: Yeah, well, it's the same thing everywhere. Why they always comin after us?

EMILIO: Cuz they're makin a better world.

MARTA: For who?

EMILIO: For us.

MARTA: Hey, how's that?

EMILIO [*going to sit down*]: Go figure.

MARTA: And what can be done?

EMILIO: That's what we'd all like to know. [*Pause.*] You got kids?

MARTA: No . . . Well, I got pregnant once, but I lost it.

[*She shrugs.*]

And also, Mario didn't want to.

[*She thinks.*]

But it must be cool to have a kid, huh? I've noticed that women never look prettier than when they hold a baby in their arms like this [*miming*].

EMILIO: It's nice, yeah . . . Specially when they ask you for food and you ain't got none for em. "The children of the poor are strong and healthy because they are raised on soil and go around naked." You heard that?

MARTA: Sure, the wives of the bosses always say that.

EMILIO: At least your husband knew the score.

MARTA [*haughtily*]: Mario wasn't my husband; we'd just gotten together. [*Pause.*] But even if he had been, whatever he'd been, I already realized that I couldn't have none cuz we dint have nowhere to raise them. Damn, God should . . .

EMILIO: Don't drag him into it. He don't hand out the stuff; at most he made it: others hands it out.

MARTA: Sure. Yeah, I know how they hands it out . . . One time they came to our house and they started to take everything out. My mom grabbed us and took us in a corner. "Go ahead and take everything, you bastards," she told em. "But don't even ask me any bullshit." She taught me not to beg. She taught me to smack myself in the mouth with a rock fore I'd beg.

EMILIO: Why'd they take your stuff? When was that?

MARTA: Awhile back, I was bout ten. [*Pause.*] But I don't like to talk about that: could make me sad. You got kids?

EMILIO: I did.

MARTA: They die?

EMILIO: Yes, an absolute death.

MARTA: How's that?

EMILIO: They forgot me.

MARTA: And you?

EMILIO: Me what?

MARTA: You forgot them too?

EMILIO: What you plannin to do?

MARTA: . . . Dunno: walk.

EMILIO: You got somewheres to go to?

MARTA: No.

EMILIO: Then you'll get there real soon.

MARTA [*gesturing excitedly*]: Look, a fire!

[MARTA *and* EMILIO *stand and watch.*]

EMILIO: What could be burning now?

MARTA: I know that smoke . . . it's from grass or wheat.

EMILIO: What doesn't burn withers.

[EMILIO *goes to sit.*]

MARTA: You know any rich guy that's got a house with a garden?

EMILIO: Garden? No, why?

MARTA: So's you could give me a lead. I fix up gardens. That's what me and Mario worked at.

EMILIO: Gardens? . . . There any left?

MARTA: Almost none. [*Pause.*] That's what makes me real mad at people: they locked themselves up in their houses and let the gardens die.

EMILIO: If only that was all they did.

MARTA: But it was the worst . . . This was the time for the carnations, for the mums, and the dahlias, afterwards came the time for the gladiolas and the giant mums. Everything looked so pretty, full of color . . . But they let the gardens dry up. And I say: what's folks gonna do when spring comes and there ain't no flowers?

EMILIO: With no soil under their feet and no bread to fill their mouths, I don't think folks is gonna trouble themselves much over that now.

MARTA: You're just like the rest. You blame your troubles on just the big things, but it's the little ones, those things so little that they almost don't exist, that go dragging you towards the desert.

[EMILIO *doesn't answer.* MARTA *takes a few steps and stands in front of him.*]

Well, thanks for everything, huh?

EMILIO: Welcome.

[*Silence.*]

MARTA [*gesturing*]: The streets are that way?

EMILIO: No, you have to go the opposite way from them [*gesturing*].

MARTA: Then they're comin from the city?

EMILIO: Maybe.

MARTA: They running away?

EMILIO [*looking*]: Don't think so. They look very calm. What I'm sayin is you gotta go the opposite way from them. Pretty soon you'll start smellin somethin rotten: after that you'll get to the city.

MARTA: And you . . . what you gonna do?

[EMILIO *takes out cigarettes.*]

EMILIO: Now I'm gonna smoke. After, I dunno.

MARTA [*after a pause, pointing to the tin can*]: Ya know? I'm gonna drink it before I go . . . I ain't got no spare change to go have no tea.

EMILIO: If you gonna drink it, put it on the fire; it's cold by now.

[MARTA *sits.*]

MARTA: Well, let's put it on a while. You gonna have some?

EMILIO: No.

[MARTA *searches for something to say.*]

MARTA: Cold, huh?

EMILIO: Sure.

MARTA: Gonna rain?

EMILIO: Dunno.

MARTA: Where you go to when it rains?

EMILIO: To where I don't get wet.

[MARTA *laughs.*]

MARTA: Right, yeah! [*Pause.*] We're far away here, huh?

[EMILIO *stands without answering.*]

   Where you goin?

EMILIO: To look for somethin for the fire; it's goin out.

MARTA [*as if about to get up*]: I'll go.

EMILIO: No, you stay here and watch the bags.

[EMILIO *begins to look, picks up a branch here and there, a paper; we lose sight of him as he looks.* MARTA *stands; she looks at her clothes, tries to smooth them, fixes her hair, and so on. Then she picks up the overcoat and carefully folds it and moves the sacks from their place. She takes a branch out of the clothesline and uses it as a broom to clean the place. The people passing by catch her attention. She stares at them and takes a few steps toward them.*]

MARTA [*shouting*]: Hey! Where you come from? Where you goin to? Answer me; answer me! Who are you? Who are you?

[MARTA *waits, shrugs, keeps raking.* EMILIO *comes in with branches, pieces of boards or any combustible object. He stares at* MARTA, *puzzled.*]

EMILIO: What you doing?

MARTA: Cleaning, see.

EMILIO: What for?

MARTA: So that it's clean, see. [*Smiling*] Us women always clean.

EMILIO: But . . . damn, how could you even think of cleaning here? This ain't no home!

MARTA: For us that ain't got no home, anywhere we is, is home.

[EMILIO *lets the scraps drop.*]

EMILIO: Hey, don't be silly.
MARTA: Hmm, you don't like it?

[MARTA *throws the stick.*]

I won't clean up one single thing!
EMILIO: You always been so good-natured?
MARTA: Sensitive. Ain't no one gonna humiliate me.
EMILIO [*happily*]: Fabulous! Now I like that about you. If I was wearing a hat I'd take it off to you, swear.
MARTA: You messin with me?
EMILIO: No, for real. They can kick you and knock down lots of your doors, and you can keep pluggin away, but if they knock down the door of your dignity, then they got ya, cuz then you ain't nothin, not even trash, got it?
MARTA: Just sort of.
EMILIO: But the thing is real simple: somewhere a door opened and all the bad that exists came in at once. Not even Christ can save you from hunger, from loneliness, from kicks in the teeth; but dignity can save you from becoming an animal. And no matter what the price, that's the only thing that matters.
MARTA: So with or without dignity, I'm just as dead? You give me so much hope, ya know. With that faith you have in life you could devote yourself to comforting the sick in hospitals; you'd earn loads of cash.
EMILIO: There's no other way. Cuz you've got so much warmth inside, I'd like to be able to offer you something better, but that is the only thing they left us.
MARTA: Offer me? Are you, like, flirtin with me?
EMILIO: Nah, it's just a figure of speech.
MARTA: You ever have a home?

[EMILIO *steps forward, looks.*]

EMILIO: Yeah, but it's been a while. [*Gesturing*] I asked one of them guys where they're goin, but he played dumb . . . He gave me a look like askin me if I was a moron or just acting like one . . . Up close they look tired, they look . . .
MARTA: You miss her?
EMILIO: Who?

MARTA: Dunno. Your wife.

EMILIO: Enough to make me scream. But can't do nothin bout it; what's lost is lost. The thing is to learn to have nothing.

MARTA: But we ain't no animals, you know. Though it's a thing that hurts sometimes, love . . .

EMILIO: Love? When a woman can't get no money, a man can't get no honey: that's love. What we thought existed don't exist: what kept us together was bread, bed, or the need for company, but we were people without love.

[MARTA *is about to protest.*]

No, don't make faces at me; go over there [*gesturing*]; go to that damn city and ask who're the ones that stayed together: the only ones are the ones that still got jobs or the ones that always had big bucks.

MARTA: Damn, you are bitter, you know! And to think that I didn't trust you cuz I thought you was a snitch!

[MARTA *laughs.*]

Don't be silly, see; I know things is bad, but . . .

EMILIO: You gonna start giving me advice? I'm young and beautiful, and I got my whole life ahead of me—isn't that right?

MARTA: No, course not. But if everybody that had something bad happen to them during this time had to set to crying, no one but the dogs would have dry eyes, man . . . And also, if there wasn't people like you, who would people like me talk to? Only someone down on his luck can comfort someone else down on her luck, see; don't be silly. And just so you know, no one can say they ain't gonna love no more, cuz the brain can't tell the heart what to do; it just rolls up its sleeves and gets down to lovin, so don't you be acting so smart.

EMILIO: How come you know so much bout love?

MARTA: Cuz I love life, see. Sometimes my heart aches with everything that happened, but I don't think love has died; what happens is that good love is like good plants; it don't come out alone, you have to plant it so it flowers. Yeah, stick with me and you'll learn a . . . [*Startled*] And this guy? Where'd he come from? Is he looking for the psycho?

EMILIO [*looking*]: Who?

MARTA [*softly*]: Him, see . . . Shhh . . .

[*From the house appears a man*—MIGUEL—*with a club.*]

MARTA [*politely*]: Good afternoon.
MIGUEL [*from below*]: Afternoon.
MARTA: Looking for someone?

[MIGUEL *watches without speaking, goes onstage, and pushes the stick on the floor.*]

MIGUEL: Weren't there more?
EMILIO: Is it yours?
MARTA: Were you looking to build a fire?
MIGUEL [*without looking at them*]: You guys from around here?
EMILIO: What's it to you?
MARTA: Nah, we ain't from round here at all. We's just passin through. Where you come from that we didn't see you?
MIGUEL [*vaguely*]: From over there . . . You gonna have tea again?
MARTA: I ain't had none . . . How'd you know we was having tea?
MIGUEL: I have to know everything . . . Take your time. [*Leaving*] It's still early.
MARTA: Early for what?

[MIGUEL *doesn't answer. He disappears from sight.*]

[*To* EMILIO] Early for what, did he say?
EMILIO: Who knows, man.
MARTA: Damn, the guy was super-scary-spooky. And you treated him bad; be more careful. Can't you see he could be dangerous?
EMILIO: I don't like people who are armed, or people who sneak up on you from the side: it always ends in violence.
MARTA: But you can't be startin somethin with everyone, ya know.
EMILIO: I don't start nothin with no one. It didn't depend on me if someone loved me or if they gived me a job or a place to live; but it do depend on me not to let nobody step on me; If they can't make me do something I don't wanna do, they won't be able to make me do nothin, and at the end of the day, that's all that matters. You get down on your knees before your shit love and your shit hope, just leave me alone the way I am.

MARTA [*angrily*]: I don't kneel down before no one; don't be a big mouth!

EMILIO: You wanted to kill yourself.

MARTA: Liar!

EMILIO: And what were you doin in the canal? You were learning to swim?

MARTA [*glancing all around*]: It wasn't me: they threw me.

EMILIO: They threw you? Who? Mario?

MARTA: Keep it down, man!

EMILIO: Don't be scared. Don't be scared no more. Who threw you?

MARTA: I don't know, I don't know who they was; I was too scared to see them good. [*Almost amused*] And besides, I was busy crying.

EMILIO: Crying? Then you lied to me: you said you don't beg.

MARTA: I didn't beg them; I just cried. It was this thing I thought of to see if they'd leave me alone.

EMILIO: And what were you doin that they went after you?

MARTA: Just living, that's all I was doing. But it was my bad luck that I passed by a street where three guys was dragging a bundle out of an alley and I froze. I hit the invisible wall . . . Know what the invisible wall is?

EMILIO: No.

MARTA: The same thing Agent 86 used to hit.

EMILIO: Who's he?

MARTA: Agent 99's partner.

[MARTA *laughs.*]

EMILIO: Oh, you're playing with me.

MARTA: No. It was a show they used to have on TV, I used to watch it while I was fixin up gardens with Mario. It was bout this goofball that used to get all crooked and stiff when he got trapped, like this.

[MARTA *does the invisible wall.*]

That's exactly how I got when I saw those guys. Then right away one of them got close to me and said: "And you, what you doing round here? You spyin?"

"No sir," I says, "just passing through."

"Where you live?"

"No, I ain't got no home," I says to him. "Ever since Mario left me I go round by myself all over."

"OK, OK," he says to me, "get outta here."

I started to go, real happy, when another one who seemed like he was more in charge says: "No, hey, we can't risk it."

"But this girlie don't know nothin bout nothin," he says to him.

"No, listen to me; we can't risk having her running her mouth out there, bring her on in."

And then they grabbed me and they threw me in the car too. And that's when I got the idea of crying, see. "What's your name?" "Which side are you on?" "How long you been getting in trouble?" And I just cried and cried.

EMILIO: What bundle was this that they throwed in the car?

MARTA: It moved, but I dint see it good; dint I tell you that I spent the whole time crying? They even kicked me so's I'd cut it out, but I dint let up. We'd been goin a long while when one of them said to the others: "Damn, this crybaby is driving me crazy with her crying fit; what are we gonna do with her? Then the guy in charge, he grabs me by the hair and he says, "Listen, loser, if you don't shut your mouth we're gonna kill you and we're gonna throw you in that canal." But there weren't no way I was gonna cut it out. Can't you see that if I didn't cry then they might make me say some bull, and then I'd really be sunk? But me, you can't put nothin over on me; they wasn't gonna get me . . .

[MARTA *falls silent.* MARTA *and* EMILIO *listen.*]

Feel it?

EMILIO: Sure. Sirens.

[MARTA *and* EMILIO *stand and look around.*]

MARTA [*fearfully*]: And they don't have nothin to do with firemen; those sound different.

EMILIO: Now what coulda happened?

MARTA: We gotta run!

EMILIO: No, wait. [*Gesturing*] It must be them they're after.

MARTA: But they're gonna come after us too!

EMILIO: So what?

MARTA: I don't want them to kill me! They've come now! Let's go!

[MARTA *takes* EMILIO's *arm and pulls.*]

EMILIO [*looking closely*]: They don't run; they ain't scared. It's like they don't hear.

MARTA: They went right on by! It dint have nothing to do with them . . . Where they goin then?

EMILIO: How should I know?!

MARTA: Why didn't they run? Why didn't they get scared?

EMILIO: Hey, I don't know. Maybe they're fed up with running and being scared, maybe they knew it dint have nothin to do with them. [*Interested*] Look . . .

MARTA [*trying to see*]: What?

EMILIO: Way over there. The guy with the stick.

MARTA: Course, he's givin em a hard time!

EMILIO [*impulsively*]: I'm gonna go see.

MARTA [*holding him back*]: No, don't go! . . . I'm scared; I don't wanna be alone.

EMILIO: Let me go; I ain't got nothin to do with you!

MARTA: And me with you neither, man, so don't go off on me.

EMILIO [*amazed*]: Damn, they ain't paying no attention to the guy with the stick neither.

MARTA: Right . . . Who are they? Who are they?

EMILIO: They might be anyone. But whoever they are, they got themselves a path . . . And some day, walking and walking, they got to get somewhere. Maybe that's how you got to be. Maybe there's no more goal than what you set for yourself.

MARTA: But they don't pay no mind to no one.

EMILIO: I like them . . . I'm liking them . . .

MARTA: Well, go on with them then, if you like them so much.

EMILIO: Why did the one I talked to before make like I already knew what I was asking? When someone tells you: "Don't play the fool, mister," they're accusing you of somethin . . .

MARTA: Why you telling me this?

EMILIO: You mad?

MARTA: No, why would I get mad? You can do whatever you want.

[MARTA *sits in* EMILIO's *place and rummages through the sack.*]

EMILIO: Want something to eat? I got some stuff there in the other bag . . . [*Meditatively*] If it has an entrance it must have an exit . . .

[MARTA *stops rummaging through the bag.*]

MARTA: What you talking now?

EMILIO [*going upstage*]: The same as always. That inevitable duty to search and search.

MARTA: You're a strange guy, huh?

EMILIO: Strange how?

[MARTA *falls to thinking.*]

MARTA: Don't know, man.

EMILIO: Don't pay me no mind. [*Rallying*] Well, you didn't finish telling me what happened to you.

MARTA: I don't wanna remember. I only told you so you wouldn't think I threw myself in.

EMILIO: So they were goin by, you interrupted them in something: they put you in the car and they went and threw you in the canal, just like that, like someone lights a cigarette or goes to throw out the garbage.

MARTA: Sure, just like that. But what happened, happened. I'm still alive: that's what's important.

[EMILIO *is going to argue;* MARTA *stands and goes to him.*]

No, don't argue with me. You are like going toward fire; you burn. I don't wanna learn to be scared; I don't wanna learn to cry . . . It's nice to live; the earth ain't to blame for nothin; Earth is like a house without walls, where there's everything you need, everything you like: sun, plants, water, fruit, birds, everything; it ain't her fault that . . .

[EMILIO *shushes her.*]

What is it?

EMILIO [*gesturing*]: He's coming this way again.

MARTA [*looking*]: Whaddaya suppose he wants now?

[MARTA *and* EMILIO *remain standing, waiting.* MIGUEL *appears. There is something darkly threatening about his politeness, something due not only to the fact that he carries a stick.*]

MIGUEL: Hello.

MARTA: Hello . . .

[MIGUEL *steadies the stick against his body, rubs his hands.*]

MIGUEL: Freezin afternoon, huh?

EMILIO: That's cuz it's winter. Would be strange if it was warm.

MIGUEL [*smiling*]: Course.

MARTA: Don't be rude.

MIGUEL [*still smiling*]: No, it ain't nothin . . . You done with your little tea break?

EMILIO: I am, but not her.

MIGUEL: Ain't you hitched?

EMILIO: Hitching is for horses.

MIGUEL: You mad, buddy?

MARTA: No, that's just how he is: he says he don't like to talk but then you gotta beat him with a stick to get him to be quiet.

MIGUEL [*rising, purposefully*]: Then I'm in great shape to make him be quiet.

EMILIO: Don't think so.

MARTA [*quickly*]: Want some tea? Was you wantin a little tea?

MIGUEL: No thanks. I was just asking if you were done . . . I dropped by before but since you were still drinkin, I didn't wanna bother you.

EMILIO: And what were you gonna bother us about?

MIGUEL: Well, I'm the security here . . . They sent me to tell you that this is private property.

EMILIO: And?

MIGUEL: And you can't be here, man.

MARTA: Course, we was just leavin . . . I mean, he's goin his way and I'm goin mine.

EMILIO: Why can't we be here?

MARTA: Cuz it's not our house, like he says. [*To* MIGUEL] But we didn't mean no harm, huh? We didn't know it was private property.

EMILIO: The truth is we didn't know that the world was private property and that's why we were born.

[EMILIO *sits.*]

If someone had bothered to tell . . .

MIGUEL: Why are you sitting? I'm serious.

[EMILIO *doesn't answer.*]

I let you be here all day; you can't complain. [*To* MARTA, *who begins to sit*] I'm serious, ma'am!

MARTA: I'm not a ma'am.

MIGUEL: Well, whatever you are. [*To* EMILIO] All right, let's go!

[EMILIO *takes off his shoe.*]

EMILIO: I can't go. I twisted my foot.

MIGUEL: Hey, how could you twist your foot when you were standing right there?

EMILIO: That's life, I guess.

MIGUEL: Don't be a smartass with me, joker. Look, I got a real bad temper. I talked to you nice, I even waited for you to finish your tea and everything, but don't push me. Don't push me.

MARTA: We ain't said nothing outta line. We was on our way already. Damn, you sure are in a hurry.

EMILIO: Why you want us to leave? This is an empty lot; we're not bothering nobody here.

MIGUEL: I dunno; it ain't got nothin to do with me: he sent me to say that he didn't wanna find you here when he gets back. I'm just the messenger.

MARTA: Who is he?

MIGUEL: The boss.

MARTA: What time does he get here?

MIGUEL [*almost offended*]: That's his business.

EMILIO: Then we still got a lot of time. [*To* MARTA] Take your time with your tea; you know there's stuff in the smaller bag.

MIGUEL: Hey no, mister, don't mess around: I don't wanna do anything to you.

EMILIO: Then why you gonna do it. [*To* MARTA] Come on, go ahead, and give me some too.

[MARTA *weighs the situation.*]

MARTA: We ain't got nowheres to go.

[MARTA *begins to poke around in the bag.*]

MIGUEL [*threateningly*]: So, I'm gonna have to run youse off?
MARTA: We ain't got nowheres to go.
MIGUEL: That's your problem, I ain't got nothing to do with that.

[MIGUEL *brandishes the stick.*]

You get out of here now!
MARTA [*frightened*]: No, whaddaya doin!
MIGUEL: But I'm trying to be nice and you don't get it. And I have to protect my job!
MARTA: Look here, Emilio!
EMILIO: He's the one who's gotta watch what he's doing. [*To* MIGUEL] It don't cost nothin to kill a person, pal; it takes a minute or two. But what about afterwards? You got a home? You got a family? Think about it first.
MIGUEL: You're on property that ain't yours; they can't get me for nothing.
EMILIO: Don't be silly, mister. If you kill us they're gonna crucify you. Can't you see that if nothing bad happens among us poor, the law dies of hunger? The law is a very strange animal, pal; it doesn't like fine steak; it likes its meat stringy and sweaty, like yours and mine.
MIGUEL: Don't give me no weird crap. I've already figured out that you're good at BS-ing, but you ain't gonna make a fool outta me. The boss has always sent word not to take no crap from no one, cuz I've got my position.
MARTA: But we ain't arguing with you about that. You've got your position and we've got ours.
EMILIO: Sure, we don't wanna make problems for you. What for, since we're equals?
MIGUEL: I've got my house and my job and I don't go getting on other people's property.

MARTA: Lucky you. I used to fix up gardens, but who's gonna ask me to fix their garden now?

EMILIO: And I was a weaver, but since they're importing everything including the thread, there isn't even any work for knitting with needles.

MIGUEL: You ain't gonna find nothin sittin here all day. [*Less belligerently*] You were a weaver? What did you weave?

EMILIO: A little of everything: blankets, cashmere, towels, whatever came in.

MIGUEL: And where'd you work at?

EMILIO: Oh, where didn't I work! I was at La Fresia, at Comandari, at Polax; even in that sweatshop, over there on Pedro Alarcón; I was there, that says it all.

MIGUEL: Yeah, I know it, I was also a textile work———. . . I mean, I am.

EMILIO: Damn, that's great; then we're colleagues.

MARTA: Only *almost* colleagues, cuz he's got a job.

EMILIO: Want a little tea? Your hands are so cold they're practically blue.

MARTA [*taking things out of the sack*]: With a little tea and a sandwich of bread and bread, you're gonna be fine.

EMILIO: Is there enough for three?

MIGUEL: No, I don't want any. I gotta get back to work. Besides security, I work on a wolf.

MARTA: On a wolf! Damn, what a dangerous job you have.

EMILIO [*smiling*]: No, see; it's a machine for ripping up rags.

MIGUEL: You know it too?

EMILIO: Sure, I know almost the whole textile business. [*To* MARTA] It's a machine for making cleaning rags. You work with nothin but old scraps that the bosses go buy from the junkyards; dirty, smelly scraps that kick up huge dust while they get ground up.

MIGUEL: That musta been where you worked: here we don't work with waste, we work with remainders from the textile mills.

EMILIO: That's how it should be, but it's not, man. Does the machine get clogged?

MIGUEL: Sometimes.

EMILIO: Don't you see? It's because of the buttons and junk that the scraps have, they get caught in the gears and they build up until the machine gets clogged. [*To* MARTA] Sometimes you can't even see yourself in the middle of all that dust. [*To* MIGUEL] Do they give you milk?

MIGUEL [*looking furtively toward the place from which he came*]: Nah, they ain't gonna give you none.

MARTA: And where's the machine at? Cuz you can't hear it at all from here.

MIGUEL [*gesturing*]: Over there. You gotta turn towards the left, by over there, sorta by where you see those dogs pokin round, and keep going straight.

MARTA: So far? And does he own all this too?

MIGUEL: And not just this. Nobody knows everything he's got.

EMILIO: Just from the rags?

MIGUEL: No. Didn't I tell you that not even I know what all he's got?

EMILIO: How could we bother him if he's so powerful?

MIGUEL: Don't know, see, but he sent me to say that he didn't wanna see you round here. [*Pause.*] So why you gonna make problems for me, right?

MARTA: Do a lot of people work at the cleaning-rag thing? Maybe he could give us a job.

MIGUEL: No, not even in your dreams; we can't take nobody now. Figure it out: from fifteen workmen we had to go down to five. I've even had to get on the machines to lower the costs. But people don't understand that, I don't know what they're thinking. I got one workman who's been out a week. You tell em they gotta watch their job but they don't listen.

MARTA: That's where this guy could fit in, see.

MIGUEL: No, cuz that's the machine I'm workin.

EMILIO: I always got into scraps with the security . . . I remember there was one they called Palomo.

MIGUEL: The one they threw in the spinner?

EMILIO: Sure, you knew him?

MIGUEL: Nah, I'd just heard talk about him.

MARTA: What's a spinner?

EMILIO: A machine where they dry the cloth after they dye it.

MARTA: And they threw him in it?

EMILIO: Sure, for being a jerk. He was a carpenter but then he ended up as a door security guard, and he was the meanest dog there ever was . . . Nothing like a pup that turns on its own litter, huh?

MIGUEL: You gotta see both sides of it. If they give you a responsibility you gotta fulfill it. For instance, the boss has told me that during work hours people can't smoke, they can't eat, and they can't make conversation, and I have to make that happen, man, cuz that's what they pay me for.

EMILIO: But it's a shitty job, huh?

MIGUEL: No, the deal is that everybody's gotta know their place, cuz when there's order there's no problem. And besides, we don't force nobody to be there. If somebody don't like their job, they know where the door is. No need to get their blood pressure up.

MARTA: I remember that when me and Mario was fixin up gardens, we charged three hundred pesos, with lunch included. But when the situation started to go downhill they took away the lunch; afterwards they started to pay us two hundred pesos, and then one . . . That was the deal and we had to take it, but goddamn, it sure hurt!

MIGUEL: And what does that have to do with what we was talkin about? Tune in, lady.

MARTA: Thing is, the bosses never showed their faces, they always sent the maids to screw with us. So, sit down a while.

MIGUEL: No, I gotta go. [*Pause.*] You gonna go, right? What we gonna fight for?

MARTA: Sure, we don't wanna fight. We wanna live.

EMILIO: The bad news is that these days you gotta fight in order to live. Sit a while; a little weak tea won't hurt you.

[MIGUEL *sits.*]

MIGUEL: Just a little while. I left the wife alone there.

EMILIO: Would you have hit us with the stick?

MARTA: We didn't do nothin to you.

EMILIO: Would you have hit us?

MIGUEL: I go around with this stick cuz you never know who you gonna meet. [*Pause.*] It was the old lady who told me to bring it . . . She's sick, screwed up by the machine dust.

MARTA: Should I take her a little tea?

MIGUEL: No, thanks, she won't open for you; she's laying down. [*Gesturing*] Besides, she's afraid of those people.

[MARTA, EMILIO, *and* MIGUEL *speak while looking at the people.*]

EMILIO: They haven't stopped goin by.

MARTA: And there's some of everything: old folks, kids . . . Where they goin?

MIGUEL: I don't know. Nobody knows.

EMILIO: But you were runnin em off before.

MIGUEL: No, I wasn't runnin em off. What happened was that I thought I saw the guy who didn't show up for work in there with them . . . But I couldn't see good if it was him, and since he didn't answer me nothing . . .

MARTA: But you had that same stick. Anyone would be scared.

MIGUEL: And anyone would be scared of them too. They don't talk.

EMILIO: They don't beg.

MARTA: They just walk.

EMILIO: I like them . . .

MARTA: I'm scared of em; I'm scared of em and I feel sorry for em. They look lonely, tired.

MIGUEL: I don't like em and I don't feel sorry for em.

[MIGUEL *looks away.*]

They're like a threat; they're getting on my nerves. [*Pause.*] And he don't like em either.

EMILIO: Who?

MIGUEL: The boss. Yesterday he sent word that if they kept going by . . .

MARTA: Yesterday? Then when did they turn up?

EMILIO: Listen . . . Didn't you say your wife was sick? Didn't you say she was layin down?

MIGUEL: Sure, the old lady's sick.

EMILIO: Then how'd she see em?

MIGUEL: How? That's right, huh . . . And there are no windows in her bedroom.

[*Brief silence.*]

MARTA: She musta felt em.

MIGUEL [*without conviction*]: Course, that musta been it. Maybe they'll give up and beat it before it gets dark, so she don't get more scared.

EMILIO [*standing*]: There's no salvation now for anyone.

MIGUEL [*almost violently*]: Why do you say that?

EMILIO: The condemned condemn.

MARTA: The condemned? Condemned by who? By God? God don't condemn, ya know.

EMILIO: No?

[*He looks at* MARTA.]

How bout you take a little look at yourself?

[EMILIO *goes upstage.*]

MARTA: And you think you're hot stuff? [*To* MIGUEL] Here's a bunch of rags, see; why don't you take them and run them through the machine? I'll sell them to you.

[MIGUEL *stands.*]

MIGUEL: I don't buy scraps; the boss buys.

MARTA: Then I'll give it to you. [*Going toward* EMILIO] Well, there's enough dirt on this guy to jam up a freight train, so it could rip up the machine.

EMILIO: No, not a chance. Poor but clean, clean on the inside and outside. And remember that I fished you out of the canal. [*Regretfully*] No, don't pay no attention to me.

MIGUEL [*going toward* MARTA *and* EMILIO]: You always talk so sweet to each other?

MARTA: No, I just found this catch now.

EMILIO: I wouldn't hook up with this one if you paid me in gold: she's a path that I know leads nowhere. Well, that's the way it should be . . . But cuz of something in her eyes, in her heart, or who knows where the hell, I think I'd travel it again . . . And I'd never get nowhere.

MARTA [*puzzled, to* MIGUEL]: Did he insult me or is he flirting with me?

MIGUEL: I think he said something really ugly to you. Give him the brush-off just like that.

MARTA [*to* EMILIO]: Did you insult me?

EMILIO [*smiling*]: No, I swear I didn't; at least I didn't mean to.

MARTA: Why are you smiling? You've changed, I still haven't figured out why, but you seem happier inside . . . Like you got some good news.

EMILIO: Course, he brought it . . . Didn't you hear?

MIGUEL: It's not my fault, don't be a wiseass with me, buddy. I follow orders. But I ain't your enemy. If I was your enemy, I wouldn't be here chatting.

EMILIO: Maybe you know someone who is our enemy? I don't. Everybody loves us a hundred or two hundred times more than their mother and their grandmother put together. They've all spent their lives fighting for us: they write books, talk on the radio, on the TV, pass laws that help us in this or that way. I swear, I never heard of any big shot that isn't supposed to help us twenty-four hours a day. Damn, if everyone agrees, if they're all on the same track, then who the hell is the enemy? Tell me, man.

MIGUEL: I don't know. I don't get involved in that. All I know is that if I don't work, I don't eat.

EMILIO: But you gotta get involved buddy, cuz this means one of two things: either they're screwing with us or our enemy is God.

MARTA: Hey, don't get carried away.

EMILIO: But sure, man. If nobody on Earth is against us, it's got to be just him that doesn't let us study, that lays us off jobs, that kicks us out of our homes, and that screws us every which way.

MARTA: Nah, I think *they're* screwing with us, cuz he isn't; God is the only one we got, the only one that listens to us.

EMILIO: Sure, for listening, he's razor sharp; it's getting him to answer that's tricky.

MIGUEL: Excuse me for sayin this, but the problem is that you're really ignorant. He doesn't answer with words, he answers with deeds, he fixes things in a way that no one else would ever think of. There's one thing I know for sure, buddy: he helped me with my old lady.

MARTA: But didn't you say she was sick?

MIGUEL: Sure, and she's gonna die. But I didn't know what to do to accept it, cuz I've always loved her more than anything, and when death came into the bedroom and started to wait for her I thought it would be the same as if it was takin the whole world. Course, cuz the death of a loved one drags a lot of deaths behind it for you: deaths in the morning, in the afternoon, and at night; the empty half of the bed is one, the half of the table is another . . . and the words that you ain't gonna hear no more, that's the death that hurts the most. That's what I was thinkin and I was desperate . . . Then suddenly she changed, she turned hateful, she turned evil; she won't let me be alone even for a second: everything hurts her; everything bothers her. "Miguel, bring me water," she says and when I take it to her she yells at me cuz she thinks it's too cold or too hot or too lukewarm. "Miguel, fix the sheets, dry my sweat, go see if you can get an appointment at the clinic. Miguel, I'm hungry, Miguel, hand me the bedpan, don't fall sleep, give me this, give me that other thing." Miguel, Miguel, Miguel, she's driving me crazy, she don't let me rest day or night. Right this second she's probably calling me for some stupid thing. Damn, and now that she's got it in her head that I should tell them [*gesturing*] to go by a different way, it's even worse, so . . . Sure, it's not that I've stopped loving her . . . But goddamn, am I gonna rest when she dies!

EMILIO: And you think that's good? Instead of making you hate her, He coulda made her get well.

MIGUEL: I don't hate her buddy; listen good to what I'm sayin. But you gotta admit it was a smart move.

EMILIO: Persecuted with no enemies, psychos, husbands accepting the deaths of their wives, people [*gesturing*] lost between earth and sky, hunger, loneliness, fear . . . Know what I'd tell God if I ran into Him out there? I'd just say this one little thing: "Hey buddy, don't do unto others what you wouldn't want them to do to you, man." That's all I'd say.

MIGUEL: Thing is you're bitter, man. You don't believe in nothin.

EMILIO: Wrong: I believe that you have to believe in somethin; the bad news is that there's nothing to believe in.

MIGUEL: Sometimes things just go downhill, mister; but you gotta keep on keepin on. Right, ma'am?

MARTA: Sure, it's only when you die that you can tell whether life is crap or not cuz as long as you're alive things could always change. OK, the water's boiled now; put it in the cans, here they are.

EMILIO [*pouring water into the cans*]: She knows what she's sayin: she is the president of the International Committee for Hope . . . Just yesterday she was so happy cuz they wanted to give her a medal that she did a backflip into the canal.

MIGUEL: For real, you threw yourself into the canal? Why?

MARTA: Just things that get into your head. Don't pay him no attention.

MIGUEL: And you got her out?

EMILIO: Sure, cuz I'm a real hero.

MIGUEL: If I'd fished her out I'd a kept her for me. Now that the other one is gonna leave me high and dry, this one woulda come in handy.

[MIGUEL *touches* MARTA's *backside with the stick.*]

EMILIO: But I fished her out man.

MARTA: Hey, do I look like a soccer ball? You just go take care of your wife.

MIGUEL: As soon as I drink my tea.

[*He touches* MARTA *again, pushing her aside.*]

Excuse me.

[*He stands where* MARTA *was standing.*]

It's been so long since I've had a second to rest . . . Now she's got this idea that she wants to die in her bed. But she heard that work's not goin good and she's thinkin they're gonna kick us out. That would really be bullshit, if she couldn't even die in her own bed. At least the boss gave me the machine job besides the security job.

MARTA: Then you're bringin in some serious cash.

MIGUEL: No, it's for the same pay, but I got an in now; you know how it is. But the boss ain't bad, as soon as he heard the old lady was sick he sent word that she shouldn't sort the scraps no more. And if we make enough at the end of this month, he's gonna fix up the paperwork so she don't have to go to the hospital as "economically disadvantaged." That's why they haven't let her stay.

EMILIO: So you're really scramblin up to the top.

MIGUEL: Considering how things are, I can't complain . . . [*Seriously*] Know something?

[MIGUEL *stands belligerently.*]

I never know whether you're laughing at me or not: why don't you say things straight out?

EMILIO: I didn't say nothin. If something's botherin you, don't take it out on me.

MIGUEL: Ain't nothin bothering me, man!

MARTA: He's doin it for his sick wife, see; don't you get it?

MIGUEL: Do what for my wife? I've always worked!

MARTA: Don't get mad. Didn't I tell you that me and Mario had to work for whatever they wanted and we had to take it? That's how life is. Whaddaya gonna do bout it? And you're even less to blame, cuz you do it for the love of your wife.

MIGUEL: But damn, blame for what? What the hell are you talkin bout?!

MARTA: No, it's OK, don't get your blood pressure up, cuz you'll age real fast. I knew a case sorta like yours. He was married and had four children. [*Pause.*] They lived in a big old house, all full of woodworm, over on San Isidro Street. Not by themselves, eh? There was about fifteen families; so the house, that had two floors, was full of kids, of clothes hanged up to dry, of drunks, and of women fighting over space on the banister to hang clothes.

MIGUEL [*drily*]: Well, then that was a slum.

MARTA [*dignified*]: No, a home.

EMILIO [*watching*]: Reminds me of the Jews . . . Watching these people reminds me of the Jews.

MIGUEL: More like the gypsies. You don't even know history and you think you're so terrific.

EMILIO: Of the Jews. The gypsies are only good for telling fortunes and making copper pans. It was the Jews that had to go wandering.

MIGUEL: Gypsies, Jews, what do I care? All I know is that if they get too close to the house, I'll bash their brains in.

EMILIO: I like Jews, they have the secret of unity in their blood. Know what that secret could be?

MARTA: Hey, I was talkin!

MIGUEL: Sure, go on, I'm not interrupting you.

MARTA [*about* EMILIO]: This guy doesn't like the stories I tell. He don't wanna know me.

MIGUEL [*aggressively*]: Just go ahead; he ain't in charge here.

EMILIO: That's what she says, not me. [*Pause.*] What's your name?

MIGUEL [*surprised*]: You don't even know her name?

EMILIO: No, what's your name?

MARTA: Marta.

EMILIO [*to* MIGUEL]: I'm Emilio, and you?

MIGUEL: No, I'm not.

MARTA [*laughing*]: Good one; he gotcha!

MIGUEL: Yeah, you gotta give it right back to him, so he calls it quits.

MARTA: And what's your name?

MIGUEL: Miguel.

EMILIO: Marta, Miguel, and Emilio: great, now we've been introduced. And we can make ourselves at home. [*To* MIGUEL] Cuz she says that anywhere you are is where your home is at. Whaddaya say?

MIGUEL: Don't get smart with me, man; don't get smart with me.

EMILIO: You don't believe in that? You don't believe that if you was born you gotta be somewhere? Cuz what would we do then if we didn't have money for the rent? Kill ourselves?

MIGUEL [*to* MARTA]: Go on, I'm listening, just so's not to be rude, but I shoulda went already.

MARTA: Nah, it don't matter; it ain't nothin.

MIGUEL: Just tell it, I told ya already: he's not in charge here.

MARTA: Nah, that was all: one time the wife of the man that I was tellin you about got sick, same as yours, and she was bout to die, when one day the man comes in loaded down with gifts and happier than a pig in mud. He had everything: clothes, food, toys for the kids, and everything brand new. Damn, what happiness! The wife was so happy, she got well . . . Or could it be cuz she had eaten? "Start learning to smile, old girl, cuz our troubles are over forever," he says, "What a long shot! What a long shot!"

MIGUEL: A long shot is at the races when the no-good horse wins?

MARTA: Sure. And from then on it was just pure happiness: well dressed, good food, sleeping in beds . . . Same as people, same as if they'd been humans . . . Damn the setup was beautiful . . .

[MARTA *falls silent.*]

MIGUEL: Well, and what else then?

MARTA [*distantly*]: Huh?

MIGUEL: What else, man? What else happened . . . I gotta be goin.

MARTA: Nothin . . . The next week they came looking for him, he hadn't won nothin at the races; he'd robbed one of the fancy houses where he went to clean floors. "So what," he says when they took him away. "We didn't wanna die without knowing what happiness is. We're people too."

EMILIO: Ah, that was your dad. You tole me bout it when they took the stuff from the bedroom. Locked up for stealing a little bit of happiness.

[*He stands and confronts* MIGUEL *deliberately.* MIGUEL *grows uncomfortable.*]

Helluva world, huh?

[EMILIO *goes upstage.*]

When did this start and why? Sure, cuz at the beginning we started off equal. There weren't no richy-rich and no stone-cold broke: we were the same and we were going to the same place.

MIGUEL: To where?

EMILIO: Don't know, man. We're finished from the start; we didn't have no say in ourselves; they made us and they told us: "Here you are, go over there," but they didn't tell us why they had made us or why we had to go over to that side that we didn't know . . . to that side where the only sure thing was that we had to die . . .

MARTA: What you delusionating bout now?

MIGUEL: Damn, the guy is strange. His elevator don't go up to all the floors.

EMILIO: No, I'm gettin it more and more all the time . . . Sure man, dying is easy, that's what we're made for; what's hard is being born; cuz you're not born when you're delivered, you're born when you're able to live . . . And if you wanna live, you gotta crack the world wide open. And if you wanna live, you gotta crack the world wide open . . . Where'd I get that from? Where'd I hear it? Damn, it's true . . . [*Lost in thought*] Me and Yola, we couldn't crack the world open . . .

MARTA: Who is Yola?

EMILIO: Yola? . . . Don't know. She didn't want to be born.

MIGUEL [*after a brief pause*]: Know what? I'm goin. I don't get involved in domestic disputes.

MARTA [*foolishly*]: You leavin?

MIGUEL [*smiling*]: Sure, didn't I just say that?

MARTA: No, I mean, in case you wanna take your wife a little bit of tea.

MIGUEL: No thanks. I've already got her up to her eyeballs in tea.

[MIGUEL *takes out cigarettes.*]

You smoke?

MARTA: Sometimes. If you want you could give me one for the road.

[MARTA *takes one from* MIGUEL.]

Thanks.

MIGUEL [*looking up*]: Sure, you gotta go soon, cuz you're gonna get soaked. It's gonna rain.

EMILIO: If you gotta get wet, you gotta get wet. God's will.

MIGUEL: I'm gonna smoke this cigarette and I'm goin. I can't smoke there. [*To* MARTA] I don't know how, listen, but the boss knows everything that happens. Well, he's right too, it's dangerous to smoke there. Cuz you see, we work with nothin but old scraps of cloth. [*Pause.*] Which way you guys headin?

MARTA [*to* EMILIO]: Which way?

EMILIO: Can I ask a question? It's been buggin me since before.

MIGUEL: Sure, what is it?

EMILIO: The machine where the boss put you to work . . . is it the same one you said the disappeared guy worked?

MIGUEL: Why?

EMILIO: You said I could ask.

MIGUEL: We couldn't leave it down. If a machine stops, production gets backed up, and if production gets backed up there ain't no profits. And in an industry, when . . .

EMILIO: Know what? I asked cuz [*gesturing*] what if they was dead, pal?

MARTA: Dead? Don't get carried away. Can't you see they're walking?

EMILIO: That's all they do. [*To* MIGUEL] Didn't you say that your wife hadn't seen them, but that she knew they were going by and that she'd gotten scared? Didn't you say you'd seen that guy? Maybe he's coming to claim his job back . . . And maybe he's coming to accuse you of something.

MIGUEL: You think I'm a little kid? The dead are buried.

EMILIO: Where? Where are they buried?

MARTA: Don't scare him. And don't scare me neither.

EMILIO: Whadda you think they are? Dead? Unemployed? Homeless? People scared of something happening to them? One of these days we could be one of them, at the end of the day . . .

MIGUEL: Whatcha askin me crap for? Don't scramble things up for me! Alls I know is you gotta get outta here! [*Vaguely gesturing*] The boss don't have nothin to do with that and neither do I. So outta here, now. You thought you were such big shots.

EMILIO: Your boss might not have nothin to do with it, but there's always someone who does have something to do with it: it's the same thing.

MARTA: Sure, you can be somewhere only at night when all the doors are shut; cuz when its daytime, they're gonna tell you, "Listen, you can't be here." "Why not?" you ask them. "Just because," they say. "You go over there." And over there they tell you the same thing, so you just gotta keep goin, and you get tired, see, you get tired as a dog, but they keep kicking you out and kicking you out . . . Damn, I didn't tell no one I wanted to be poor, I didn't tell no one I wanted to live; if they made me live they have to put up with me somewhere, see!

MIGUEL: Sure, I see your point, but don't make trouble for me. I don't have nothin to do with this.

MARTA: You're here, see; you're tellin us we gotta go.

MIGUEL: But they sent me, please understand!

EMILIO: Who?

MIGUEL: Whaddaya mean who? The boss, man.

EMILIO: Which boss?

MIGUEL: You screwin with me? [*Aggressively*] On top of everything else, you wanna screw with me?

MARTA: Nah, that's just how he is. He's just joking. But he ain't bad, he ain't bad . . . I know him already.

EMILIO: I'm asking who your boss is cuz since you got here you've been sayin that he sends messages to you.

MIGUEL: And that's the way it's gotta be man. How's he gonna come and hang out in the dust and commotion?

EMILIO: But who is he? Have you ever seen him?

MIGUEL [*after a brief pause*]: No. [*Pause.*] What for?

EMILIO: What for? They've got you buried in the darkest corner of the world, in between machines that grind and grind without stopping, belching dust and stench; your wife is dying thrown away in a corner and workers suddenly disappear . . . But the machines can't stop, so you have to guard and work, guard and work . . .

MIGUEL: Shut up! Shut up, mister!

EMILIO: Who are you obeying? Who are you guarding all this for like a dog? . . . You're gonna die thrown away, same as your wife.

MIGUEL: He pays me . . . he pays me! You . . . you gotta have a boss . . . I'm like everybody else, like everybody else . . .

EMILIO: But who is your boss?

MIGUEL [*harassed*]: I don't know, don't know: leave me alone! Don't screw with me no more! Don't screw with me no more! I know what I'm doing. I have to follow his orders; the old lady's sick; she's dying; if he gets mad and fires me we ain't got nowhere to go! Leave me alone, leave me alone, mister, for God's sake!

[*After a moment of indecision,* MIGUEL *picks up the bags.*]

MARTA [*frightened*]: Whaddaya doin? Whaddaya doin?

[MIGUEL *violently places the sacks behind the stake that supports the rope.*]

MIGUEL: Here's where you can put your crap!

[MIGUEL *grabs the stick and approaches* EMILIO.]

I'm sick of this shit! You goin or not?

[MARTA *moves between them.*]

MARTA [*more surprised than frightened*]: Listen . . . Where'd you say? [*Gesturing*] Here?

MIGUEL: Sure, that over there ain't got nothin to do with us.

MARTA [*incredulous*]: Here? Here?

[MARTA *takes a few steps and stands behind the sacks.*]

If we're here you can't do nothing to us?

MIGUEL: No, that belongs to the other owner; ours is just up to here.

[MIGUEL *points out the stake.*]

I always put in sticks to mark it, [*looking at* EMILIO] but there's no shortage of jerks that takes em out.

MARTA: How come you didn't tell us sooner?

MIGUEL: What did ya want, a written notice?

MARTA [*happily*]: Look, Emilio: we just have to move over a few steps. [*Smiling*] Excuse me, huh?

[MARTA *goes to* EMILIO.]

Get up then.

EMILIO: So that's the Promised Land? Whose is it?

MIGUEL: Don't know, I ain't never seen [*passing to the other side*] the owner of this side.

EMILIO: The frying pan or the fire.

MIGUEL: What did you say?

MARTA: Nothin, he didn't say nothin. [*Smiling*] You're on our side.

MIGUEL: Oh, pardon me.

[*He crosses back.*]

I'm not one to take liberties. I respect private property. [*Gesturing*] Need any help?

EMILIO: No, I'm not gonna be able to go over there: I'm too tired.

MARTA: Cut it out. It's only two steps.

EMILIO: Two steps towards where? No, thank you very much; I thank you from the bottom of my soul. I swear, I'm so touched that if I could, I would cry like a baby, but listen to me: so many times already, I've been forced to take two steps, so many times I've been forced to say yes when I wanna say no; so many times I've had to choose to be nothing . . . No, pal, I'm not moving from here.

MIGUEL: Oh, so you're not goin? So you're gonna keep playin the tough guy with me?

[MIGUEL *brandishes the stick.*]

MARTA: No, hey, no! Just leave us here; the boss ain't gonna notice nothin.

MIGUEL: I can't, he knows everything; he always knows everything I do! And besides, this jerk is laughing at me all the time! I'm not a piece of trash. I ain't sold out to nobody: I just take care of what's mine, what I've earned! I've been working there for years, they're not gonna fire me because of you! I'm a man, you loser; I ain't no garbage, I ain't no garbage!

[MIGUEL *knocks* EMILIO *over with a single blow.*]

MARTA: Get up, Emilio! Get up!

MIGUEL: You goin or not, jerk? You goin or not?

[MIGUEL *clubs* EMILIO *until he kills him. Once the act is consummated, the absurdity of the situation becomes clear; when confronted with it, only a remote, pathetic babbling of homeless inhabitants rises to the surface.*]

MARTA: You bastard . . . you bastard . . . You didn't have to do nothin to him. Who was gonna know if we was two steps this way? Who was gonna know?

MIGUEL [*mechanically*]: I had to protect my job . . . I had to protect my job . . .

MARTA: We're crazy . . . We're all crazy . . .

MIGUEL: I ain't no garbage . . . I ain't no garbage . . .

MARTA: What did they do to us? What the hell did they do to us?

BIBLIOGRAPHY

"A Francia Viaja 'El tor por las astas.'" *La segunda,* March 1, 1983: 26.

Albornoz Farías, Adolfo. "Veinticinco afanosos años entre textos y escenas." In *Crónicas del amor furioso,* by Juan Radrigan, 7–15. Santiago: Ediciones Frontera Sur, 2004.

"Anoche debutó un nuevo dramaturgo." *La segunda,* March 24, 1979: 23.

Beverley, John. "The Margin at the Center." In *The Real Thing: Testimonial Discourse and Latin America,* edited by Georg M. Gugelberger, 23–41. Durham: Duke University Press, 1996.

———. *Testimonio: On the Politics of Truth.* Minneapolis: University of Minnesota Press, 2004.

Boyle, Catherine M. *Chilean Theater, 1973–1985: Marginality, Power, Selfhood.* Cranbury, N.J.: Fairleigh Dickinson University Press, 1992.

"'Las brutas': Tres mujeres que conmueven." *El sur,* August 18, 1982.

Burgos-Debray, Elisabeth. Introduction to *I, Rigoberta Menchú: An Indian Woman in Guatemala,* edited by Elisabeth Burgos-Debray, translated by Ann Wright, xi–xxi. New York: Verso, 1984.

Collier, Simon, and William F. Sater. *A History of Chile, 1808–2002.* 2nd ed. New York: Cambridge University Press, 2004.

Comisión Nacional sobre Prisión Política y Tortura. "Informe de la Comisión (10 November 2004)." http://www.comisiontortura.cl/inicio/index.php (accessed March 8, 2006).

"Con exito se presentó a Radrigán en Nancy." *El mercurio,* June 3, 1983, sec. C: 11.

Constable, Pamela, and Arturo Valenzuela. *A Nation of Enemies: Chile Under Pinochet.* New York: W. W. Norton, 1991.

Denegri, Francesca. "*Testimonio* and Its Discontents." In *Contemporary Latin American Cultural Studies,* edited by Stephen Hart and Richard King, 228–38. London: Arnold, 2003.

Dillard, J. L. *Towards a Social History of American English.* New York: Mouton Publishers, 1985.

Drake, Paul W. Foreword to *Victims of the Chilean Miracle: Workers and Neoliberalism in the Pinochet Era, 1973–2002,* edited by Peter Winn, ix–xiii. Durham, N.C.: Duke University Press, 2004.

———. "Historical Setting." In *Chile: A Country Study,* edited by Rex A. Hudson, 1–57. Washington, D.C.: Federal Research Division, Library of Congress, 1994.

"Elogian obra 'Las brutas.'" *La nacion,* August 5, 1980, sec. C: 15.

Farías, Roberto. "Tres muertas inquietantes." *Paula* (May 2005): 80–85.

Felman, Shoshana. "Education and Crisis, or the Vicissitudes of Teaching." In *Testimony: Crises of Witnessing in Literature, Psychoanalysis, and History,* edited by Shoshana Felman and Dori Laub, 1–56. New York: Routledge, 1992.

Giella, Miguel Ángel. *Teatro Abierto 1981.* 2 vols. Colección Dramaturgos Argentinos Contemporáneos. Buenos Aires: Corregidor, 1991.

Graham-Jones, Jean. *Exorcising History: Argentine Theater Under Dictatorship.* Lewisburg, Pa.: Bucknell University Press, 2000.

Halperín Donghi, Tulio. *The Contemporary History of Latin America,* edited and translated by John Charles Chasteen. Durham, N.C.: Duke University Press, 1993.

Hendrickson, Robert. *American Talk: The Words and Ways of American Dialects.* New York: Viking, 1986.

Hersh, Seymour M. "Censored Matter in Book About CIA Said to Have Related Chile Activities; Damage Feared." *New York Times,* September 11, 1974: 14.

Human Rights Watch. *Human Rights Overview: Chile.* March 8, 2006. http://hrw.org/english/docs/2005/01/13/chile9846.htm.

Hurtado, María de la Luz. "Conjugation of Identities in the Dramatization of Chilean Reality." Paper presented, conference of Stanford University and Fundación Frei, De frei a frei: Política, economía y cultura en los últimos 30 años en Chile, Stanford, Calif., April 25, 1997.

Johnston, David. "Valle-Inclán: The Meaning of Form." In *Moving Target: Theatre Translation and Cultural Relocation,* edited by Carole-Anne Upton, 85–99. Manchester, U.K.: St. Jerome Publishing, 2000.

Kafka, Franz. *The Trial.* Translated by Willa and Edwin Muir. 1937. Reprint, New York: Schocken Books, 1992.

Kornbluh, Peter. *The Pinochet File: A Declassified Dossier on Atrocity and Accountability.* New York: New Press, 2003.

Laub, Dori. "Bearing Witness, or the Vicissitudes of Learning." In *Testimony: Crises of Witnessing in Literature, Psychoanalysis, and History,* edited by Shoshana Felman and Dori Laub, 57–74. New York: Routledge, 1992.

Lefevere, André, and Susan Bassnett. "Where Are We in Translation Studies?" Introduction to *Constructing Cultures: Essays on Literary Translation,* by Susan Bassnett and André Lefevere, 1–11. Philadelphia: Clevedon, 1998.

Lepeley, Oscar. "Avatares del teatro chileno contestatario durante los primeros años de la dictadura militar." In *Resistencia y poder: Teatro en Chile,* edited by Heidrun Adler and George Woodyard, 113–24. Madrid: Iberoamericana, 2000.

Levi, Primo. "The Gray Zone." In *The Drowned and the Saved,* translated by Raymond Rosenthal, 36–69. New York: Summit Books, 1986.

Levine, Suzanne Jill. *The Subversive Scribe: Translating Latin American Fiction.* St. Paul, Minn.: Graywolf Press, 1991.

Matta, Fernando Reyes. "The 'New Song' and Its Confrontation in Latin America." In *Marxism and the Interpretation of Culture,* edited by Cary Nelson and Lawrence Grossberg, 447–60. Urbana, Ill.: Illini Books, 1998.

Montgomery, Michael B., and Joseph S. Hall. *Dictionary of Smoky Mountain English.* Knoxville: University of Tennessee Press, 2004.

Newby, Rick, ed. *The Rocky Mountain Region: The Greenwood Encyclopedia of American Regional Cultures.* Westport, Conn.: Greenwood Press, 2004.

Nigro, Kirsten. "Getting the Word Out: Issues in the Translation of Latin American Theatre for U.S. Audiences." In *Moving Target: Theatre Translation and Cultural Relocation,* edited by Carole-Anne Upton, 115–25. Manchester, U.K.: St. Jerome Publishing, 2000.

Partnoy, Alicia. Introduction to *The Little School: Tales of Disappearance and Survival in Argentina.* Translated by Lois Athey Partnoy and Sandra Braunstein, 11–18. Pittsburgh, Pa.: Cleis, 1986.

Piña, Juan Andrés. *Teatro chileno contemporáneo: Antología.* Teatro ibero-americano contemporáneo 1. Madrid: Fondo de Cultura Económica, 1992.

Popkin, Louise B. "Translator's Note." In *The Letters That Never Came,* by Mauricio Rosencof, translated by Louise B. Popkin, xvii–xx. Albuquerque: University of New Mexico Press, 2004.

Presidencia de la República, April 6, 2006. http://www.presidencia.cl/view/viewBiografia.asp?seccion=Biografia.

Radrigán, Juan. *Crónicas del amor furioso*. Santiago: Ediciones Frontera Sur, 2004.

———. *El día de los muros*. Santiago: Impresora Bio-Bio, 1975.

———. *La contienda humana*. Santiago: Ediciones Literatura Alternativa, 1989.

———. *Los vencidos no creen en Dios: Cuentos*. Colección Sísifo 2. Santiago: Editorial Entrecerros, 1962.

———. *El vino de la cobardía*. Santiago: Impresores Guerrero y Recabarren, 1968.

"Un Radrigán Juguetón." *Ultimas noticias*, December 26, 2000: 40.

Rettig, Raúl. *Report of the Chilean National Commission on Truth and Reconciliation*. March 8, 2006. http://www.usip.org/library/truth.html.

Rojo, Grinor. *Muerte y resurrección del teatro chileno, 1973–1983*. Madrid: Ediciones Michay, 1985.

Rulfo, Juan. "They Gave Us the Land." In *The Burning Plain and Other Stories*, translated by George D. Schade, 9–16. Austin: University of Texas Press, 1967.

Scott, James C. *Domination and the Arts of Resistance: Hidden Transcripts*. New Haven, Conn.: Yale University Press, 1990.

Silva, Angélica Lavados. "Crítica de teatro: 'Testimonios sobre las muertas de Sabina.'" *El Cronista*, March 27, 1979: 30.

Sommer, Doris. "No Secrets for Rigoberta." Chap. 5 in *Proceed with Caution, When Engaged by Minority Writing in the Americas*. Cambridge, Mass.: Harvard University Press, 1999.

Spivak, Gayatri Chakravorty. "The Politics of Translation." In *The Translation Studies Reader*, edited by Lawrence Venuti, 397–416. New York: Routledge, 2000.

Stern, Steve J. *Battling for Hearts and Minds: Memory Struggles in Pinochet's Chile, 1973–1988*. Durham, N.C.: Duke University Press, 2006.

———. *Remembering Pinochet's Chile: On the Eve of London 1998*. Durham, N.C.: Duke University Press, 2004.

Timerman, Jacobo. *Chile: Death in the South*. New York: Knopf, 1987.

Valenzuela, Tita. "Shanty Town Theatre." *Index on Censorship* 14, no. 1 (1985): 9–10.

Venuti, Lawrence. *The Scandals of Translation*. New York: Routledge, 1998.

Williamson, Edwin. *The Penguin History of Latin America.* London: Penguin Books, 1992.

Winn, Peter. *Victims of the Chilean Miracle: Workers and Neoliberalism in the Pinochet Era, 1973–2002.* Durham, N.C.: Duke University Press, 2004.

Yocelevsky, Ricardo A. *Chile: Partidos políticos, democracia y dictadura, 1970–1990.* Santiago: Fondo de Cultura Económica, 2002.